T0196631

MEET MEH UNDAH DEH BONGOLO & TARK LIKE WE NO

A Case for Virgin Islands Creole Den An'
Now & A Socio-Cultural Lexicon

CLEMENT WHITE

authorHOUSE®

AuthorHouse™
1663 Liberty Drive
Bloomington, IN 47403
www.authorhouse.com
Phone: 1 (800) 839-8640

Cover courtesy of the Department of Interior, United States Government Printing Press, Washington 1939.

Published by AuthorHouse 01/12/2018

ISBN: 978-1-5462-1846-3 (sc)
ISBN: 978-1-5462-1845-6 (hc)
ISBN: 978-1-5462-1844-9 (e)

Library of Congress Control Number: 2017917915

Print information available on the last page.

CONTENTS

For: The strong, resourceful, and resilient residents of the Virgin Islands, US and British, who endured the wrath of a relentless Irma and the ire of a defiant María

Remembering my mother's dear friends, Miss Iona Henry and Miss Eulalie "Lopie" Lopez

For Dr. Gilbert Sprauve, Professor Emeritus, University of the Virgin Islands, and Dr. Lezmore Emmanuel for their passionate defense, affirmation, and promotion of our language and its legitimacy. These pioneers were laboring virtually alone against a backdrop of suffocating ideologies, and negativity. Their contributions and respect for Virgin Islands Creole have been instrumental in forging a better understanding and appreciation of our language and thus of our Virgin Islands traditions, culture, customs, and ultimately of ourselves. This is in recognition and honor of their uncompromising commitment.

ACKNOWLEDGEMENTS

Heartfelt recognition and honor to my dear mother, Marjorie "Miss Maggie" Asta White Stevens for endless, uncompromising, unconditional love and support. She never had the opportunity to attend school, never read a book, but was my first teacher. Now even as her work on earth was ended on October 10, 2014, I know that she will continue to guide and inspire me, so remarkable a woman, mother, and human being she was. Listening to my extraordinary mother speak for so many years exposed me to the richest linguistic field possible.

Infinite credit goes to my wife, Dr. Jeannette Smith White, who always supported and encouraged me and continues to be a source of inspiration. She believed in me to the fullest extent, and I would never undervalue her important role in all my literary projects. Her constructive critiques with respect to writing and literary analysis have been unmatched. To our sons Sekou "Chike" and Asha, our grandsons, Amari and Ahsir, and granddaughter Avani, you mean the world to me.

To my sister Cheryl A. White, because of your dedication to our mother, I was able to continue writing. I recognize and appreciate your sacrifice and dedication to our beloved mother. Your rewards will be great, far greater than you can imagine. Your sacrifices have not gone unnoticed! My brothers and I will never understate them. Your attention and care of our mother symbolize a lesson in love and commitment.

Shirlene Williams Lee from the very beginning in the 1960's you played a pivotal role in the transcription of my work, typing my manuscripts with your inimitable professionalism and expertise. Thanks for your numerous reminders of words and phrases. Your constant questioning as to whether or not I had a particular word or saying was priceless. Thanks for finding the most appropriate book cover in your archives, and those of your brother James. Words are not sufficient to express my gratitude to you. Critic, poet, photographer, analyst, sounding board, artist, designer, advisor, commentator, photographer, motivator and more importantly, friend— from the first grade at the extraordinary Dober School until now!

You have been there every step of the way. Everything you do, you do it well. Without your assistance this project would have never been completed.

Charles A. White and Celestino A White, you have the memory of our dear mother, "Miss Maggie." Even having lived in New York for decades has not dulled Charles' recollection of words and phrases. Thanks to my sister-in law Sally White, New Yorker and converted West Indian, under the influence of my Virgin Islands family. Dr. Marta Rodríguez, thanks for your interest in our language; I am impressed by your ability to decipher so many local expressions. Thanks to Delaun Mercer for her encouragement and her keen comments and inspiration in the primary stages of this project. Mona Freeman I appreciate your interest in this project and your inquiring as to whether I had included certain words or phrases.

Fiolina Mills, you have helped to shape how I view languages. Thanks for your lessons and guidance; so much gratitude. There is no true way to measure your impact on my life. My high school Spanish teachers, Mrs. Carmen Encarnación and Mrs. Alicia Ortiz I will always remember you. Miss Ruth Thomas, your influence is far-reaching, having touched the lives of an infinite number of Virgin Islanders.

Thanks to my colleague Professor Susana de los Heros, linguist/ sociolinguist, but more importantly friend for her valuable scholarly references that have served me so well in the formulation of the theoretical foundation for this work. Karla Crispin I appreciate your timely input, technical and organizational support. Thanks for being an extra pair of eyes.

Larry Sewer, a staunch supporter of Virgin Islands culture, thanks. Carol Henneman, I admire your love for Virgin Islands traditions. Kwabena Davis, Edwita, "Tin Tin" Hart, Irvin "Brownie Brown", and Edwin Davis, advocates for Virgin Islands language and culture, thanks. Elaine Warren and Edgar Lake my literary collaborators for decades, thanks so much. Dr. Vincent Cooper, professor of English at UVI, thanks for your valuable insights on issues of West Indian and Caribbean languages. To the people of the Virgin Islands, of the West Indies, thanks for giving me such a rich tapestry of language, traditions, customs—of culture.

Dr. Gilbert Sprauve, Professor Emeritus, University of the Virgin Islands, I recognize, value, and honor your lifetime of remarkable work and the respect that you have demonstrated for Virgin Islands Creole. Your dedication to this theme and your contributions have helped me and countless other Virgin Islanders to embrace our language and culture, and to respect and accept who we are. Your commitment to exploring the issues surrounding our Virgin Islands Creole has served as a motivation for me to undertake this most awesome, but rewarding task. You have done the important groundwork and beyond, inspiring me and numerous others seeking to better understand the rudiments of our language. Our Virgin Islands are indebted to you for your immeasurable service.

So much inspiration for this project came from my many years as summer faculty and Faculty Coordinator at the Institute for the Recruitment of Teachers in Andover, Massachusetts (**IRT**). I thank the many students, faculty, administration and staff over the two and a half decades for their motivation and encouragement. Special thanks to my former students at the Institute: Dr. Reginald Wilburn, Curriculum Coordinator (&faculty), Dr. Besenia Rodríguez, Curriculum Coordinator (&faculty). Dr. Alexandra Cornelius, former Director (& faculty). No less gratitude for Dr. Asabe Poloma, former Executive Director (&faculty) and Dr. Kelly Wise, founder of the Institute, (former Director, Faculty, and Executive Director).

Mrs. Bernice Louise Heyliger, everyone now knows that without you, I would not be writing anything. Endless thanks and appreciation.

PREFACE

The idea of a book on United States Virgin Islands Creole had been brewing in my head for decades. In fact, I still have that yellow notepad from the 1980's on which I had begun to scribble words and expressions, with the dream that someday, in a book length manuscript, I would comment on our rich linguistic heritage. Even before the decades of the eighties, while writing poetic verses, for example "*Jumbie Jubilee*," in <u>Islands Jewels</u> (edited by the venerable Valdemar A. Hill, Sr.) I was always intrigued by the special nature of United States Virgin Creole, and often thought about how an exploration of this vernacular undoubtedly would be a rewarding undertaking. Of course, for decades I also listened in awe to my dear mother's words, and the way in which she orally conveyed her ideas through a colorful orality. Indeed, I am most fortunate to have been an inheritor of this unique personal and oral cultural legacy. Moreover, I also am the beneficiary of being raised in a community in which the medium of speech was part of a vibrant cultural tradition. I always knew that on a personal level I wanted to honor the way we spoke, but there was more—I wanted to uphold, affirm, and defend it!

Three pivotal moments occurred many years after my initial inspiration, confirming that often what seems to be quite simple can prove to be most significant. They were the moments that moved my idea closer to a concrete reality. Several years ago Bernard "Tony" Belle, a St. Thomian living in Rhode Island, asked if I knew what a "*shak shak*" was. It was an expression with which he was familiar, but after many years living in the United States he had not heard it for a long period of time. In responding to my friend, it occurred to me that the opportune moment to begin that book on Virgin Islands Creole—words, expressions, and structure—had arrived.

Shortly after this episode my niece Shané Rhymer became a student at one of the local universities in Rhode Island. During her residence in the state she and I engaged in numerous enlightening discussions on language and culture, and in one moment she asked, "Uncle, when are you going to write something about Virgin Islands language and culture?" That was a question that further reminded me of my own intention and mission.

It was shortly after this that I asked two of my younger nephews (ages 6 and 8) from my large, extended family if they knew what a "Bonkonko" was. One of them responded in the most beautiful way, in the manner of a child: *"Wa kin' ah stuiepid language ah yoh use' to tark, Uncle?"* His cousin supported his position with a simple, "Yea." It was a response that symbolized that our medium of communication had undergone changes. Unquestionably, some of the expressions from my generation sounded foreign to them. Out of the mouths of babes!

Reflecting on those three simple but pivotal moments **MEET MEH UNDAH DEH BONGOLO & TARK LIKE WE NO—A CASE FOR VIRGIN ISLANDS CREOLE DEN AN' NOW & A SOCIO-CULTURAL LEXICON** was born. It is a kind of a hybrid work, nurtured from an academic and perpetual personal curiosity. This project, an exploration of our language within a complex U.S.V. I. society was finally launched thanks to Bernard "Tony" Belle's timely curiosity, my niece's inspiring question, and my nephews' innocence of expression.

INTRODUCTION

My initial disclaimer is that this book does not purport to be exhaustive, nor does it even have as its principal mission the tracing or social contextualization of all of the expressions included here, and their linguistics rudiments. That would be the job for linguists and socio-linguists, and I make no such claims; notwithstanding from time to time I have referenced linguistics scholars such as Noam Chomsky, Fernand de Saussure, R. A. Hudson, Francisco Moreno Fernández, Dr. Gilbert Sprauve, Dr. Robin Sabino, Dr. Vincent Cooper and others[1]. At its core, however, this project, has two very simple objectives that are not at all mutually exclusive. The first is to highlight the unique nature of selected words, expressions, and proverbs currently or formerly in use in the Creole of the United States Virgin Islands[2]—some of which have barely survived, and others that are still in full vogue.

Beyond being merely a glossary of Virgin Islands words and phrases, this work is by its very nature a defense of the United States Virgin Islands Creole. So that, in the final analysis, as my second objective, I will argue that we should recognize and honor the Creole of the United States Virgin Islands as a legitimate mode of speech, with its nuances, regulations, and well-established structures. This is not a scientific study, nor does it pretend to be one, but instead represents the product of a kind of institutional memory growing out of decades of listening to family, friends, and neighbors; in other words, generating from countless communicative exchanges with Virgin Islanders. To be sure, though, this work does not presume to be all encompassing, nor an indisputable representation of United States Virgin Islands Creole.

It is a given that no collection on this topic, no matter how ambitious, can ever corral the thousands and thousands of local words, phrases, or proverbs, or even more unreachable, the endless subtle nuances. Naturally, some word usages and expressions once endemic in Virgin Islands Creole have been lost not only through the process of the natural evolution of language, but also because of overt or tacit censorship, that was not in any way fortuitous. Virgin Islands Creole is so rich and vibrant with respect to pronunciation, inflection, various borrowed words, and the use of hyperboles that it would be impossible to capture in a few pages all of the various machinations that serve as components for oral elaboration. In point of fact, no amount of pages would be able to perform such a herculean task. I write simply as witness, listener, observer, inheritor and participant of a rich linguistic heritage. I am reminded of the great Inca Peruvian writer, Garcilaso de la Vega, who in arguing for the authentication of his Incan culture, posits that the "easiest and more even path to follow is to relate what in my childhood I would hear my mother, her aunts, uncles, and other elders say"[3]{*my translation*}. To be sure, this work is not confined to experiences in "my childhood," but Garcilaso's declaration is very pertinent because of its emphasis on orality—"I would hear." This is the model for the simple, most direct path, which I myself have opted to follow here.

Indeed, it is my wish that all Virgin Islanders might appreciate and respect the richness and uniqueness of our language, even in its continuous and inevitable process of transformation. Moreover, perhaps those unfamiliar with the Virgin Islands speech patterns, once exposed to them may get a better sense of what they are hearing, and that they too will appreciate and respect the islands' orality, and in effect, attain an appreciation of a vital cultural component of the United States Virgin Islands. Whether or not certain words and expressions are recognizable will depend to some extent on such factors as the age of the person, the historical time frame, and the length of time residing in the United States Virgin Islands, on which island, and of course, his or her individual interest in the Creole itself as a viable mode of communication. But no matter the time period, United States Virgin Islands Creole, through its multiple filters, has always represented an indispensable link of our socio-cultural legacy, and should be acknowledged as such.

I must stress that this work is about the entire United States Virgin Islands and not only about any particular one of the islands. The main thrust of this discussion *is not* to compare and contrast utterances from St. John,

St. Croix, and St. Thomas. Some of my most memorable and cherished moments spending summers in St. Croix during my youth were the spirited, fun-filled "debates" with friends and family as to whose way of speaking was the "*best*;" lively exchanges about who spoke "*funny*" and who spoke "*good*." As might be expected, my brothers, sisters, and I defended St. Thomas' turf. My family and friends in St. Croix launched their own staunch defenses. Similar debates were popular between friends and families from St. John and St. Thomas. Indeed, even as children we had a sense that there were aspects of our speech that differed from one island to another, but also everyone knew that the commonalities abounded. So unquestionably, in this work there will be words and expressions that are more, or less, prevalent on one island than on another, and indeed cases where pronunciation may vary marginally, or greatly, along with other nuances. This should not be surprising. In the end, however, the discussion still centers on speech regularly spoken in our islands, or at one point that was the norm.

This book project, in essence a kind of socio-cultural reminiscence, in part speaks to my own nostalgia as I think of the cultural wealth garnered through our language. For this reason, a major part of this explorative task is the section of individual entries included here, a lexicon of sorts—words, phrases, expressions, characteristic of the language heritage of the United States Virgin Islands. In essence, many of the entries were "chosen" primarily because of my unabashedly subjective attraction to them. And this was so in some cases for reasons that I understand, but quite honestly, at times I was simply victimized or cajoled by a vague subconscious process of subjectivity. I readily confess that in the process of undertaking this work, many words and expressions frequently uttered by my mother rang incessantly in my head; hence, assuring that this project has as an essential component of its cornerstone an undeniable personal journey. Her fingerprints may be undeciphered and even indecipherable, but I do attest that they are omnipresent. Sentimentality and subjectivity have unwittingly imposed themselves on me.

With respect to the entries included, there are cases where I give explanations, sometimes only to clarify some ambiguity or ambivalence of some words or expressions: example, *<disgustin'>*, under the later section titled **Words, Expressions, Maxims, Proverbs—A Virgin Islands Cultural Lexicon.** In other cases, I simply offer a brief definition or explanation of an entry. At other times, however, the explanations may be much more extensive, especially with regard to fading expressions, unusual syntactic structures, or unique or varied usage (see *"ting" "dem," "self," "garn,"* and *"meson"* in the section **Words, Expressions, Maxims, Proverbs—A Virgin Islands Cultural Lexicon**). Many references bring with themselves a particular type of historical time frame and linguistic usage. For example, the once popular phrase, *"undah deh Bongolo"* (this book's cover; see later Section, **Words, Expressions, Maxims, Proverbs—A Virgin Islands Cultural Lexicon**) referred to the heyday of the market place in St. Thomas, and the social contacts and contracts that people enjoyed especially in the 1950's and 60's.

The common utterance, *"Meet meh undah deh Bongolo,"* may well be heard occasionally but is no longer universally recognizable in St. Thomas. Similarly, *"He live 'roun' deh coas' "* had a particular meaning in St. Thomas that is now virtually lost (See entry "**roun deh coas'**" in the section titled **Words, Expressions, Maxims, Proverbs—A Virgin Islands Cultural Lexicon**). In other situations, I felt it imperative to make reference to the historical context of the word or expression, and in so doing inherently suggest why the particular expression is no longer used. Often, though, a brief and simple definition or description suffices. Other times I opted to write some expressions without explication as a deliberate strategy to help us to reflect on their uniqueness or creative nature. Ultimately, though, the words and expressions included in the entries capture tenets of beliefs, suspicions, traditions, customs, world view, and ideology. And also, they are often encased in molds of humor, irony, and biting satire—endearing and enduring staples of the United States Virgin Islands.

In highlighting the erosion of language I will also reference some landmarks of the Virgin Islands of the United States because with the disappearance of some of these referents the language associated with them also became virtually nonexistent. By referencing language and places, I hope to pay homage to Virgin Islands Creole and in the process embrace our linguistic heritage and legacy. Optimistically, it is my dream that this work might reconnect with those disconnected due to migration from our islands and thus have been out of contact with the language for quite some time; hence, the words, phrases, or proverbs might rekindle a spark. Furthermore, it is my hope that some words and expressions which are no longer popular may very well bring back cherished memories, in addition to reaffirming a sense of Virgin Islands identity.

I have included a section on Virgin Islands Dutch Creole (Negerhollands), this intriguing precursor of contemporary United States Virgin Islands Creole. That inclusion is **not** designed to suggest an extensive examination of that past Virgin Islands language. Dr. Gilbert Sprauve, Dr. Robin Sabino, and other scholars have dedicated a life's work to this linguistic phenomenon.[4] My reference to this language is to honor it as part of the linguistic trajectory that has landed us where we are today as current speakers of a unique Creole, which bears linguistic imprints of our forefathers and foremothers. It is my hope that members of our community will reflect on that moment in history when Virgin Islands Dutch Creole flourished and will begin to cherish it as an essential cog in the evolution of present day Virgin Islands speech.

Virgin Islands Creole is also a language of sounds, wordless expressions that are at times even more expressive and impressive than any verbal utterance. Some of these have been identified in this work under the heading, "**Special Sounds.**" Common examples are the sounds made from the "*suckin' of teet*'," along with several other examples listed in the entries. Because many of the words have no "official" spelling I try to recreate the sounds as phonetically as possible, recognizing that writers or interpreters of culture may very well render the spellings somewhat differently. One might write "*de ting*," another, "*deh ting*," and yet another individual may well render the same thought as "*dey ting*." The aim here is not to ignite an endless and meaningless quarrel with choices of orthographic renditions. Ours is primarily an orally transmitted Creole that is still waiting to be transcribed (by consensus) in writing. That may be another project, maybe the task of another writer, a linguist or socio-linguist.

In the unfolding of this project, I also discuss the grammatical structure of the Creole spoken in United States Virgin Islands and examine how various parts of speech function in this system. The choice of examining grammar and syntax was a natural one because I wanted to give our Creole the serious scrutiny and analysis that it deserves. Much credence can be given to a language if those who speak it also validate it. By opting to explore issues of grammar and pronunciation as they relate to United States Virgin Islands Creole, I am essentially affirming the integrity of this medium of communication. At various points, I have included a few charts mainly as a convenient way of summarizing some of the topics presented. At the end, I also compiled these diverse charts into one group in order to offer the reader a site for reference or consultation.

In a few cases, the current inapplicability of the historical context renders an expression extinct, or virtually so. For example, no one today would speak of the *"Nite Soil Truck,"* the vehicle that once carried away human waste in the early hours of dawn. It certainly would be anachronistic to employ such a phrase in contemporary Virgin Islands society. Or even if we made reference to this vehicle, it would not resonate with listeners unfamiliar with the historical period. Yet, it is important for our residents to be aware of the phrase because those who labored performing that task sacrificed their health in many ways. The least we can do is honor and respect these Virgin Islanders by acknowledging the language associated with their commitment. Undoubtedly, industrialization and modernization have caused the displacement of these laborers, and along with this, the disappearance of the once popular expressions, *"Nite Soil"*/ *"Nite Soil Man,"* / *"Nite Soil Truck,"*— a direct erosion of the language due to inevitable and predictable, or often unpredictable, socio-economic transformations in the United States Virgin Islands community. Language eroded or loss, comes accompanied with an equal loss or erosion of knowledge, a logical reality that is often too understated. This type of loss inevitably leads to cultural erasure.

Because of the particular historical juncture at which they were in their heyday, many of the words and expressions included in this collection have unfortunately now lost their functionality. Some are on life support, endangered— still used, but with much less frequency than in past decades. But, in spite of this dire truth, their place in the annals of our linguistic trajectory must never be minimized. To do so would be to undervalue and discredit the many protagonists whose creativity has given rise and real meaning to our narratives. Like the hall of famer who will never recapture that lost athletic prowess but has contributed to the evolution of his or her sport, the fading or now extinct word and phrases have been integral in the formulation and elaboration of our contemporary United States Virgin Islands Creole. Symbolically they represent a sort of blueprint, guiding us to understand who we are as a people.

THE ENGLISH BACKLASH

I recognize that often in our islands when one advocates for the legitimacy and the affirmation of our Virgin Islands Creole some opponents misconstrue, or at times purposely recalibrate this to mean a denunciation of "*Standard English.*"[5] There is often a contentious, (or even at times, contemptuous) interpretation of the advocate's "intent" as that individual promotes the local tongue. The argument, non-syllogistic by its very nature, posits that anyone who embraces the idea of a *United States Virgin Islands Language* discourages Virgin Islanders from learning "proper" English.[6] It is an egregious argument with no basis in fact, but one that has persisted for years with no regard to its fundamental flaw, its false premise—that the mere advocacy of one language implicitly disavows another. A most blatant fallacy is that promotion of our language is motivated by a desire to discredit or minimize other languages spoken in the United States Virgin Islands. I affirm without reservation that Virgin Islanders who learn and master several languages will increase their chances of entry into universities, of acquiring jobs or of advancement in their particular fields. So in this work, I argue for the promotion of Virgin Islands Creole, but simultaneously with a clear sensibility and sensitivity of the strategic and pragmatic importance of English and within a well-established framework of its potential role as catalyst in personal, economic, and social development, mobility, and stability.

In addition to recognizing the importance of English, I have always advocated that Virgin Islands residents take advantage of our unique socio-linguistic community—- our numerous languages in a relativity small geographical space, within the context of a now expansive and interconnected global market. In point of fact, however, mine is not an "*either/or*" proposition but one that sees no inherent contradiction in the advocacy for our local speech and the mastery of English, or indeed of other languages. In the same way, when I encourage students to master Spanish, I am not inferring that they should then reject other languages that they may speak, or hope to learn. This is not an incitement of some kind of language rivalry (competing and conflictive modes of communication) but a matter of the coexistence of multiple ways of speaking. Underlying it all, however, is also a call to respect and honor U.S. Virgin Islands Creole as an endemic component of Virgin Islands culture, and by extension, its identity.

Hence, herein lies my second disclaimer: It is not the agenda of this book to ignite an irresolvable quarrel concerning whether the learning of English should be supplanted by United States Virgin Islands Creole. Since this writer has already affirmed that this is not his position, it would be nothing more than a specious squabble.

A plan to eliminate English as the de facto official mode of communication[7] in the Virgin Islands and insist on Virgin Islands Creole only would be untenable and lacking vision, and I can never subscribe to such a project. Yet, I am not so naïve as to think that there are not those who would arrive at the conclusion that this is the goal of this work, in spite of my own overtly explicit and unwavering stance in favor of English mastery. An advocacy for *Virgin Islands Creole only* would conveniently play into the hands of the detractors who would be only too happy to embrace a false pretext as a basis for the rejection of our Creole, seeing it at best as a crude and improper misrepresentation of English. It would provide a pathway to those paralyzed by language trepidation and those subsumed by an idea that there exists some kind of anti-English agenda. Opting to pursue the present project should not be seen as some sort of nefarious conspiratorial plot, but as simply a commitment by one articulator to embrace one important element that signals who he is as a Virgin Islander.

The aborted movements in the United States of America to establish an "English Only"[8] society failed miserably and will continue to do so for a simple reason—the United States is a country made up of a multiplicity of cultures. The sheer numbers of Latinos and the exponential increase of this important group[9] and others over the past few years have made the quest for a monolithic linguistic society non pragmatic, and illusionary, in essence, a linguistic hoax. In the same vein, it would be illogical and frankly, nonsensical and folly to promote the use of some sort of *Virgin Islands Creole Only Movement*. The argument for the embracement of our Creole does not in any way impinge on, nor inveigh upon the viability and legitimacy of the English language, which occupies its own linguistic space in the Virgin Islands sociological context. Moreover, this is not an advocacy for the creation of a new language, but one for the support, maintenance, and sustenance of a language that already exists. Unequivocally, I am not a disciple of any school of thought that argues for a replacement language in the United States Virgin Islands. To be certain, though, neither am I an apostle of the creed of linguistic heresy—the idea that English should be the only "legitimate" *language* of the Virgin Islands, a rather elitist position that defies the reality.

If we are willing to accept that our battle is not with English, or against any other language, but with ourselves (U.S. Virgin Islanders) then we would at least set in place an essential stepping stone for future serious debates about our language. Above all, an argument for a Creole as substitute for English would be the highest form of hypocrisy, disingenuousness, and intellectual dishonesty given the fact that in the present project I am enlisting the same language (English) that I would be purportedly condemning. There has never been any serious scholar in the U.S. Virgin Islands who has ever suggested such a proposal; yet, some have been unjustly accused of doing just that.

UNITED STATES VIRGIN ISLANDS CREOLE: A PERSPECTIVE

Issues of language are inextricably intertwined with ideology, societal norms and personal inclinations, and in the United States Virgin Islands we have always been at the center of a language debate. Without doubt, this is due to our linguistic restlessness, being as we are a community that continues to live in the shadows of the United States. The territorial arrangement opens the door for the imposition of American English with its own multiple forms of expressions.[10] In addition to this, the United States Virgin Islands represent a culturally diverse, highly pluralistic society, a reality that creates opportunistic moments for language influences. In essence, when we speak of the United States Virgin Islands we are thinking of a true melting pot, a kind of cultural mosaic that envelops a wide array of peoples and cultures. This is not a nativist project; hence, in my mind, the idea of a Virgin Islander is *not* necessarily and arbitrarily linked to place of birth. The fact that a person was born on one of the three islands does not insure that that person will be familiar with U. S. Virgin Islands Creole. The converse is also true: Having been born outside of the U.S.V.I. is not a guarantee that an individual will not be able speak the local Creole—here I allude to my grandparents, uncle, aunts, countless other relatives and friends. I respect and honor the fact that there are those who would challenge this position; yet, I strongly affirm and embrace it.

In our islands one hears English, Arabic, French, Haitian Creole, various East Indian languages, Spanish, Chinese, and several French based Creole languages spoken on a regular basis. Hence, inevitably projects such as this one are imbued with philosophical, socio-political, and ideological implications that thrust us into a fundamental question as to who or what is a Virgin Islander, and what is Virgin Islandness, questions that may seem superfluous to some. Yet, they force us to expand our periphery as we ponder these perennial challenges.

I admit that this book does not provide a response to those inquiries; as important as they may be, such determinations are well beyond the reach of this manuscript's limited focus. Consider the fact that one can speak of Brooklynite speech, without denying the plethora of national and international forms of speech in that great New York borough. We can make a similar argument for Bostonian speech. This is also true for cities such as Madrid where the *Madrileña*[11] speech patterns subsist, in a cauldron of linguistic diversity, emanating from multiple Latin American nations, Africa, and other places in the world. In much the same way we can speak of *"el habla cubana"* in that huge and vibrant island-nation with its infusion of people from other nations in our Caribbean hemisphere. Hence, while I do concede that there are various modes of speech heard in the U.S. Virgin Islands, ultimately my position is that there does exist a United States Virgin Islands Creole language. This is a brand of speech that is identifiable and discernible, linked to the Dutch Creole once prevalent in the Virgin Islands, and numerous other languages overlapping during the Danish colonial era and subsequent to that period. This project affirms its existence and advocates for its recognition and uncompromising and unapologetic promotion as a viable language of the United States Virgin Islands.

United States Virgin Islands Creole is sufficiently distinct in its structure, unique vocabulary, and syntactic arrangement to be classified as a language and not just some alleged vulgarization or bastardization of American English. I am intrigued by the goal of CEDAGR[12] in France, the French acronym for *Center for Solidarity and Study of Antilleans, Guyanese, and Reunion Islanders.* This association is committed to eradicating prejudices against Creole languages spoken in France, and advocates for their official recognition. The organization's position is unequivocal and well-affirmed:

> Speaking Creole is a fundamental part of who we are...
> Our goal is to put an end to the subordination of Creole

to other languages, including French and to show that it can be used in all contexts (Beriss 124).

If in the United States Virgin Islands we can arrive at this level of social and linguistic consciousness, we will undoubtedly begin a process of unseating long-held negative sentiments with respect to the Creole spoken in our territory.

Virgin Islands Creole if nothing else is a *language* that is quite performative, and, yes, we are speaking here of a language, and not of a "*mere dialect*"— this should not be such a radical, nor revolutionary position. Yet, I concede that I am entering into a bruising battle of interpretation with respect to these two notions, and their overlapping points of convergence and inherent contradictions. Nonetheless, I am not at all hesitant to confront this issue. The linguist Francisco Moreno Fernández acknowledges the challenge of separating the two concepts positing that "the definitions that have been proposed with respect to the concepts of 'language' and 'dialect' have been numerous and diverse. From a strictly linguistic point of view there is no evidence to justify the distinction between language and dialect" (Fernández 86)[13][my translation]. Probably the challenge of legitimating the concept of "dialect" is "the difficulty of marking the boundaries" (Fernández 87)[14][my translation]. This notwithstanding, however, Moreno Fernández references the highly respected and prolific Spanish philologist, sociolinguist, and dialectologist Manuel Alvar López in trying to achieve a working distinction between the two notions. Alvar López views <language> as "a linguistic system on which a speech community relies and is characterized by being markedly differentiated...by being of an important literary tradition... and on occasions having imposed linguistic systems from its own origin" (Fernández 88)[my translation].[15]

By contrast <dialect> is defined as "a system of signs that have been ruptured from a common language, active, or extinct, normally with a concrete geographical demarcation, but without a strong differentiation from other signs of the same origin" (Fernández 88)[my translation].[16] The fundamental truth is that these are concepts that are superimposed. No wonder R.A. Hudson asks the basic question, "What then is the difference, for English speakers, between a language and a dialect?

There are two separate ways of distinguishing them ["language" and "dialect"] and this ambiguity is a source of great confusion...on one hand, there is a difference of size, because a language is larger than a dialect...The other contrast between 'language' and 'dialect' is a question of prestige, a language having prestige which a dialect lacks" (Hudson 31-32). Too often we became enamored with the idea of status and prestige and thus categorize modes of speech according to our own ideological positioning.

I do not mean to infer that the term "dialect" is somehow inherently a pejorative term. I am especially intrigued by Moreno Fernández's response to the issue—"language" vs "dialect." As noted before, his position is that from the point of view of linguists, there is no real distinction. He does acknowledge, however that depending on the language in question, the interpretation of what is <dialect> may vary greatly. For example, this critic recognizes that in English sometimes the word <dialect> "*could* [emphasis mine] be equivalent to *sub-standard* or *non-standard*"[17] (Fernández 86) [my translation]. In this light, when the notion "dialect" is referenced in the context of the English language and Virgin Islands Creole, the local parlance is often seen by some as merely an obscene derivative of English. And, in point of fact, in the minds of too many, the notion of "dialect" simply becomes transformed into a dismissive terminology. As Hudson rightly observes: "It is part of our culture to make a distinction between 'languages' and 'dialect' " (Hudson 31). Moreover, Hudson emphasizes, "there is nothing absolute about the distinction which English happens to make between 'languages' and 'dialects.'"

In the larger sense, I know that when we speak of a "language" we think of a system that is institutionalized, supported, for example, by governmental and social structures in a community. Inherent in this are not only socio-political implications, but also the inference of the "natural" or "logical" subalternity (with exceptions in some societies) of that speech that varies from the established, "official" and "authorized" standard of speech. Virgin Islands Creole clearly represents that type of speech variety that goes against the grain, being as it is, far removed from so-called "normalization" and "standardization." Yet, as we will see later, it has its own structure and its grammatical rules, just like the "Standard language" has its particular linguistic nomenclature.

In view of the ambiguity and ambivalence of the two notions my primary thrust is to take a stance against the routine and categorical condemnation and prevailing mischaracterizations of the way we speak in the United States Virgin Islands, a mode of articulation that has been under attack for many years. The idea of Virgin Islands speech as "substandard" or "primitive" is an unmitigated misnomer crafted in an ideology of superiority and inferiority. My refusal to employ the term "*dialect*" in relationship to our Creole is NOT because I consider the notion inapplicable to our way of speaking, but more as a counter ideological stance against a predominant ideology that recasts "dialect" as somehow "perverse," while privileging "language" as legitimate. Opting for the term "language" is my way of affirming our own linguistic space, and challenging the idea of "*dialect*" as being subordinated to a more standard variety.

Language itself, the notable linguist Ferdinand de Saussure affirms, is "a system of interdependent terms in which the value of each term results from the simultaneous presence of the others" (Saussure 9). We also know that individual languages are interdependent in the sense that they are nurtured and filtered through other languages. Yet, at some point, in spite of the similarities and points of contacts, each language has its particularity and its level of independence. Analogous to this is the fact that Children are dependently tied to their parents and to others in society, but they still eventually learn to navigate life as independent, separate beings. When we argue that the Creole of the United States Virgin Islands is an independent language, this does not mean to infer that speakers of Creole do not use English words and expressions. We know this to be a given, and to pretend that United States Virgin Islands Creole and English are somehow unequivocally disjointed would be at best vain and ludicrous posturing.

SO-CALLED LANGUAGE PROBLEM

In part, our "language problem" stems from the confusing understanding, or perhaps misunderstanding, of what truly constitutes the debate on Virgin Islands Creole. Often those who engage in discussions on our language do so without clearly identifying the parameters of the debate. In this regard, for example, there are those whose mission is "*to teach others the correct mode of English speech.*" Simultaneously, however, the notion to "correct," itself rests on an unstable premise. The axiomatic declaration embedded in the process of "correcting" is tied to an English language seen as privileged. I am yet to hear a person "correcting" another for speaking "*incorrect Virgin Islands Creole.*" The reason for this is simple: The notion of "*incorrect*" intuitively assumes that there is an established standard that is acceptable; it implies axiomatic legitimacy of that standard.

The problem is that for too many of us the Creole itself as a mode of communication is considered "incorrect;" it is seen as an inarticulate variety and hence invariably "inappropriate." Therefore, for this group, debates surrounding Virgin Islands Creole tend to center themselves around judgment on pronunciation and grammatical patterns as linked to the rules of English, principally "American English." The debates need to shift to the process of assessing and evaluating our Creole as an independent entity, in order to ensure its viability and its sustainability. If someone were to argue that the Creolized question, "*Way pa' dem boys garn?*" is wrong, the response to this critique should depend on what the critic means by "wrong." If the argument is that the statement violates rules of English grammar and morphology (if an individual is speaking English), there can be no serious challenge, nor objection, to such a contention.

9

The criticism of the Creole begins with and proceeds from the assumption that the "official" *language* of the United States Virgin Islands is in fact only English. But if the basic premise is interrogated, then an opponent would be formulating a counter ideological position that would challenge the stated position of the critic. Hence, the counter position would be advocating for a kind of linguistic independence, a position that affirms the legitimacy of the Creole as the default language[18] of the United States Virgin Islands. It would simultaneously accentuate the importance of our Virgin Islands language as part of our cultural identification.

In his insightful work on the question as to whether English should ever be used as the medium of communication in production of literary works by African authors, Ngũgĩ wa Thiong'o rightly contends:

> The choice of language and the use to which language is put is central to a people's definition of themselves in relation to their natural and social environment, indeed in relation to the entire universe" (Thiong'o 4).

This critic's observation is on target, for indeed language is at the epicenter of who we are as Virgin Islanders in the broader, more encompassing Caribbean and West Indian context. Privileging our Creole would be an affirmative sign that we recognize its substantive socio-cultural and linguistic legacy. It is worth emphasizing Thiong'o's cogent commentary that "[l]language is the collective memory bank of a people's experience in history. Culture is indistinguishable from the language that makes possible its genesis, growth, banking, articulation, and indeed its transmission from one generation to the next" (Thiong'o 15).

"Language is such a great instrument of communication" posits the great Spanish linguist Rafael Seco, that it is now a point of discussion as to whether language was born out of society, or if in fact that society resulted from language.[19] (my translation). Unquestionably, culture is revealed through language, and simultaneously is complicit in its production and evolution.

No one would deny that some of what we say in the Creole of the United States Virgin Islands would be understood by speakers of English since in point of fact we employ some vocabulary and morphological, and syntactical patterns characteristic of that language. At the same time, however, most of what we articulate and the manner in which we do so would be beyond the reach of comprehension for English speakers unfamiliar with our Creole. An analogous situation is that of Spanish and Portuguese. Consider the fact that a knowledgeable speaker of Spanish (with no independent knowledge of Portuguese) would *at times* be able to communicate with a speaker of Portuguese, whether that person is from Bahia, Lisbon, or Mozambique. Conversely, a person adept at Portuguese (with no independent knowledge of Spanish) should be able to engage in a conversation with another who is speaking Spanish, whether that individual is from Puerto Rico, Spain, Costa Rica or Equatorial Guinea.[20] The main challenge would be for the speaker of Portuguese or Spanish to proficiently express his or her thoughts using the other person's target language. Certainly, there are many expressions of one target language that would be unintelligible for the speaker of the other language, and vice versa.

The truth is that even though Portuguese and Spanish share many words, there are also numerous words and expressions that are markedly different in these two languages. Both, for example, share the following words: *casa (house), comer (to eat), ver (to see)*, and many others. On the other hand, there are many words that are dissimilar. Hence, whereas aural skills may enable each communicator to understand the other with varying levels of inconvenience, spoken articulation would often prove to be more difficult, operating within a sphere of linguistic guesswork. A parallel observation can be made with respect to American English, for example, and United States Virgin Islands Creole. While there is no denying the shared words, there are countless disparate expressions that would present formidable linguistic hurdles for the English speaker unfamiliar with Virgin Islands Creole. That individual would not know in all cases what constitute the shared words and expressions in both languages, and what the points of divergence are. Undoubtedly, U.S.V.I. Creole with its blend of English and local parlance will present linguistics obstacles for those not sufficiently exposed to the language.

In effect, the speaker of English (the person unfamiliar with Virgin Islands Creole) could easily become confused, and perhaps even frustrated, as that person tries to navigate the grammatical and social nuances of our Creole. Compounding this is the fact that in our islands there is a considerable amount of code switching[21] between American English and Virgin Islands Creole, a process that is not at all surprising. Most Virgin Islanders do this with impunity, even though I suspect that for some residents the switch may not be as natural or as fluid. To borrow W.E.B. Dubois' insightful terminology and apply it liberally here, we possess a kind of "double consciousness," in a sense straddling two worlds.[22] Within this conflated linguistic paradigm Virgin Islands Creole needs to be honored as it represents a major marker of the islands traditional and cultural DNA.

ENGLISH "GONE BAD?"

A crucial question is: Can infractions themselves result in a new mode of communication that in some ways may resemble English, but in more significant ways be a departure from it morphologically and syntactically? An examination of the Creole spoken in the United States Virgin Islands would quickly confirm that this in fact has been the reality. I find the prolific critic, Noam Chomsky's postulation to be especially relevant here, as he discusses what he terms language performance: "A record of natural speech will show numerous false starts, deviations from the rules, changes of plan in mid-course, and so-on" (Chomsky 40). There is no question, as James and Lesley Milroy argue, "that non-standard forms are not simply debased variants of standards and that they can be shown to be 'grammatical' in their own terms" (Milroy 7). Language is not pre-packaged or pre-arranged, hence our Virgin Islands Creole did not follow a linear trail in its evolution and development. How we arrive at those words and expressions—trial and error, derivation, chance, linguistic osmosis, missteps etc.—is always relevant, but the means cannot, nor must not undermine the importance of the end.

In essence, I reject the posture of those within and without our community who summarily dismiss many of our words and expressions as simply "*bad pronunciation and bad English structure.*" But even if we were to concede to such an accusation, I would argue that the consistent and fixed usage of particular words and phrases in our speech over time makes them self-sustaining and legitimate modes of articulation. In essence, then, the Virgin Islands Creole word, "*tarmon,*" is a separate word from the English "tamarind," just like "*coisa*" in Portuguese and "cosa" in Spanish are different words even though they may signal the same referent.

Similarly, the Portuguese "*livro*" and the Spanish "*libro*" may refer to the same object, but are different morphemes. Therefore, I am comfortable in asserting, that the English word "tamarind" is a translation of "*tarmon*," a deliberate inversion that speaks to the legitimacy of our own denomination of the fruit.

The reality is that *tarmon*, and *ponguana* for that matter, are linguistic reflections of our cultural realities. Even though both speaker and listener may be familiar with the English word "*tamarind*," it would be most unnatural to say, for example, "*stewed tamarind*," (or *tamarind stew!*) despite the fact that this may be conveying the same image. Such an expression would be forced, pretentious, and patently artificial in the Virgin Islands context. This is not to contend that no one ever says it; but such a pronouncement, at least at that moment of articulation, would signal a means of communication not emblematic of Virgin Islands Creole. As is the case with "*tarmon*," the persistent usage of the word "*ponguana*" over decades signals a clear creolization that defies the simplistic classification of "*mis pronunciation*" of the word *pomegranate*.

The Virgin Islands word, *Ponguana*, born out of the socio-cultural milieu of our islands, is now deeply embedded in our linguistic tradition. Hence, the word *pomegranate* essentially is the English translation of our Creole word (*ponguana*), and not the so-called "corrected" spelling of that word. The frequent assertion that Virgin Islands Creole is nothing more than English "gone bad" is not only an overreaction, but also an unsubstantiated generalization. Opting to use the word "*ponguana*" results from our linguistic socialization over a protracted time period and reflects a part of the firm establishment of a rich Virgin Islands linguistic tapestry. The notion that the local language is primarily a system of grammatical and pronunciation mistakes ignores the existence of numerous words, expressions, and grammatical patterns that are barely tangential to English usage.

Against this backdrop, when we think of an expression such as "*so' foot*," for example, (See this expression later in the individual entries) we see it as one that through various generations has attained its own particular and peculiar character, very much like "*tarmon*" and "*ponguana*" cited earlier. The expression is so creolized that the use of the English word "*sore*" would sound non-authentic in our islands if someone were to use it in describing an individual's physical condition. Hence, the expression,

"*He is ah so' foot man*" has a connotation that extends well beyond the English rendition - -"*He has a sore foot.*" In the first place, in Virgin Islands Creole the reference to "*foot*" may not even necessarily be a reference to this particular part of the individual's anatomy. In fact, it may well be an allusion to the person's leg. Significantly, however, no one would say in Virgin Islands Creole, "*So' leg man!*" Hence the entire expression, "*so' foot,*" has a much localized uniqueness. Secondly, and equally important, is that taken in its entirety, the coinage, "*so' foot*" is used as an adjective in Virgin Islands Creole. Think of the peculiarity of the construction!

The word "sore" in English is itself an adjective and "foot" is a noun. When combined in Virgin Islands Creole with "self," the expression "*so' foot*" is uniquely adjectival, "*so' foot self.*" Of course, in Virgin Islands Creole one can also say, "*He geh ah so' foot.*" In this case, the English *grammatical structure* dominates, i.e. in our Creole, "*foot*" is a noun modified by "*so.*'" In English, however, there is no adjectival equivalence to the Creolized expression "*so' foot*;" for example, no one would say in "standard" English: "*He is a sore foot man.*" It is not only an ungrammatical and unnatural utterance to the English speaker, but would be equally culturally unintelligible.

There are many who contend that Virgin Islands Creole represents a kind of language corruption achieved over time, and they point to a persistent lack of education, or miseducation as the underlying cause of a kind of contrived intergenerational tragedy. Those detractors maintain that we are dealing primarily with a type of linguistic barbarism that needs to be confronted in order to rescue American speech, to restore it to its level of "authenticity." After all, these pundits contend, we are American territories. They maintain that we should be no different than the various states, even though the same people unquestionably accept the political differences, for example, the fact that United States Virgin Islanders are not allowed to participate in the national electoral process.[23] With regard to language, however, they staunchly abhor and denounce the reality that our speech patterns vary significantly from that of the contiguous states. As citizens of the United States of America we need to "sound like Americans," would be a typical argument framed by some.

Unfortunately also, there are even those who expend much energy trying to change their speech patterns. Some people once they leave the

United States Virgin Islands vow consciously, or maybe even subconsciously, never again to speak like a Virgin Islander and feel fortunate and privileged if told: *"You do not sound like a St. Johnian, Crucian, nor St. Thomian."* For some, this is the supreme compliment for what they may perceive as the ultimate measuring stick of assimilation and confirms their transformation in the process of becoming a "complete American."[24] If a United States Virgin Islander's only sense of nationalistic identity is in relationship to the United States mainland, then the attainment of a local consciousness becomes highly problematized. The idea of a "national" identity must include a sense of connection to the local culture and traditions of the islands, a kind of reconfiguration of the notion of "nationalistic identity" that has as its center these islands geographical location—in the Caribbean, in the West Indies.

There are those who are even reluctant to employ the terminology, United States *Virgin Islands Creole,* patently rejecting this concept. In other words, there is a detectable level of discomfort and hesitancy in embracing the very notion of the way we speak as "a language." It would be as if they were "condoning" and "authenticating" a pattern of speech that should not be encouraged, but rather "corrected." Rather than subscribe to the use of the word "Creole," they would readily accept the term "dialect" as an appropriate and more palatable substitute. Then, there are many traditionalists, or in some cases purists, who see the local mode of communication only in relationship to American English. Hence, for them, Virgin Islands Creole is seen as a violation of the established morphological and syntactic rules and norms associated with so-called *"Standard American English"* linguistic models. They are quick to apply the "deficient" label to the Creole speaker, a brand that intrinsically calls into question the individual's ability to manage the English language. But what happens if we challenge or reject the premise that suggests "violation," "infraction," and "breaking" of the rules? Then at that point we would be unraveling that linguistic space of prohibition in our contestatory quest to affirm our language viability and legitimacy. There is a site of contention that allows for constant challenges of the various anti-Virgin Islands Creole sentiments, and the incessant uneasiness and protestation even against the mere appropriation of the terminology, *United States Virgin Islands <u>Creole</u>.*

The idea that we are merely speaking a defective brand of American English when we speak Virgin Islands Creole is one that flies against our linguistic realities- - the confluence of multiple African and European languages operating in our sphere over a prolong period of time in our history. Words are not the only evidence of language borrowing; there are also inflection, gestures, intonation, and other components that have been passed down to us from the prevalent multilingual and multicultural Virgin Islands societies of previous centuries. Unquestionably, "language …has a dual character; it is both a means of communication and a carrier of culture," (Thiong'o 13), an important point missed by too many critics of our Creole.

If we conveniently choose to ignore our history, or in fact choose to falsify it, then we would be forcing ourselves to accept no other recourse but the various negative categorizations of the way we speak in United States Virgin Islands. In essence, we would be transforming ourselves into partisans of scurrilous attacks aimed at Virgin Islands Creole, while simultaneously becoming resigned to our categorization as *"Violators of the English language."* Critics would continue to ignore Virgin Islands traditions, culture, and customs and set up their own systems of "comparative languages," hence judging the islands for what they would consider to be language inadequacies and shortcomings.

There are those who would cringe whenever there is a breakdown in communication and bow their heads in apologetic shame because of what they may perceive as a linguistic barrier created by the Virgin Islander himself, or herself. After all, they would argue, he or she is the one who refuses (or is incapable) to subscribe to the tenets of the English language, and hence is primarily responsible for the failed communication. Naturally, because for many critics "American English" is in fact the default, Virgin Islands Creole in their judgment can only fall short of the "appropriate" measuring stick. When this position is invoked as a kind of counter response to the argument for legitimacy of Virgin Islands Creole, many of us recoil in our world of concession, convinced by the linguistic antagonists that we have suffered generations of language miseducation.

We begin to echo with regularity and without hesitancy the "broken English" characterization. I have heard it countless times- - a Virgin Islander residing on the United States mainland is asked, for example:

"Do you speak English in the United States Virgin Islands?" The answer is often a qualified one: *"Yes, but we speak broken English, jus' a dialect."* There is an immediate false equivalence made with this formulaic response, i.e. *"Virgin Islands dialect= broken English."* In accepting and regurgitating the antagonists' posture, we subconsciously (sometimes even consciously and very deliberately) then set in motion strategies to "better ourselves," to "correct the way how we speak," to reconfigure our speech patterns; in effect, to begin to recognize ourselves as linguistically fractured—we become complicit in the process of our own linguistic disfigurement. This response reflects how ideology functions at its very best. It is precisely at this juncture of concession that the socio-linguistic acrimony is born and nurtured.

Language acquisition falls within a complex system of communication that includes, among other features, hearing, listening, speaking, comprehension, mimicry, and retention. Members of the same language community have acquired the skills necessary to communicate with others within the particular community, largely through a pattern of repetition and imitation. Indeed, there is a kind of familiarity arising from constant contact with the group members, and the resulting modes of communication reflect the level of linguistic consent. As a whole, the United States Virgin Islands boast a high population density, and as acknowledged previously, within this demographic framework various languages and accents co-exist. But contrary to some alarmists, this social and sociological phenomenon does not corrupt, contaminate nor defile what we know as Virgin Islands Creole.

Can we speak of alteration or modification of the language? Certainly, such eventuality is normal. Hence, trying to forestall external linguistic influence is tantamount to attempting to curtail our perennial trade winds from blowing. So the fight is not (or should never be) a blind resistance against outside influences on United States Virgin Islands Creole, but rather against any calculated effort to discount the validity of that language itself. The struggle is not to try to maintain the language as static; this would be a useless goal, because we can only do so much to preserve a language intact since it is constantly exposed to a variety of socioeconomic, and other catalytic factors. Any expectation of maintaining the "purity" of any language is illusionary, and any such aim would be encased in mythical dreams. The major battle, as I see it, is to bring people out of the shadows; convince them of the importance of fighting to establish the right to language legitimacy. Even though many may not recognize it as such, it is a civil rights issue, as well as a humane and ethical one. Perhaps over a period of time such a struggle *could* be embraced by subsequent generations that just might be seeking ways to authenticate themselves. I am optimistically referring to those who in the future would feel a need to connect with a culture that in some ways might have been lost to them. I emphasize "could" because the effort would have to be a monumental one. Later on, I offer some thoughts that could serve as a basis for the fight for the legitimation of our Creole.

We readily acknowledge here that the evolution of language and speech is a natural process tied to such realities as immigration, emigration, economics, and politics. Hence, our changing Virgin Islands Creole *in part* is due to this naturalness of the shifting patterns of language interconnected with these realities. Students of modern Spanish would often hardly recognize some medieval Spanish words and phrases; similarly, students of present day English may well struggle with some aspects of Chaucerian English. This is so because of the changes over the years that are connected to social, historical and cultural currents. In a similar vein, U.S.V.I. Creole has been transformed over the years with the loss of words and expressions and the acquisition of others. Consider the fact that the American English vernacular is now replete with words and phrases not even heard 10, or even 5 years ago. This is partially because of the rapidly changing technological world. For example, the internet with its unique and specialized vocabulary has imposed itself on the global community, generating words and permutation of words that have become embedded in the fabric of the English language, as well as in that of Virgin Islands Creole. If culture is never static, then it follows that language, itself a subset of culture—or itself culture— can also never be classified as immutable. Admittedly, I am operating within a kind of schizophrenic paradigm in which I welcome the natural evolution of language, but still yearn nostalgically for those oral elaborations of the United States Virgin Islands Creole of yesteryear.

During the first decade of the 20th century my Nevisian grandmother, Mary Moving Barrow, and her cohorts brought to Grove Place, and to

St. Croix in general, a pattern of speech that was in many ways uniquely Nevisian. I often recall my numerous exchanges with her and the special manner in which she articulated and narrated stories. The fact is, language becomes even more enriched through its interweaving and interlocking mode, its communication with other cultures and traditions. That has certainly been the case between American English and the Creole of the United States Virgin Islands. Simultaneously, and unfortunately, however, a large portion of the struggle to legitimate Virgin Islands Creole has been the fight against a linguistic patrol that charged us with various language crimes and confiscated our will to utter and translate our morays and unique experiences through our own mode of articulation. The arrest left little room for rehabilitation as we were summarily sentenced to a life of *de facto* language censorship and its subsequent humiliation.

VIRGIN ISLANDS CREOLE: A CASE FOR LEGITIMACY

Ultimately, the "problem" with Virgin Islands Creole does not lie in the language itself, but in the negative projected images associated with it. For example, there has been a perennial insistence on the "rawness," or the "broadness," or the "wrongness" of Virgin Islands Creole.[25] Such characterizations speak for themselves and give us a sense of the depth of rejection in some quarters. Interestingly, though, the language does not need to be revamped, nor rehabilitated. Primarily, it begs for its articulators to extend our arms and welcome it to the community of legitimate languages within the wider global society of communicators. In a sense, we have a monumental task principally because it is irrevocably linked to a need for systemic attitudinal changes.

Our Virgin Islands language not only signals our geographical position, but also through its various configurations over the years signifies us as an ever evolving community. It is a component of what Yara Yosso introduces in her valuable study as "community capital wealth" (Yosso 70). In the context of United States Virgin Islands Creole, this refers to the cultural and social capital gained and shared over the years through communication in the local language. Yosso's use of the term "linguistic capital"[26] as one aspect of cultural wealth is applicable to the United States Virgin Islands where English and Virgin Islands Creole continue to jockey for space in the social and cultural sphere.

In any time frame where ideology raises its divisive head, challenges surmount and solutions are naturally more protracted. If someone were to say, *"Deh people dem gon come wen dey don fini*sh," they would be uttering a very creolized sentence, made even more complex in its oral utterance because of its localized intonation, inflection, and accentuation. The person unfamiliar with United States Virgin Islands Creole might do an analysis that would render the sentence as patently nonsensical. But, this simple creolized sentence is infused with three distinct grammatical structures that highlight its peculiarity: 1) *people dem*—the word "people" is already pluralized, but is nonetheless reinforced by "*dem*," a kind of quantifier that gives it redundancy (This is discussed in more detail under the section on pluralization). 2) *Gon come*—an expression that indicates a future moment, commonly used in place of "will." 3) *don finish*— an expression that exaggerates a result.

The English statements, "*I am done*" and "*I am finished*," essentially express the same basic fact. When these two notions are hinged together in United States Virgin Islands Creole, the resulting redundant nature of the sentence achieves a heightened level of emphasis and peculiarity. Of course, the words are easily recognizable as common English words, but what happens when words are linked together in a seemingly "illogical manner"? In the case given here, the expression "*people dem*" is a construction that is uniquely local. Moreover, the idea of "*don*" and "*finish*" as consecutive words in the syntactic order goes against established syntactical norms in English. Yet, for the listener intimately familiar with our Creole the meaning is unmistakable. In effect, what to the English speaker may seem most irregular and dysfunctional, in our Creole comes across as emphatically normalized. The three features cited underscore how distinctive grammatical structures often are in Virgin Islands Creole. (More on grammar in a later section).

I sense that there will always be a number of Virgin Islanders who will probably never adjust to the idea of United States Virgin Islands Creole as an acceptable mode of speech, except under rare circumstances, for example in informal gathering. Then, there are those who are even more extreme in their views, and for them the idea of Creole as a category of languages in the United States Virgin Islands should never be seriously entertained. They are absolutists in their stance and often emit a kind of acquiescent attitude with respect to what they consider "correct English." Moreover, there is a rather fawning disposition when referencing American English. And even though they understand and can speak Virgin Islands Creole, many in this group ostensibly feign that they do not, and are even offended if someone were audacious enough to speak to them using that medium.

The feeling of being offended results when we assign primacy to English, declaring *"that it is the official and only language of the United States Virgin Islands."* Such advocacy negates the recognition of the existence of a second Virgin Islands language. If we subscribe to this type of philosophy, then we will consistently believe a ubiquitous myth promulgated in our community for far too many years. Some detractors in the Virgin Islands wage war against any meaningful attempt to elevate the stature of the language. It is clear that they miss an important point—there is no contradiction inherent in the acquisition of two related, yet distinct languages. The task of convincing this group is a challenging one because its members do not stray too far from the premise of "appropriateness" (or "inappropriateness") of languages. Or perhaps more accurately, they do not stray from their own interpretation of what "appropriateness" portends.

When we speak of "appropriateness" of the language this must never be confused with "rightness" or "wrongness." As I see it, the idea of whether an utterance is "appropriate" or not should only be linked to the idea of effective communication. If an individual utters a word or expression in Virgin Islands Creole and is told that the utterance is inappropriate, such a rebuff might be interpreted as a verbal rebuke or reprimand for incorrect speech. The use of the word *"appropriate"* should infer that there exists a community of language speakers who are able to follow the conversation and participate in meaningful communicative exchanges. In effect, the *utilization* of Virgin Islands Creole should be considered *inappropriate*[27] *(not appropriate)* primarily if the Creole speaker is using the language to communicate with someone unfamiliar with it and who is, therefore, incapable of following the vocabulary, syntax and nuances of the thoughts being expressed. *The Creole language itself, however, must never be deemed or judged as inappropriate.*

Language does not emanate from knowledgeable linguists sitting in some ivory tower formulating arbitrary rules; in point of fact, "the bond between the sound and the idea is radically arbitrary…the community is necessary…" (Saussure 8). Moreover, this critic attests, "[w]ithout language thought is a vague, unchartered nebula. There are no pre-existing ideas, and nothing is distinct before the appearance of language" (Saussure 7). In fact, argues Saussure, "if words stood for pre-existing concepts, they would all have the exact equivalents from one language to the next" (Saussure 10). To be sure, the Virgin Islander does not express himself/herself in the same manner as a mainland American, not as a Trinidadian, nor as a Guyanese. There are many socio-cultural factors that guarantee significantly marked differences. Rules themselves are born out of empirical oral realities. At some point later linguists, etymologists, philologists, dialectologists, grammarians and others are able to recognize, decipher, and compile the rules within the established system of speech. Infractions themselves often become interwoven in the fabric of a language becoming normalized in the well-established patterns of that language. Henry Louis Gates cites Mikhail Bakhtin in the opening of Gates' groundbreaking work, Race, Writing and Difference, a quotation worth co-opting here:

> Language, for the individual consciousness, lies on the borderline
> between oneself and the other. The word in language is half someone
> else's. It becomes "one's own" only when the speaker populates it with
> his own intention, his own accent, when he appropriates the word,
> adapting it to his own semantic and expressive intention. Prior to this
> moment of appropriation, the word does not exist in a neutral and
> impersonal language.. (Gates 1)

The pervasive internal battles of how to speak, or how *not* to speak continue to characterize, or perhaps more accurately, mischaracterize us. In reality, questions of language inadequacy and incompetence have always been at the forefront of discussions of U.S. Virgin Islands Creole. For many, this created a subliminal mode of self-consciousness with respect to our accent, pronunciation, and word choices. For example, it is not at all uncommon to hear some Virgin Islanders residing on the United States mainland express their reluctance to speak publicly for fear that someone might laugh at, or otherwise belittle their accent. This self-deprecating stance, social uneasiness, and awkwardness could only result from subtle lessons learned over time. If past language censorship had not occurred, then the United States Virgin Islander living abroad would communicate instinctively without fear of questions regarding the validity of Virgin

Islands Creole and with the unmitigated confidence in our local mode of communication. This clearly is not the case for some.

To many people, the mere suggestion that our Creole be considered in the same vein as the English language is blatantly blasphemous and even seditious. Even the most cursory glance at our history would shed light on why this has been the case. Traditionally, the speaking of "standard" English was associated with status and upward socio-economic mobility, and conversely far too often people were branded as "lower class" and "ignorant" when they spoke primarily in Virgin Islands Creole. In essence, they purportedly suffered from the "Broken English Syndrome." Thus, any attempt to equate the two languages was also seen by many as quite audacious. This tendency toward value judgment persists today as too many of us continue to relegate Virgin Islands Creole to a secondary status.

The idea that there was (is) some inherent relationship between the utilization of "*standard English*" and intelligence is patently baseless. This was, and continues to be a contrived association and concocted deduction that undoubtedly resulted from a perverted ideology. Similarly, there exists absolutely no relationship between the speaking of our *Creole language* and ignorance. Frequently, being categorized as one who could only communicate in Creole created socio-economic obstacles and limitations principally for the individual who fell in that category. That person was too often prejudged. The unspoken, false association between language utterance and one's behavior was a prevalent way of falsely branding and characterizing Virgin Islanders. There is no question that vestiges of this negativity still overshadow our linguistic reality.

I look at St. Martin with much admiration as there are many people on that island who speak not only French or Dutch, but English and Papiamentu as well. In fact, there are others that, in addition to all this, speak Spanish fluently. Undoubtedly, the island has to make a constant effort to ensure that it preserves its linguistic legacy. Their challenge in some ways is similar to that of the United States Virgin Islands— how do you encourage your residents to "hold on" to their language in the face of globalization and massive international social and economic upheavals? At the same time there is a unique situation in St. Martin, dealing as it were with two nations sharing one small geographic space. Hence, the task is compounded by the nationalistic divergence encased within one island.

But, my sense is that in spite of the complicated nationalistic/political arrangement,[28] St. Martin and other areas are intent on preserving their linguistic heritage. This begs the question, why are we in the U.S. Virgin sometimes so hesitant and even fearful to embrace our Creole?

Throughout this work the intersection of various Creole languages will be evident; in other words, there are patterns of speech that coincide with that from many other regions of the West Indies and the Caribbean. Chomsky's citation of James Beattie in his <u>Theory of Language</u> highlights this natural sharing of languages:

> James Beattie remarks that 'Languages, therefore resemble men in this respect, that, though each has peculiarities, whereby it is distinguished from every other, yet all have certain qualities in common. The peculiarities of Individual tongues are explained in their respective grammars and dictionaries (Chomsky 41)

As referenced earlier, I am a proud product of my Nevisian grandmother, and my speech has been influenced by her in ways that I cannot even begin to quantify. Mine is a story that is prevalently replicated throughout the United States Virgin Islands. I vividly recall her blend of Nevisian and Crucian expressions, a juxtaposition that was far beyond the capacity of a young boy to grasp. So that arguing for a Virgin Islands Creole does not preclude the concession of points of contact with forms of speech on other islands. In fact, underlying my argument is an acknowledgement of the existing commonalities between our various West Indian Creoles. Perhaps one day we can begin to think of **a** "West Indian language," maybe "speaking in West Indian," an imagined linguistic discursive practice with its infinite variations. That argument would open a theorizing space for a linguistic, ideological, and philosophical project that would very well be a point of contention among scholars for time to come. That is certainly far beyond the scope of the present work.

In much the same way as we can speak of "British" and "American" English as similar, yet distinct, so too can we speak of various West Indian Creole languages and Virgin Islands Creole as overlapping, yet diverging patterns of speech. Commonalities notwithstanding, we realize that different historical and social moments have converged to carve distinctively unique oral elaborations in various countries of the West Indies. Affirming a Virgin Islands language is not a mutually exclusive position from the recognition of the fact that ours is also a West Indian Creole, emanating from the various cultural and historical wells of our Caribbean. In fact, we speak here of the Virgin Islands of the United States, but we are part of an extensive island chain that includes our neighboring islands—the British Virgin Islands. The Virgin Islands, American and British, are inextricably and irrevocably tied through our histories, families, traditions, and customs, in essence, our cultures. There is no question, however, that residents under both nationalities would essentially draw the same conclusion: *we recognize the intersectionalities, but each still has its distinctive mode of speech.*

It is also true that the United States Virgin Islands owe some of their linguistic evolution to many other islands of the leeward and Windward Islands chain. In essence, our language is constantly being nourished by the springs of West Indian philosophies and ever changing social, political and economic realities. Any Language undergoes a natural metamorphosis when coming in contact with others; it cannot be frozen in time. All this notwithstanding, the fact is that that U.S. Virgin Islands have followed their unique historical pathways and contours, entangled with the Dutch, Spanish, French, British, Irish, Danish, American milieu[29] and of course, various African patronages. Indeed, the fact that some words and expressions uttered in the U.S. Virgin Islands are also popular in St. Kitts, St. Martin, Antigua, Trinidad, or Nevis does not negate their particularities and applicability in the U.S. Virgin Islands context. The reverse is also true, that a United States Virgin Islander cannot discount the localized application of words or phrases commonly heard in the islands mentioned above, and others, simply because one might be familiar with some of the same phrases in the United States Virgin Islands. It would be outright social and linguistic perjury to assert that U.S. Virgin Islanders speak the Creole of Jamaica, or that in Barbados they also speak Virgin Islands Creole. Such ludicrous assertions would fly in the face of common sense and the linguistic realities.

VIRGIN ISLANDS LANGUAGE—
THE STRUGGLE AGAINST DECREOLIZATION

For many years now I have heard the complaints of U.S. Virgin Islanders that "in the Virgin Islands we are losing our mode of speech." Underlying that fear, they insist, is the greater, far more ghastly truth— that we are losing ourselves. This thinking has been part of the prevailing narrative for many years, and people are quick to conclude that this "colossal loss" is due to population shifts, migration, and economic influences, among other variables. As noted earlier, language naturally responds to these mitigating factors and many others. This is a universal constant. But while we are readily inclined to accept the role of some social determinants, we tend to exclude another important reality: our own complicity. In some ways we were, (and in fact continue to be) unindicted coconspirators who genuflected obsequiously to the sanctimonious acrimony of a kind of unofficial linguistic surveillance patrol, as referenced in the previous section. We bowed our heads in shame as they passed the sentence of *DEFICIENT LANGUAGE*, and we became branded from one generation to another. As a result, we have struggled perennially trying to accommodate ourselves to our Virgin Islands Creole, and have continued to question its legitimacy.

Why do we no longer utter certain words and expressions? Many of them were, I believe, banned and outlawed by the guardians of linguistic elaboration and so-called cultural "purity"—and all done as most of us stood silent. They regularly inveighed against Virgin Islands Creole, spewing their venom. Among family and close friends we articulated our ideas, sentiments, exchange jokes, adages, and beliefs using our Creole as the target language, but were at times discouraged from its use in the broader public sphere. This resulted sometimes in a kind of negative self-consciousness and sensitivity when we spoke. As indicated earlier, many saw and still now envision United States Creole as a restricted language without the range of engagement inherently expected in Standard English.

The capricious classification of languages as "beautiful," "harsh," "complicated," "strange," or "ugly" is purely subjective and ideological, and we must proceed from that basic truth in order to comprehend what has happened in our Virgin Islands community. There is nothing innate about language; there is a kind of indifference associated with it that dispels the idea of some inherent "goodness" or "badness." Furthermore, contrary to what some might argue, there is no language "better" or "more worthy" than another. It is pure mythical fabrication that the so-called Shakespearean English is the "best" or "most correct" English. With respect to our islands, there were those who walked the beat, and in fact some continue to do so, delegitimizing Virgin Islands speech patterns: *"Learn to speak the American way; to pronounce American."* In essence, we were encouraged and even warned to disassociate ourselves from the linguistic "corruption" and "contamination" that our people were supposedly imposing on the English language. Such declarations and ideological sermons ignored our multiple intersections of language and culture, and generations of colonization, decolonization, and re colonization. Too often we acquiesced to the patrol's linguistic slander, defamation, and its vitriolic and vociferous dismissal of the notion of a Virgin Islands language.

Unfortunately, because of the relenting language defamation, for far too many of us Virgin Islands Creole became "barbaric," "uncivilized," "vulgar" and was thus branded impure; subsequently, linguistic sanctions were imposed. In effect, it was assessed as "unworthy" of being considered among "authentic" languages. *"That is not a word"* or *"That is not how you pronounce that word"* were typical verbal reprimands and aspersions cast by those on constant and self-appointed patrol. Over a period of time we accepted the derisions as axiomatic, maybe because they were uttered with systematic impunity. In essence, a discourse[30] was created over time. If we were to accept the commentaries of the critics of Virgin Islands Creole as a kind of collective "text," (in the broadest sense) then we could say like Edward Said that such "texts" create the "very reality they appear to describe. In time, such knowledge and reality produce a tradition"

(Said 877). In this case, we speak of a tradition of rejection, a discourse fomenting over decades.

Interestingly, the so-called "language problem" in the United States Virgin Islands really can only be resolved in one way. However, the irony is that this "one way" solution is due to the fact that the "problem" is not how we speak, but rather how we view the way that we speak. It is a distinction worth pursuing here. Hence, the resolution lies in the establishment of an unyielding position that affirms that no "real" problem exists in our language itself, not in its vocabulary, nor in its grammatical structure. In more unequivocal terms, our Virgin Islands speech *is not* inherently problematic, nor is it some linguistic anomaly. We have been dwelling in the obscure alleys of perceptions, clearly operating under the unsparing influence of ideology. The argument that Virgin Islanders are inept articulators of the English language loses its steam when cast within the context of a more overarching interrogation of that premise itself. Ultimately, then, we can begin to see the "Virgin Islands Creole language problem" not only as ideological, but also as blatantly concocted.

The idea is not to promote the way that we speak as having some kind of supremacy over any other language, but rather to argue for the promulgation of our form of speech in the private and public domain. This represents an unwavering move toward the de-stigmatization of Virgin Islands Creole. In some ways, the antagonists have passed judgment with such rancor that we often have responded to this with our own sense of language inferiority. Think of a person being "trained" to respond to certain stimuli; there comes a time when the response to that training becomes patently automatized. Hence, at times when we tried to establish a firm posture, affirming and embracing our speech, we were forced by societal pressures to recoil, and reminded to purge ourselves of the oxidized grime built up over years of linguistic perversion.

Considering this on a pure human level, let us take the case of an individual who views himself or herself in a mirror each day and who, in spite of his or her "normalcy," consistently sees a distorted image. The fact is, the individual is looking at himself or herself; that is the reality. On the other hand, it is the perception and the interpretation of the image that are distorted. Often times in any society distortions result from internalized negative characterizations about a person's physical appearance. That is to say, the person viewing herself or himself might well conclude that there is some deficiency in that individual's appearance. A faithful analysis could prove the invalidity of such a conclusion. Analogous to this is the fact that for too many years our community has been looking in the mirror, and believing the distorted linguistic image that is reflected. The good news, however, is that in much the same way as the individual can be made whole, so too can a linguistic community; once we are brought to the level of basic understanding of "the real problem," that of false representation (Althusser 241).

This is, as we have made clear, a battle that cannot be waged solo. And this is so because it is a fight against years of ideological entrenchment. Despite this fact, it is still possible to be victorious in the perennial war against self-deprecation. It must be understood that such battles (as with the individual viewing himself/herself in the mirror) cannot be won if waged decontextualized from the underlying problematic. For example, if a therapist were to tell the person assessing himself in the mirror that merely "fixing" his hair would solve "your deep-seated problem," then that professional may have ignored more potentially profound causes of the underlying issues. That person would be proposing a cosmetically superficial approach to a situation that requires a more in-depth analysis and understanding. If as members of our linguistic community we consider only the mere peripheral as remedy, we would be headed down the path of delusion and self-deception. This is the fundamental recipe for self-rejection and self-hate. In essence, our tendency to reject our Creole is not necessarily because we ourselves discern some "abnormality" in the way we speak. But rather, it is because someone peddling an ideology has convinced us of the inferiority of our language. Subverting prevailing negative interpretations of Virgin Islands Creole would be a major step in debunking the myth of language subordination.

Franz Fanon complained about a similar situation in Martinique and other areas of the French West Indies, a lament that resonates in the United States Virgin Islands. As he praises those who embrace the local Creole, Fanon derides the Antillean (West Indian) who creates a distance between himself/herself and the Creole language: "Nothing of that sort [creolization] in the Antilles. The language spoken officially is French. Teachers keep a close watch over the children to make sure that they do not use Creole" (Fanon 28). This echo can be heard in our Virgin Islands; for while it may be true that we are proud of being Virgin Islanders, this expression of pride too often does not extend to our mode of communication. Or even in cases when we do identify with our language we do so with restrictions. For example, some are happy speaking Virgin Islands Creole as long as it is confined to the backrooms, in secret. But the speaking of this language should not and must not be a clandestine activity. Such an attitude reduces it to the level of the carnivalesque, the trivial, and the banal. Furthermore, this encourages a kind of *de facto* ban on the way we speak, and ultimately promotes an attitude of resignation to the unwritten prohibitions.

Virgin Islands Creole, because of its multiple inversions, ironic twists, and often duplicitous patterns lends itself to much humor owing to the creative play on words. There is nothing at all repulsive about this truth, nor about the appreciation of our language on such a level, nothing vile or distasteful. If because of some idiosyncratic utterance in our Creole, laughter is evoked, this should not be by any measure an affront to the way we speak. This is a totally innocuous situation. However, this could be problematic if we allow the Creole itself to become the joke, and because of our attitude help to ensure that it never supersedes its prescribed level of secondary status. Frequently we subscribe to a type of language validation that relegates our speech to certain venues where there is an implicit sense of relaxed regionalism. We envision our Creole enclosed in such "safe spaces" in which the medium of communication assumes a light-hearted tone. The inference is clear; often in our minds there has to be a special space, but only a second tier place carved out for Virgin Islands Creole. Such thinking naturalizes our own resistance to U.SV.I. Creole and causes some to seek new language configurations that lead us away from ourselves.[31]

The notion of Virgin Islands Creole as exclusively, or even principally colloquial, conjures up images of informality, resulting in the normalization of the idea of our language as superficial. Reflecting on Francisco Moreno's observation referenced earlier, such a relegation guarantees a particular conceptualization of our Creole as "nonstandard," or in fact, "substandard." This designation assumes the existence of a fixed mark which is the measuring stick that we tend to use as the basis for comparison. Unless this basic assumption is challenged, United States Virgin Islands Creole will continually be seen as indisputably ordinary and banal, when viewed in the context of American English. Such a presumption would automatically promote such adjectives as "flawed," "defective," and "deficient" when we are referencing our Creole. Accepting the classification of U.S.V.I. Creole as primarily a colloquial tongue is submitting to a persistent dismissal of the language as being on the same tier as English. By this I do not mean that it should be used as a substitute for English, but given the same respect as a language.

The dilemma is to embrace the utilization of Creole at every level, while steering away from the idea of our language as somehow second class. When I myself opt for the use of Virgin Islands Creole in short stories or poetry, this decision itself infers the primacy of the Creole language without apology. The resistance needs to be against the propagation of a premise that forces us to see Virgin Islands Creole *only* portrayed in the context of the light-heartedness and banality. Meanwhile "Standard" English with its supposed superior vocabulary and purportedly sophisticated grammatical structures is expected to occupy a space within which it operates on multiple levels from the banal to the sublime. The truth is, it always operates from the vantage point of presumed legitimacy and viability. On the other hand, however, United States Virgin Islands Creole, never has had such a presumptive luxury, its peripheral status emanating from a kind of a priori justification. It has never been universally affirmed (even within our own islands) in such a way as to be recognized and elevated to socio-linguistic prominence. We must insist that our Creole language be used to also express the philosophical, historical, psychological and other realities, both on a local or global level. To assume that it cannot accomplish such a task is to concede to a primordial myth that has percolated in the underbelly of our community for far too many decades.

CREOLE AND THE CLASSROOM SPACE

It is important to keep in mind that Virgin Islands Creole is not officially inscribed in the various school curriculums of the United States Virgin Islands. It is not incorporated in any of the educational structures of the public, private, parochial, or charter school systems. This fact alone, however, does not impede the "intrusion" of the language in the formal classroom setting. The question is, in these circumstances where the Creole language imposes itself on the prescribed plans of the instructor how does the teacher "correct" a student without a rebuke that would cause the student's feelings of self-confidence to decline? I am attracted to the idea of "feedback" versus "correction" (Hadley 83)[32] as a means of instructing the student if there is a possible infraction, grammatical, morphological, or syntactical. A space for a sensible discussion can be opened in which the student is given an adequate explanation as to why the word choice or phrase (ex. "*Deh man dem*") is problematic, within the context of the stated objectives of the particular class.

It would neither be sufficient nor beneficiary for the teacher or individual in authority to simply exert his/her own power to reject or dismiss Creole word usage or structure, but rather to clarify, amplify, or comment on the issue, perhaps even creating an auxiliary classroom exercise. Just informing the student of a rule violation would be nothing more than depositing information in the individual's head, a process of "banking" to employ Paulo Freire's coinage. The more "humanist" approach would be a dialogue that would create what Freire calls the "problem-posing method" (Freire 53-67).[33] This means that the student will be better able to understand the intervention of the teacher, and moreover could appreciate the relevance of the instructor's intervention, and not just see it as disciplinary. It is a double-edged sword. The dilemma raised by this issue is how to ensure that in the schools Virgin Islands Creole is not ostracized as somehow detrimental and inhibitive to a student's academic, personal, and professional growth. The teacher, through judicious and conscious actions, can avoid a spectacle and in so doing shield the innocent student.

Under no circumstance should Virgin Islands Creole, an important medium of communication in the United States Virgin Islands, be a source of embarrassment. But if we are not careful, what we might perceive as an innocent commentary could have a lasting negative affect. In this context, for example, a young child may interpret the word "*inappropriate*" as punitive. Therein lies a major problem. Once the position of linguistic judgment is firmly established and entrenched, nudging people away from their own subjectivity becomes arduous at best. We must find the necessary language to speak about our language — United States Virgin Islands Creole. The argument for the legitimacy of this language is one that is not only important, but also essential in order to steer us away from the need to self-deprecate.

Many years ago a teacher offered a "Speech," course and students at first confused it with a course on the development of oratory skills. This course, however, was markedly different because the instructor's mission (only one particular individual ever taught this course) was to approximate an American linguistic model for his "deficient" students, in the context of language proficiency. As students we went through hours of grilling in a vain attempt to help us to adapt to a mode of articulation antithetical to our own. Not surprisingly, this was an exercise in futility primarily because it proceeded from a false premise—that U.S. Virgin Islanders (in general, West Indians) spoke incorrectly. There was an ideological fallacy that set the tone for the class, the intent of which was to save us from our fractured linguistic selves. That course incarnated the misguided notions of language and the misunderstanding of the indispensable role of culture in the crystallization of our linguistic identity. Creolization was clearly seen as an abrasive affront and even more so, an obstacle to intellectual engagement. The tacit message could not be more pronounced and unequivocal in that classroom with its misguided objective, and an agenda of one individual who mis recognized the students.

Undoubtedly, there has been a more pronounced effort by some who tend more to gravitate toward the Americanization of the local parlance. Of course it would be blatantly inaccurate to pretend that this "appropriation" of American English is only done by a particular group. The fact is that there is a wide array of individuals who prefer to distance themselves from the local speech. The explication of this phenomenon cannot be succinctly expressed in this work with its limited objectives. In point of fact, it may very well be that the explanation of such a profound socio-psychological situation is beyond the reach of anyone to adequately articulate. However, it is obvious that the penchant for linguistic distancing exists and continues to challenge the nature of our Creole language. Is the distancing a result of shame, self-deprecation, and fear, or is it a more profound psychological need to self-identify with the superior economic power?

The fact is, the categorization of our way of speech as simply "*poor grammar*" and "*perverted pronunciation*" represents a facile dismissal that discounts history, tradition, and customs and is by its nature a reductionist argument. When we ourselves insist on the rejection of the notion of linguistic ineptitude, then we are not only asserting our language legitimacy, but also our basic right of free expression in the public and private spheres. But the "struggle" should not be centered merely on the "correctness," or "incorrectness" of words or expressions, but should challenge a basic stance: *The English language used as the scale for judging the local language.* Refuting this model as axiomatic opens up the space of the freedom that we have sought for many years. Breaking out of the confines of restrictive characterizations also means engaging detractors and critics in the most rudimentary ways—rejecting, for example such descriptive words as "bad," "backward," "uneducated" when referencing our Creole. A categorical rejection of such modifiers is likewise an affirmation of the refusal to succumb to the potent ideology with its markers of social determinism.

The good news is that there are members of the Virgin Islands community who are committed in their support of the promotion of Virgin Islands Creole. They argue with the same fervor and spirit as the antagonists, but of course, in favor of the propagandization of our language as a serious mode of articulation. Moreover, I am optimistic that we can have an increasingly steady language conscious alliance of local and diasporic Virgin Islanders who will be willing to stand up and fight for our linguistic space. However, while it remains true that there are strong advocates for Virgin Islands Creole, it is equally true that the numbers are overwhelmed by those who are firm opponents of the promotion of our mode of communication as a language. The ultimate moment of enlightenment will be the recognition that the manifestations of our culture are embedded within the framework of our language itself. Failure to accept this as fundamental would be paramount to losing our essence, and straying further and further away from our identity as Virgin Islanders.

Human beings react to language in much the same way as we react to ourselves, individually and collectively. This means that we can be self-complimentary, self-critical, or resentful toward ourselves. And this can be for reasons that are not always easily explicable or discernible. Similarly, when we assess our Creole, we respond to it with a wide array of sentiments and behavior. In some cultures the local language (or languages) is embraced, respected, and idealized as a viable means of articulation. In fact, at times the community in question may well consider its particular language as sophisticated, exemplary, and even often superior to all others, or others within a prescribed geographical space. In general, speakers of United States Virgin Islands Creole do not see such a level of sophistication associated with our speech. Furthermore, while we may speak the language with ease, our acceptance of it may not necessarily come so readily. It is a confusing situation that is far too common.

In communities where language is honored, there is a long established tradition that has edified and maintained the status of the particular language. Subsequent generations therefore naturally accept and follow the model firmly set in place. Embracing the way one speaks is an outgrowth of accepting oneself, language clearly being an extension of the individual and the collective society. Certainly, it is not that all Virgin Islanders reject or are uneasy with our form of speech; that would be a mischaracterization and misrepresentation. What is more accurate is that many of us have not attained a level of linguistic comfort with respect to our Creole. Often, for example, we express much joy in what past generations habitually uttered. We seem to relish in this, and there is frequently a sense of pride as we boast, *"Ah rememba wen deh ole people dem use' to say...."* Such expressions undoubtedly speak to a sense of identification and a clear recognition of one's culture. The problem is, however, that such expressions of connection are far too fleeting and limited and are often far too superficial.

In an ironic twist, many of the same people who recall the days of the colorful expressions with fondness, are often the same ones who may consciously distance themselves from the language as a whole. There is without question a pathway that can lead us to a level of more acceptance of our language, but that trail is laced with challenges. Among the first and most important of those challenges is the ability to see our language not only as an integral component of Virgin Islands culture, but also as an outgrowth of earlier linguistic building blocks that have been the cornerstone of our contemporary speech.

VIRGIN ISLANDS DUTCH CREOLE (NEGERHOLLANDS) AND THE DANISH WEST INDIES

The evolution of language in the former Danish West Indian colonies—St. Thomas, St. Croix, and St. John, is linked to a long legacy that fused European languages with various African languages: Yoruba, Fula, Akan, among others. At the epicenter of the geographical and linguistic restlessness was the Dutch vying for first place in the market place of human exploitation during the 18th century. Established as a power house in the slave trade, they imposed their language on the populace, eventually resulting in a kind of new hybrid language based in part on Dutch. The new mode of articulation emerging as it were in a crucible of competing nations was also infused with various African languages, reflecting the "diversity" of the new African diaspora as subject. Virgin Islands Dutch Creole, then, took shape in the heyday of the trafficking of human cargo in the lucrative business of the slave trade. It is unfortunate that most of us today have not been privileged to hear this language articulated at any level.

Dr. Gilbert Sprauve and Dr. Robin Sabino are two of the pioneers who have studied this linguistic phenomenon, still largely unknown in our contemporary Virgin Islands community. We know that during its heyday the language was spoken in all three of the Danish West Indies, but clearly most prominent on St. Thomas. Indeed the Moravian Church felt it necessary to translate the Bible into Dutch Creole, strong evidence of its prevalent usage during the 18th century. That the language is extinct does not preclude the fact that there are still remnants of it in the vocabulary, pronunciation, inflection, intonation, and popular adages and sayings endemic in Virgin Islands Creole. We are, as part of the natural cultural and linguistic process, a subset of our ancestors. We can never be completely separated from our past (nor should we want to be!), thus it is expected that echoes of words and sounds of our predecessors would still resonate within us.

The precursors of contemporary Virgin Islands[34] language, the earlier articulators of our traditions and customs, should always be revered as significant contributors to the development of our language today. Certainly to minimize their input is to dishonor and discredit their historic and linguistic relevance. Language does not emerge from a vacuum, from some vague vacuous space. Hence, it should neither be surprising that present day Virgin Islands Creole owes much to the speech patterns of our ancestors who revolutionized a language out of necessity and a basic will to survive. The fact that we as Virgin Islanders do not have a clue of this language, or worse, may not even care to know about it, does not change the influence that it has had on the current manner in which we speak. The Moravian missionaries in their efforts at evangelization, accomplished a secondary, maybe even accidental task—the immortalization of our ancestors' mode of communication in writing.

The urge to cling to and learn more about a language that was reflective of the very essence of exploitation, colonialism, and colonization, speaks to the complexity of these kinds of paradoxical relationships. The will to learn more about the language spoken by the victims of the most horrific system of dehumanization presents an internal conflict for this writer; yet, it is a conflict that in some ways resolves itself in the earnest quest to understand our linguistic evolution, to identify with it, and to respect those who spoke a language often under the weight of socio-economic and political duress.

Let us not fool ourselves; those ancestors who were speakers of Virgin Islands Dutch Creole were also subjects of a dominant culture whose linguistic imposition forged new modes of articulation. What should we as Virgin Islanders do with respect to learning more about this language? Or maybe the question is whether we can investigate it further while simultaneously remaining conscious of the fact that there must have been much pressure to have a language common to the various African groups in order to ensure the economic prosperity of those in power. The subjugation of our ancestors was for the financial and social benefits of the hegemonic structure. Within the framework of this multiple prong imposition Virgin Islands Dutch Creole, so-called Negerhollands, emerged and thrived, and 21st century U.S. Virgin Islands has within its linguistic veins the DNA of this language.

There can be no neutrality in this matter because as I seek to discover more about this linguistic phenomenon I am consequently implicated in the debate. Negerhollands could not have been part of our linguistic patronage for more than one hundred years without leaving its markers willed to us by our creative ancestors. But here we are today in the twenty-first century still struggling to understand our linguistic lineage. The lesson is crystal clear: *there is no neat, sanitized pattern of language patrimony.* We know, of course, that the rich tapestry of Virgin Islands Creole is not linked only to our Dutch Creole but owes its uniqueness also to a long legacy that includes influences from Ghana, Nigeria, Senegal, the Congo, other countries in Africa, and of course Denmark and the United States. This socio-economic reality, combined with and compounded by a variety of imposing international languages, uniquely positioned the Virgin Islands as a crucible of languages. All have played a pivotal role in the development of what is today our mode of speech.

In the 21st century with its proliferation of social media and easy access to communication, the internet is having its own massive influence on language, not only internationally, but locally as well. Nonetheless, in the final analysis I still do believe that the foot soldiers, those committed to forestalling a radical shift—, (for example from Virgin Islands Creole, to just another speech pattern akin to that the contiguous states) can help to ensure that we respect the language genealogy and embrace our language as emblematic of our culture. No one can say with 100% certainty what percentage of present-day Virgin Islands Creole emanated from what specific European or African languages; it is safe to conclude, however, that numerous languages and cultures converged to create our linguistic particularities and idiosyncrasies.

The big question is what happens to our language in the next fifty years? The next 100 years? Is our present way of speaking destined to go the way of Negerhollands and Latin with their extensive written records but extinct oral articulation? Or is there a way to honor and embrace our language and in the process help to guarantee its survival? The quest for stabilization of our Creole does not in any way infer some kind of imagined immutability of the language, but it does refer to our appreciation of our modes of speech. If we are ever able to successfully encourage our populace to engage in this sort of linguistic embracement brought on by an awareness of our language as a reflection of who we are, the possibilities become endless.

This awareness and embracement would extend to our Virgin Islands Dutch Creole and our appreciation of its undeniable impact on our contemporary Virgin Islands mode of speech. Dr. Gilbert Sprauve and Dr. Robin Sabino have led the way on the important explorative journey of this most intriguing language. Their insightful and impactful investigative labor has opened the door for more of us to better know ourselves by learning more about how our ancestors spoke. The question is, what are we as individuals and as part of the collective society willing to do in order to ensure that the articulators of that Virgin Islands language are never obliterated from history? Maybe the first step is an earnest recognition of the crucial role of United States Virgin Islands Dutch Creole in our development socially, culturally, and linguistically.

PRONUNCIATION: A NOTE ON SUPPRESSION OF CONSONANTS "g", "d", "t" and "r" IN SELECTED POSITIONS

At some point we have all heard people say, *"Man, it was so embarrassin' listenin' toh 'im."* Moreover, the expression *"speakin' so broad,"* or *"Ah carn' believe she went toh college tarkin' like dat"* are common reactions of disgust for what some consider serious pronunciation violations of the English language. Apart from the startling irony gleaned in some of these typical reactions (very often the critics are also speaking in Virgin Islands Creole!), they also suggest a well ingrained pattern of speech, so established that it causes some chagrin for some. Pronunciation is very often a target for detractors when they are dismissive of United States Virgin Islands Creole and are looking for a pretext for its rejection.

Perhaps no letters provoke more consternation than the letters *"d," "t"* and *"r"* with their complicated unwritten rules of suppression. These consonants present a very interesting case not simply because the sounds are often suppressed, but because there is remarkable consistency in the "managing" of this feature. For the speaker of Virgin Islands Creole there is never any doubt as to when this suppression is allowed. Unquestionably, if provided with a list of words, the individual, the speaker of the language, would be able to tell when these consonants can be eliminated in pronunciation. It is important to highlight the fact that this is never done arbitrarily, but instead is part of a well-organized system of speech.

In this section I will supply numerous examples of words in order to examine how this phenomenon plays out in our everyday utterances. Once again the rules are unwritten but are subconsciously known by those who are members of the speech community. The argument is, though, that the suppression is indeed a popular feature of the language. The following pages explore this phenomenon with its unwritten rules and regulations. The discussion comes accompanied with summary charts.

SUPPRESSION OF THE FINAL "d" IN VIRGIN ISLANDS CREOLE

There is no question that the speaker of Virgin Islands Creole knows that he or she can suppress the "*d*" in the following words: *pretend, understand, bold, mold, could, command, hand, land, understand, comprehend, kind, lend, bend, around, round, send, sound, mind, wind (verb), wind (noun), friend* (and many more). To the linguistic outsider, a particular deduction may seem logical— *when pronouncing a word in Virgin Islands Creole, simply eliminate the "d" if it occurs in the final position of the word."* Such a rule, however, cannot serve as a viable universal linguistic guide for governing this feature because the exceptions are too numerous. In fact, not only would the Creole speaker be aware of the silencing of the "*d*" in the list above, but that person would also know those words in which it is *no*t permissible to eliminate the final "*d*" in pronunciation.

The samples given are a subset of a wide array of words that would fall under the same category. The specific words chosen are commonly used in our daily speech, but beyond that, their selection has no particular significance. People speaking in Virgin Islands Creole are consistent with the suppression of the final "*d*," and it is most remarkable to note that the speakers, both children and adults, are faithful to this rule of pronunciation. Would a speaker of English unfamiliar with the Creole of the U.S. Virgin Islands be able to discern the English words in the Creolized pronunciations? The likelihood is that that individual would, in some cases, know the equivalent word. However, it is improbable that the person would be able to accurately predict those words in which the "*d*" is always enunciated. Such a task is reserved for members of the community of the shared language—U.S. Virgin Islands Creole.

The fact is that generally the suppression of the "*d*" is applied when the letter is preceded by the consonants "*n*" and "*l*." However, when the final "*d*" is preceded by the consonant "*r*," the suppression is never allowed. For example, the following words and similar ones would never be pronounced without the final "*d*": *awkward, coward, forward, lard, leopard, regard, reward, ward, word, yard.*

The *Chart I* below addresses the rule for pronunciation with respect to the final "*d*" when immediately preceded by "*n*" and "*l*":

I. EXAMPLES OF THE APOCOPATION OF FINAL "D" WHEN PRECEDED BY "N" OR "L"	
"N"	
Standard English	**USVI Creole**
hand	han'
understand	understan'
comprehend	comprehen'
pretend	preten'
wind	win'
"L"	
Standard English	**USVI Creole**
mold	mol'
cold	col'
hold	hol'
fold	fol'
Leopold	Leopol'

Furthermore, in our Creole *generally* speaking we do not think of suppression in words when the final "*d*" is preceded by a vowel- -as in "ad," "ed," id," "od," "ud": *bad, mad, sad, pad, head, lead, bed, fed, red, Ted, wed, bid, hid, kid, lid, rapid, rid, cod, nod, rod, Tod, bud, dud, mud, sud.* In each of these cases the "*d*" must be pronounced. But, the caveat is that this *general* rule does have some exceptions, as we see in the statement "*I ha' don' tark toh deh man befo' yoh come.*" [The English equivalence is *"I had already spoken to the man before you came."*]. Another rendition of the sentence would be the use of the first person singular subject pronoun, *"Ah,"* in place of "I" which provides a unique Creolized construction: *"Ah ha' don' tark...."* In each of the cases the "*d*" in the word "*had*" is suppressed with regularity, even though the "*d*" is preceded by the vowel "*a.*" With the other words ending in "*ad,*" the pronunciation of the "*d*" remains quite a rigidly consistent rule. The explanation as to why this is so is very likely irrevocably lost in the diffused evolution of our language, but it is important to note that speakers of our Creole language strictly adhere to these rules. With no preexisting architectural linguistic design for language, no a priori regulations set in stone, rules are generally developed after scrutiny of the practical application of the language. In other words, theory follows practice, rather than some theoretical notion governing the practical articulation.

Another exception to our rule with regard to the letter "*d*" preceded by a vowel of course is related to the use of some predicate adjectives, which, as in the case of the past tense, we tend often to suppress the "*d.*" (See the later discussion under *"A Note about the Grammatical Structure of the Language,"* where the use of the creolized past tense is addressed). Following are just some examples of when the "*d*" is suppressed even though a vowel immediately precedes this letter: *"He was force' toh do it." "De food wusn' cook' today." "Smokin' ain allow' in heh."* This should not at all be surprising since we generally eliminate the final "*d*" when using the simple past. (Again see the discussion on this feature under *"A note about the grammatical structure of the language."*). So that, when we think about exceptions to the rule of suppression of the "*d*" with respect to the vowel, the main exception is in the word "*had.*" I prefer to see the suppression in words above such as *"allow(ed)"* and *"cook(ed)"* as primarily affiliated with the rule of the formulation of the past tense. In the final analysis, when we think of the countless number of words ending in "*d,*" it is important to point out that the speaker of Virgin Islands Creole has no problem in consistency with the application of the multiple regulations.

SUPPRESSION OF THE FINAL "t"
IN VIRGIN ISLANDS CREOLE

With respect to the final "*t*" of words as written in English, a frequent feature in Virgin Islands Creole is the silencing of that consonant. But again, this must be considered with much caution. For example, in the following words this consonant is suppressed in Virgin Islands Creole: *cas(t)*, *dus(t)*, *fas(t)*, *fis(t)*, *firs(t)*, *gus(t)*, *jus(t)*, *las(t)*, *lis(t)*, *mus(t)*, *pas(t)*, *rus(t)*, *tes(t)* *wris(t)*… In this particular <u>*lis(t)*</u> the pattern is clear, that in each case the final consonant is preceded by the letter "*s.*" There are, of course, numerous other words of the same nature, and the rule is quite consistent with respect to pronunciation. So that, in Virgin Islands Creole it would be most logical to hear: "*I doan <u>trus'</u> 'im atarl*," "*Ah <u>jus'</u> finish*," or "*Dis ting ain gon <u>las'</u> larng.*" In these cases the speaker of Virgin Islands Creole does not pronounce the final "*t*"- - "*trus*," "*jus*," "*las*." One should not infer from this that the suppression of the final "*t*" is only allowed in the combination "st." A crucial question is what happens in those words in which the letter preceding the "*t*" is not "*s?*" The answer is not a simple one and speaks to the complexity of our Creole.

Like all other languages, U.S. Virgin Islands Creole has unwritten grammatical norms. But "*unwritten*" does not mean that no rules exist. With respect to the final "*t*" of a word, the fact that the speakers of the language are themselves consistent with the elimination of that last letter, is proof that there are rules. Rules and regulations are dictated by our linguistic tradition, by an established protocol.

Very much like other languages, mimicry and imitation are the guidelines for the production and reproduction of the speech patterns in our community. We will explore other combinations in which the apocopation of the "*t*" is not only permissible but also prevalent.

There is a clear pattern with a series of words, not only ending in "*st*," but also in "*ct*," "*ft*," "*pt*," and "*xt*." With each combination given here, any speaker of Virgin Islands Creole faithfully follows the rule that the "English" word is rendered without recognizing that final "t." The combination "*nt*" presents a different situation; at the same time, however, the Creole speaker adheres to the rules of exceptions as well as those of application. *In general*, when the final "*t*" is preceded by "*n*," the "*t*" is pronounced: *cement, rent, hunt, dent, lament*, and many more words.

Even though it is true that this stated rule is the norm, it must also be noted that there are notable exceptions to this, as seen in the words "*don't*," "*can't*," "*won't*," "went" and the *verb* "want." As will be seen in the vocabulary entry section of this book, with these words the speaker of Virgin Islands Creole eliminates the final "*t*," and hence we have renditions such as "*doan*," "*carn*," (or "ciarn"), "*woan*" and "*wan'*." It is important to note that with respect to the word "*want*," the rule varies depending on whether one is employing a noun or a verb. As seen above, I specifically mentioned "the verb *want*" because in Virgin Islands Creole when utilized as a *noun* the "*t*" must be enunciated, as in the expression later in the entries, "**dying' fo' want**." In other words, even though a Virgin Islander would say *"Ah ain wan' toh eat now,"* no one would say, *"dying' fo' wan'."* The application of such a subtle distinction can only come from years of speaking and hearing the local parlance. If not, the individual outside of this linguistic sphere would very likely deduce that the word is always pronounced the same.

When certain other consonants immediately precede the final "*t*," the "*t*" is enunciated in *almost* all cases, as in **"cart," "heart,", "start," "fight," "height," "might," "belt," "felt," "melt," "Halt."** There is a noted exception; the phrase "*light bill*" in United States Virgin Islands Creole is often pronounced "*ligh' bill*." (Please see explanation of this phrase in the entries.). As is explained in the entries, this is a unique case because used in isolation the word "*light*" is pronounced much like "*fight*." Hence, in other contexts the "*t*" must be pronounced as the word is uttered.

Let us now consider the following words in which the "t" is preceded by a vowel: *cat; fat; pet; pat; pot; cut; foot; loot; mat; gut; pit*. When exposed to such a list, one may hastily conclude something like the following: *"It is obvious that in such words where the vowel immediately precedes the "t," the "t" can never be suppressed."* However, even though it is true that the general tendency in such cases is to pronounce the final *"t,"* there are noticeable exceptions: three verbs stand out (*let, get, put*), the conjunction, *"but,"* and the preposition *at*. The unwritten rules are tricky and mastery can only come from repeated oral application. How would someone know, for example, that in the words *"what,"* and *"that"* the suppression of the final *"t"* is not only acceptable but natural? *"Wa' he wan'? "Da' is mine."* However, extrapolating from this the permissibility of *"ha' "* instead of "hat" would be a gross violation of the pronunciation rules of the language, as would be the suppression of the *"t"* in *"pet,"* or *"cut."* The following pronunciations are accepted in Virgin Islands Creole: *"Le' meh do it." "Geh' deh book." "Pu' deh plate heh." "He say bu' he gon sell he house." "Who ah' de do'?"* ("Who is at the door?"). Often with the word "it" the *"t"* is not recognized in pronunciation. *"Eh gon be good,"* a popular expression roughly equivalent to the English expression: *"It is going to be interesting."*

As a final note, when the *"d"* or *"t"* appears in the middle of a word, at times these consonants are suppressed, in line with the grammatical rules mentioned. In this context, in Virgin Islands Creole, it is common to hear *"tesin"* instead of *"testing"* or *"holin,'"* instead of *"holding"* etc. In other words, the rule for the suppression of the *"t"* when preceded by "s" is applicable to the use of the present participle and gerunds as well. Consider the following sentence: *"Dey home resin' up fo' wok lata'."* Every Virgin Islander knows that the equivalent English participle is *"resting."* This rule, however, cannot be sufficiently generalized to include all words ending in <*sting.*> As an example, in the popular word *"disgustin' "* the *"t"* must always be pronounced, unlike with words like *"tes(t)in,'" "las(t)in,'" "dus(t) in"* etc.; hence, the expression, *"He so disgusin'"* would be inadmissible in Virgin Islands Creole.

In an ironic twist, however, the suppression of the *"t"* is allowed when *"disgus(t)"* is used as a verb or noun—*"Man, Ah disgus' ah 'e wid he rude self." "She was de watchin' im wid disgus'."* It is interesting that in speaking to several people they were surprised that they were actually adhering to rules of the language, without being aware of the congruity of its utterance in our community. It must be emphasized in these discussions that we are referring to general rules of pronunciation; indeed, exceptions and variations are also part and parcel of the patterns of our localized speech patterns.

The two charts that follow, *Chart II and Chart III*, summarize the main features of the rules of pronunciation with respect to the suppression of the final "t."

II. EXAMPLES OF THE APOCOPATION OF FINAL "T" WHEN PRECEDED BY "C," "F," "P," "S," "X"	
Standard English	**USVI Creole**
fact	fac'
lift	lif'
accept	accep'
trust	trus'
next	nex'

III. EXAMPLES OF THE APOCOPATION OF FINAL "T" WHEN PRECEDED BY A VOWEL: EXCEPTIONS	
Standard English	**USVI Creole**
let	le'
get	geh'
put	pu'
but	bu'
at	a' (pronounced "ah")
it	e'
that	da'
what	wa'

SUPPRESSION OF THE FINAL "r" and "g" IN VIRGIN ISLANDS CREOLE

With respect to the final "r" of most words in U.S.V. I. Creole, the suppression of this consonant is typical as in the following words, and certainly in countless other words ending: *car, far, tar, sir, Jennifer, spar, number, November, ever.* [*ca,' fa,' ta,' sa', Jennifa,' spa,' numba,' Novemba,' eva'*]. This is very consistent. The rules of pronunciation regarding the consonant "*g*," present us a distinct situation, depending on whether the word is a gerund, participle, verb, or noun. This "*g*" is frequently suppressed in pronunciation in the endless categories of gerund and participles—"*cookin*," "*runnin*," "*dancin*'," "*playin*." This rule, however, does not automatically apply to words *not* in that category, for example, "*ting,*" in U.S.V. I. Creole, a noun or verb (See extensive discussion of this multifaceted word in later lexicon entry). Other examples are "sing," "fling," "bring," and "ring" in which the "*g*" must be enunciated: "*Man, bring deh ting, no.*" In other words, the statement, "*Man, brin' deh tin', no*" would **not** be an admissible sentence in Virgin Islands Creole. The moment that such a statement is rendered it would be immediately recognized by the Creole speaker as being a departure from the accepted speech patterns. In summary, the "*g*" can be eliminated in every case where the gerund or participle is used. This popular feature of U.S.V.I. Creole allows for that suppression in every case of the categories referenced (gerund/participle).

THE SURPRISING SILENCE OF THE H

We readily recognize that the suppression of the letter "h" is not a feature that we generally associate with the Creole spoken in the United States Virgin Islands. In point of fact, various people with whom I have spoken informally indicated to me that there were absolutely no circumstances in which the sound of "*h*" is suppressed in pronunciation. This is not the case, however, and as alluded to before, in general, language is spoken without regard to rules and regulations. Speakers do not have at their disposal a grammatical compass that guides them as they speak. And this fact helps to substantiate the point made earlier; that is, the consensus community may not necessarily be able to respond instinctively to the question, *"Is the "h" ever suppressed in Virgin Islands Creole?"* Nonetheless, the community adheres to the tacit rules governing the application of this sound, confirming its consistency and inherent regulatory pattern.

A careful examination of United States Virgin Islands Creole would reveal that we do have several cases in which the "*h*" is silent. It would also be readily clear that the practice is not a pervasive one, in the sense that one cannot assume this suppression in every case. Unquestionably, though, the evidence in the daily oral elaboration of the language, clearly confirms this feature as an established pattern. Consider the following English sentence: *"The ball hit him in his head."* In the Creole of the U.S. Virgin Islands this would be translated as *"Deh ball hit 'im in 'e head."* In this case the "*h*" is silent in the objective pronoun —"im," instead of "*him.*" In addition, the word, "'*e,*" functions as a possessive, with the "*h*" suppressed. It is important to also recognize that with the verb, "*hit,*" often in daily speech the "*h*" is not recognized. However, with the word, "head,"

53

the "*h*" sound is acknowledged, though not very emphasized. Hence, in that one sentence the treatment of the "h" varies. It would not be possible to know when this is allowed without being a part of the community of speakers, or a very astute observer of this group.

In the Creolized questions, "*Who 'e is?*" And "*Who 'e fa'*? [Respectively, "Who is he? // "*Who does he belong to?*]³⁵" The "*h*" is not acknowledged in pronunciation. The following sentences would be typical expressions for speakers of Virgin Islands Creole: "*We gon wake 'im up late.*" "*Ah gon buy it fo' im.*" "*Ah gon call 'im today.*" The answer to the question, "*Way 'e live?*" can elicit the response: "*Ah tink 'e̲ live Wata'gut.*" We can also hear, "*Wa' 'E Name dem*" and numerous other expressions in which the "*h*" in the pronoun "he" is not heard in the enunciation of the word. This must not be seen as an "error" in pronunciation, but as part of the nomenclature of the Creole language. "*Me ain geh ah ting toh tell 'e, meson.*" Again, this must be approached with much caution. For example, consider the following: "*Who toh give it toh, **him**? In this case the "H" as part of the isolated pronoun has to be pronounced* (versus, the above sentence, "*Ah gon call 'im̲ today.*").

There are, however, far more cases in Virgin Islands Creole where the silencing of the "*H*" does **not** occur. If, for example, someone were to translate the English sentence, "*He is my friend,*" into Virgin Islands Creole, the local rendition would maintain the "*h*" sound—"*He is mey frien'.*" Similarly, "*He speaks Spanish*" would be rendered as "*He duz speak Spanish,*" the "*h*" in the pronoun being fully recognized. Interestingly though, as seen previously the suppression can occur when the word does **not** begin the sentence: "*Ah know 'e duz speak Spanish.*"

In addition to the silencing of the "*h*" with "*him*" and "*he,*" we also see this feature with the objective pronoun "*her*"— "*Doan tell ha (ah) mey business!*" "*We duz see ha (ah) eveyday.*" In addition to this, the word "*hey*" is equally rendered as "'*ey*": "*Ey, wa' goin' on?*" "*Ey meson, da boy doan hea' atarl.*" While it is true that the "h" disappears in some cases, in Virgin Islands Creole no one would eliminate it in the following: '*ome'* for "*home,*" '*erman*' for "*Herman,*" '*ulk* for "*hulk,*" nor '*elp,*" for "*help,*" '*ell,*" for "*hell,*" "*ear*" for "*hear,*" just to mention a few cases. In these particular cases, due to the tacit rules of the language community the individual would be prohibited from suppressing the "*h*". The fundamental truth is, however, that even though the suppression of the "*h*" is not applicable in most cases in our Creole, it would be incorrect to dismiss this phenomenon as merely incidental. The suppression of that letter ("*h*") is a popular characteristic in the Creole languages of some of our Caribbean neighbors. The Creole of the United States Virgin Islands while not totally following the extensive pronunciation protocol of other islands with respect to the "*h*," has its own rules that certainly certify that the feature is an integral component of our language.

THE SUPPRESSION OF THE "TH" SOUND IN U.S. VIRGIN ISLANDS CREOLE

In Virgin Islands Creole the "*h*" in the "*th*" combination, as a dental fricative, is always suppressed; indeed, I would argue that if in fact the "*th*" is discriminately enunciated the person is utilizing another means of articulation other than United States Virgin Islands Creole. In other words, in the language of our islands the sound achieved by the combination of "*t*" followed immediately by "*h*" is not audible as a "th" sound. Of course, children in school were and are summarily reprimanded for failing to "properly" enunciate that sound. Naturally, it is understandable that in the formal classroom setting where English is being utilized that students be made aware of the rules of pronunciation and their applicability. The only problem (the error that we have committed over decades in this regard) is that we have failed to assure the student that the suppression of the "*th*" sound is not some kind of linguistic blasphemy. The truth is that what might be considered a mis pronunciation in English is a staple in Virgin Islands Creole. My view would be that the student be accorded an explanation and not a simple categorical rejection of a socio-linguistic norm.

Should a student in Virgin Islands Schools be told, for example, that in "standard" English the "*th*" has a unique sound that should be clearly distinguishable from an isolated "t" sound? Those who advocate for our Creole would not argue against this obligation on the part of the teacher, or guardian. However, herein lies an important teaching moment where the instructor can seize the opportunity to explain the differences between the two languages—English and Virgin Islands Creole. In this scenario the teacher or guardian would insist that in English the correct "*th*" pronunciation must be emphasized. At the same time, both individuals (teacher/guardian) would encourage that student NOT to see his or her pronunciation as a mortal flaw, but as one that should be reserved while communicating using Virgin Islands Creole as the medium of exchange. If this approach is taken, then the student will not feel a sense of shame, but in essence will learn more about the English language, one of the components of his or her bilingualism. Simultaneously, the individual can feel a sense of pride embracing the local vernacular as emblematic of his or her culture. Through the guidance of the teacher the student comes to understand the value of his or her own pronunciation as a cultural and traditional feature of the Creole language spoken in the United States Virgin Islands, in contrast to being a mere violation of English rules. (See discussion in the section **CREOLE AND THE CLASSROOM SPACE** earlier).

The chart that follows highlights some typical words in U.S.V.I. Creole in which the "th" is not enunciated. Because of the consistency of this rule, the chart does not need to be extensive. Thus, the words were chosen at random, but we know that in Virgin Islands Creole the "th" sound does not exist. This is so whether the "th" appears at the beginning ("*theology*"), middle, ("*withstand*") or end of a word ("*uncouth*"). It would be as if the spelling of the word discounts the "h" as an essential characteristic. *Chart IV* offers a few examples; of course, in the case of "*this*" and "*them*" the sound is transformed into a "d" sound—"*dis*" and "*dem*" respectively. This sound is also heard in words such as "widstan" ("with"), "brudda," (bro*th*er), "ladda'" (la*th*er), and "bade" (ba*th*e).

IV. EXAMPLES OF THE SUPPRESSION OF THE 'H' IN WORDS WITH 'TH' COMBINATION	
Standard English Word	**USVI Creole Word**
This	Dis
Them	Dem
Three	Tree
Toothache	Tootache
Marathon	Maraton
Faith	Fait
Math	Mat

In each case where the "th" is not fully enunciated the resulting word is a new word. We can no longer speak of the second list as *words that are incorrectly pronounced.* Instead, we must see them as a series of creolized words that in context the listener has absolutely no problem in deciphering. If an individual were to say, *"Ah have tree brudda,"* no one who speaks and understands Creole would ever confuse this with the wooden structure that we know as *"a tree."* In the statement, *"She know ah lot ah mat',"* there is no possibility of misunderstanding on the part of the listener. In sum, failure to enunciate the "th" has always been frowned upon by educators and parents trying to teach *"proper English"* to those in their charge. Rather than dismiss or discredit this as an abomination, we should accept it as a representative feature of our speech, just as *"tarmon," "gongolo,"* or *"ponguana."*

A NOTE ON THE GRAMMATICAL STRUCTURE OF THE LANGUAGE

During the past years when I have spoken to Virgin Islanders about "grammatical structure" of Virgin Islands Creole, the reaction has often been one of genuine surprise. The fact is that people do not think consciously of the way they speak, and this is true in all languages. In cases where I have pointed out to friends the "rules" of grammar, they acquiesced, admitting that they had never really thought of our language as having a grammatical structure. This points to my argument that contrary to what critics may argue, Virgin Islands Creole is not some casual inversion of English, nor is it a random rendition of words and patterns. Instead, there is an ingrained systemic mode of speech that has its roots in the collective linguistic legacy of our islands. We are speaking of a well-organized system that speakers follow intuitively as they communicate within the consensus community. As Chomsky puts it, "every speaker of a language has mastered and internalized a generative grammar that expresses his knowledge of his language. This is not to say that he is aware of the rules of the grammar or even that he can become aware of them, or that his statements about his intuitive knowledge are necessarily accurate" (Chomsky 43). [36] If as United States Virgin Islanders we accept as axiomatic that the way we speak is *"corrupt English"* (a popular designation), then the idea of rules would seem, at the very least, an outlandish one. Within the framework of this reasoning the only rules would be those set forth by the language model use as a guiding post for our speech—"Standard English," primarily as spoken in the United States.

The basic truth is that there are viable grammatical rules and regulations[37] that govern our Virgin Islands Creole, and this Section explores how these function. They are noted for their consistency and the extent to which they are adhered by the consensus language community of the U.S. Virgin Islands. The section examines a number of fixed grammatical patterns that are used on a daily basis in the process of communicating in Virgin Islands Creole. The grammatical examination will center primarily on most of the parts of speech, specifically, nouns (their pluralization), adjectives, adverbs, prepositions, pronouns, and verbs (present and past conjugations), in addition to the possessive, demonstratives, and reflexives.

The idea is to demonstrate the frequency and consistency of these grammatical patterns in our Creole and to understand how they are utilized in communication. It is important to make clear that it is not possible to exhaust all of the grammatical rules with all of their nuances and complexities. Nonetheless, the "rules" show a pattern of utilization that confirms the assertion made here of the well-established nature of our Creole. It is also extremely important that speakers of Virgin Islands Creole do not dismiss this simply because they may not be able to identify the rules in a given moment. Interestingly, while words have changed, or simply disappeared over the years, the grammatical structure of the Creole of the U.S. Virgin Islands has remained relatively intact—over the past 5 decades. Virgin Islanders growing up in the 90's and in the 2000's might not recognize some of the vocabulary from the generation of the 50's, 60's or 70's. Similarly, the 50's and 60's generation might find it very challenging to understand some of the terminologies heard in contemporary U.S. Virgin Islands Creole. However, the grammatical patterns would be easily recognizable from one generation to another. The pluralization of nouns, for example, continues to follow a pattern that has been in place for generations. The same holds true for many other regulations, for example, with respect to the use of the simple past tense, prepositions, possessives and other grammatical categories when employing Virgin Islands Creole.

NOUN PLURALIZATION

Rules for pluralization of nouns are not that simple because there is an array of situations that would determine how to proceed grammatically. But, there are three distinct categories under which pluralization falls. The *first* and most prevalent of these is performed by placing the suffix "*dem*" after the noun (see the word "*Dem*" in the entry on vocabulary later in this study), for example, "*Deh book dem,*" "*Deh house dem big.*" "*He son dem tall.*" "*Deh people dem.*" "*Mommy, deh people dem heh….*" In this statement, the subject of the sentence, *people*, is already pluralized; yet, in our Creole we would still add the quantifier "*dem.*" The construction itself, "*Deh people dem,*" defies all logic. But who says that language has to follow logic? This is clearly for emphasis, especially in a language such as ours with its numerous hyperboles. It must be pointed out here that the phrase, "*Deh person dem,*" even though it would be readily understood if uttered, would sound rather unnatural, if used as a substitution for "*Deh people dem.*" The speaker would have to be guided by linguistic protocol in order to recognize that such an utterance is not part of the vernacular of Virgin Islands Creole. Such intimate knowledge attests to the many subtle and tacit intricacies of our language.

There is an innate rule that guides the speaker as to when to use the singular or the plural of the subject. So that, one can say either "*Deh darg dem barkin'* " or "*Deh dargs dem barkin',*" even with an already pluralized subject. In this case, as part of the formula the linking verb *(is/are* etc.) is suppressed (more on this under the Section, **Verbal Suppression**). Ultimately, the choice of whether to add "s" would depend on the speaker's preference, since essentially there would be no conflict of comprehension, nor cultural indiscretion if one were to choose one expression over another. However, the same logic cannot be applied to "*child*" and "*chiren*." The statement, "*Deh child dem heh*," would not flow naturally, even though it would be easily grasped; however, this would not be an acceptable sentence in Virgin Islands. The most natural rendition would be, "*Deh chiren dem heh*." Also, the phrase, "*Deh boy dem heh*," does not present the awkwardness of the previously stated sentence that uses the noun "child." Speakers of the language easily move between the annexation of the "*s*" and its elimination, in a manner that signifies a sense of adherence and compliance.

In addition to the rules for pluralization discussed above, there is a *second* category: on some occasions a noun can be made plural by leaving it in its original singular form regularly used in English. Emphasis must be placed on the fact that the pluralization without "*s*" is not by any means universal, and hence would not work in many cases. We are speaking here of limited usage. Clearly, this is an area that would present a great challenge for the uninitiated who might be trying to decipher when such a formulation is allowed. Below, I have supplied some examples of some of the grammatical situations that govern the use of the singular to express the plural. Only through mimicry and constant usage can one know what is allowable and what is not. For example, in cases when expressions such as "*ah bunch ah*," "*ah lat ah*," "*ah set ah*," "*ah giang ah*" (the Creole "*ah*," instead of the preposition "*of*") are used, the noun is often written without the "*s*" or "*es*." These are just a few examples, not intended to represent the wide scope of possibilities. The key here is the use of the prepositional phrase, even though as will be seen later this is not a prerequisite.

Let us look at several English sentences and see how they would/ could be translated or interpreted in U.S.V. I. Creole. For example, the English statement, "*There are a lot of books on the table*" in Virgin Islands Creole **can** be rendered as "*It geh ah lot ah book on deh table*." Other examples are the following: "*We see a lot of roaches in this place*" would be represented as: "*We duz see ah bunch ah roach in dis place*." Also, "*There are a lot of men (women) on the beach*" could be interpreted as "*It geh ah giang ah man on deh beach*" or "*It geh ah giang ah woman on deh beach*." However, under no circumstances would it be permitted to say, "*It geh *ah giang ah <u>chile</u> on deh beach.*" (In English the word "gang" would not be used in this context.)

With respect to pluralization, the challenge is that in some situations the elimination of the "s" as a feature will not function at all. The familiar speaker can only follow the well-established linguistic blueprint. For example, the statement, "*Deh <u>ca'</u> pretty,*" if used to convey the thought that "*The cars are pretty,*" would not only miss the mark, but would be undeniably inadmissible in U.S.V.I. Creole. Yet, in the utterance, "*It geh so much ting[s] on deh table,*" it would be just as natural to pluralize the word "ting" as it would be to leave the word in the singular form. The following sentences attest to the use of the singular as a plural as normative in the Creole of the U.S. Virgin Islands: 1) "*E geh so much man in deh street.*" Incidentally, in this sentence one cannot replace the word "much" with "many." The explanation of "much" and "mo" are addressed in the vocabulary entry later in the book. 2) Also, the sentence, "*E geh mo' woman ova' de.*" Leaving the nouns "man" and "woman" in the singular does not present any kind of a challenge for the speaker of the Creole.

The *third* category is the use of "dem" as a kind of demonstrative adjective (more on this later under the section on *adverbs* and *adjective*). Rather than having the word as a suffix, it would immediately come before the noun that it modified. The following sentences would demonstrate how this operates grammatically: "*Dem house pretty.*" "*Dem type ah cellphone doan wok good.*" "*Dem boy cou' swim.*" "*Meson, dem people is sometin' else.*" "*Man, dem guirl geh some strenk, yoh hea'.*" "*Dem darg mangy.*" "*Dem man was heh las' night drinkin an' ting.*" The point is that the demonstrative "*dem*" inherently signals a noun as plural, whether or not an "s" or "es" is added to the noun. The reality is that in the Creole of the U.S. Virgin Islands such a construction is not only permitted, but is prevalent. Again, another advisory is necessary here with respect to the two nouns referenced earlier: "*person*" and "*chile.*" The singular usage of these words to convey plurality would not be allowed in our Creole. But this fact, in and of itself, confirms the point that we are dealing with a language with its regulations, but with its numerous exceptions with which its articulators are intimately familiar. In this regard, the following sentences would be considered highly irregular in USVI Creole: "*Dem person know me,*" or "*Dem chile duz play too much.*" Chart *V* summarizes the three broad categorization of pluralization in Creole.

V. SUMMARY OF NOUN PLURALIZATION	
Standard English	USVI Creole
The books	Deh book (s) dem
A lot of men	Ah latah man
Those houses are pretty.	Dem house pretty.

VERBAL SUPPRESSION

The suppression of the linking verb ("to be") is very West Indian, and is frequently used in the Virgin Islands Creole. This is one of the many cases where reaction from purists could be severe: "*She cannot speak English properly.*" "*That is pure corruption of the English language.*" Even if we accepted this as axiomatic, we would do well to also accept as true that languages evolve from other languages. The English spoken today in the United States of America evolved from a series of other languages, but today survives as an "independent" language. It is important to note that patterns established in our Creole language, whether by design or by customary usage, have become ingrained and have contributed to a structure that is grammatically normalized and consequently an intrinsic component of our speech. Following are a few expressions where the linking verb is eliminated: "*How yoh mudda'?*"—"*How deh chiren dem?*" "*Wey yoh ca'?*" "*Pauline home now.*" ["*How is your mother?*"—"*How are the children?*" "*Where is your car?*" "*Pauline is home now.*"]. The linking verb is also suppressed when origin is suggested, for example: "*Wey he from?*" "*Wey pa' Rachel from?*"

The practice is also frequently used with adjectives. The idea here is that the adjective in a particular sentence is self-sufficient to insure the desired meaning: "*She nice.*" "*He tall.*" "*Dey too rude.*" "*She fas(t), meson.*" (A reference to her speed as an athlete). ["*She is nice.*" "*He is tall.*" "*They are rude.*" "*She is fast.*"]. The omission is also prevalent with present progressive expressions: "*Ah tellin' yoh deh trut.*" "*She sleepin'.*" ["*I am telling you the truth.*" "*She is sleeping.*"]. In other words, there are many cases in Virgin Islands Creole in which there is the subconscious knowledge that the linking verb would add nothing new to the interpretation of the utterance.

It is important to point out here that even though this verbal suppression can be a feature in the present progressive as indicated above, it should not be extrapolated that the same *always* holds true for the past progressive. Therefore, using the examples given above in the past progressive the sentences must be rendered with the linking verb explicitly stated: *"Ah wuz tellin' yoh deh trut."* *"She wuz sleepin.' "* In addition to the examples described above we also see the elimination of the linking verb in the construction with the word, *"gon,"* a kind of creolized future. *"Ah gon tark' toh ha' " lata'." "Dey gon call yoh wen dey geh home."* [*"I am going to talk to her later." "They are going to call you when they arrive home."*]. In this type of construction, the expression *"gon' tark"* renders the linking verb (*"am"*/ *"are"*) grammatically nonfunctional.

In the first paragraph of this section I have supplied several examples of the suppression of the linking verb in relationship to a noun: *"How yoh mudda?"* and the other examples. However, even though the response to this question and others like it can be done without the linking verb (*"She fine"*), there are situations where such an omission would be inadmissible. For example, the English sentence, *"She is Karen,"* cannot be rendered in Virgin Islands Creole simply as *"She Karen."* Nor can one say in Creole, *"Mabel American."* Both of these representations of identity must use a form of *"to be."* This is not only true for personal, religious and professional identity, but that of nationality as well. In sum, none of the following sentences would be considered correct in Virgin Islands Creole: *"She Tyrone." "He Catholic." "She ah mechanic." "Christie St. Johnian."*

There are caveats, however, with respect to age, a testament to the complexity of the language. That is, although a sentence such as *"Karen 20 years ole"* is not common, if a pronoun is used in place of the proper noun (Karen), then the construction is not only allowed, but is also popular. Therefore the answer to the question, *"How ole she is?"* [More on this syntactic arrangement later] can have as a response, *"She 'bout 20 yrs. ole."* Or *"She only ten years ole."* Contrast *"Winston is only 10,"* with *"He only 5;" "I only 10"* etc. Determining when such constructions are permitted results from years of living in the community of the shared language. It also speaks to the breadth of Virgin Islands Creole, its variety and richness. Moreover, it confirms that there is no whimsical or capricious approach to grammar usage in our Creole.

Chart VI below synthesizes how the verb suppression functions with its various categories.

VI. SUMMARY OF THE SUPPRESSION OF THE LINKING VERB	
Standard English Statement	**USVI Creole Statement**
Location: *I **am** here.*	*Ah heh / I heh.*
Origin: *They **are** from New York.*	*Dey from New Yark.*
Adjective: *Ellie **is** tall.*	*Ellie tall.*
State of being: *He **is** fine.*	*He fine. (He good*)*
Present Progressive: *Sandy **is** eating.*	*Sandy eatin'.*
Future: *We **are** going to call you.*	*We gon call yoh.*

*With respect to state of being, "good" and "fine" are used interchangeably.

VERBAL CONJUGATION, THE PRESENT TENSE

A conjugation chart of Virgin Islands Creole would look quite simple, and this is because of the use of "*duz*" in all constructions in this category. In general, in our Creole we use an emphatic present instead of the regular indicative present commonly employed in the typical declarative English sentence. No matter the subject pronoun, once the sentence is affirmative the word "*duz*" is employed. The following examples illustrate this popular creolized construction: "*I duz wok in town.*" "*You duz wok ah lot.*" In "standard" English a construction such as, "She **does** work in town" suggests a contrast, i.e., "She **does no**t work in the country." This is referred to as "the emphatic present." In U.S.V.I. Creole, this is a normalized construction in which the negative of "**duz**" shifts to "*doan.*" For example, "*Judy doan' wok' here; she duz wok' in town.*" No matter the subject pronoun these two verbs never change. Of course, sometimes the present tense is formed by simply using the regular indicative of the principal verb: "*She wok' in town.*"

The English rule for verbal conjugation, *add an "s" to the verb* when using a singular subject, or eliminate the "s" in case of plural subjects, has no applicability in Virgin Islands Creole. An understanding of this inapplicability must be in context with the position discussed earlier— that our language cannot, in fact must not be assessed under the umbrella of English rules and regulations. As a means of clarity, let us conjugate the infinite "*to sing.*" This is chosen at random and not because of any inherent feature of the infinitive itself. The conjugation of this verb is typical of the pattern of conjugation of regular verbs used in English. *Chart VII* gives the conjugation of this selected verb through all persons, first, second, third—both singular and plural. Following *Chart VII* is another one, *Chart VIII*, which focuses on the creolization of the same conjugations.

The idea of "standard" does not imply "correct" versus "incorrect" but rather is used as a designation to distinguish the pattern from that which would be considered more colloquial or regional. In addition, the idea of "standard" is in relationship to the English spoken in the United States, and accounting for regional and ethnic differences. As far as conjugation of verbs is concerned, we are referring to the grammatical protocol followed, for example, in the schools and universities in the United States. It is most revealing to see the contrast between this approach to English conjugation and that utilized in U.S. Virgin Islands Creole.

The contrast is provided in the two distinct charts provided below, *Charts VII* and *VIII*:

VII. STANDARD ENGLISH CONJUGATION	
I sing	We sing
You sing	You sing
He, she, it sings	They sing

VIII. USVI CREOLE CONJUGATION	
Ah (I) duz sing	We duz sing
You/yoh duz sing	Ah you/Ah yoh duz sing
He, she, it duz sing	Dey duz sing

As an alternative to the above U.S.V.I. Creole Conjugation, *Chart VIII*, Virgin Islanders might choose to eliminate the emphatic word, "*duz*" in which case the conjugation would look very much like that illustrated in *Chart VII*. It would be, however, an infraction in the third person singular if this were judged by the rules of "Standard English." In addition to the use of "*duz*" there is an alternate series of conjugations as shown in *Chart IX*. Again, it is important to highlight the fact that there is often overlapping between the English and the Virgin Islands Creole versions, but this reality does not, or at least should not, reduce the independence of the latter as a vibrant language. Following is the conjugation of the selected verb without the emphatic, "**duz**":

IX. ALTERNATIVE USVI CREOLE CONJUGATION	
Ah sing	We sing
You/yoh sing	Ah you/Ah yoh sing
He, she, it sing	Dey sing

Following this rubric the speaker of Creole would say "*He sing in deh choir,*" an equivalent expression to "*He duz sing in deh choir.*" One major difference between the two is the power of the word "*duz*" to highlight the situation: "*Boy, he duz sing good!*" This would not work if the speaker simply said: "*He sing good.*" Certainly, this second sentence does not capture the full essence of the utterance. Another example, "*Boy, she duz act stuiepid!*" Even though the alternative Creole statement ("*She act stuiepid*"), conveys a similar meaning, it lacks the emphasis inherent in the use of the verb "*duz.*"

One interesting subject/verb combination is the association of the subject "*you*" or "I" with the verb "*is.*" For some inexplicable reason some Virgin Islanders insist that no one ever uses this combination. This assessment results from the fact that many are thinking in terms of general patterns. For example, hardly anyone would say when speaking Virgin Islands Creole, "*You is tall,*" nor "*Wey is you from?*" Similarly, no one would ever say, "*I is goin' lata'.*" However, it is common to hear: "*Yoh is ah real nice man.*" If one person is waiting for another, and they are communicating by phone, the question might be posed: "*Wey you is so larng, man? Hurry!*" [Or "*Wey yoh is so larng, man?*"].

Language is so ingrained in us that we are often unaware of its usage, but this itself speaks to the naturalness of the oral elaborations. The popular statement, "*Meson, you is something else*" is a clear illustration of the combination of the subject (*you*) and the verb (*is*). We are unable to deduce from this, however, the cases where this particular subject "*you*"/ "*yoh*" can be combined with the verb, "*is.*" The creolized sentence, "*Man, you/yoh is ah big joke*" is popularly used, and it is unlikely to hear someone say: "*Man, you are a big...*" The only other option in our Creole is the elimination of the linking verb: "*Man, you/yoh ah big joke.*" In Virgin Islands Creole the following statements are acceptable: "*I is ah man who doan like toh talk.*" // "*I is the fus'one toh come heh.*"/// "*I is he cousin.*" On the other hand, the following sentences would be unacceptable statements in Virgin Islands Creole: "*I is home arl day.*"/// "*I is workin' today.*" When this combination is allowed and when it is not, depend on the islands' linguistic and cultural road map because these "rules" are totally confusing, and hence cannot be applied indiscriminately.

PERSONAL SUBJECT AND OBJECT PRONOUNS

In the Creole of the U.S.V.I. English object and subject pronouns are substituted for each other in particular situations, but this is very tricky grammatically because only through traditional consent does the speaker know exactly when this substitution is allowed. I will supply examples to show how the subject pronouns (*I, he, she* etc.) and object pronouns (*me, him, her*, etc.) function and the peculiarities associated with their usage. The pronouns that are provided below are the subject pronouns that are used in English. Thus, it is not a question of whether or not these are employed in Creole speech. The most important factor is the manner in which they are utilized, often inverted in their usage. The subject and object pronouns in English are listed in *Chart X* below:

X. Subject Pronouns	Object Pronouns
I	Me
You	You
He	Him
She	Her
We	Us
You	You
They	Them

The statement, "*Dey duz speak Creole*," follows the pattern *subject-verb-object*. In some cases, however, the use of the **object** pronoun functioning as subject of the sentence is also frequently allowed: "*Dem de 'ain know ah ting*" is an example of the object pronoun being used as a subject. In this case "de" is an adverb and is *not* a reference to the personal subject ("they"). Very often "*de*" is used for emphasis; for example, it is common to hear "*Dem de garn larng time man.*" This sentence might be responding to a question such as the following: "*Tony dem home?*" However, in United States Virgin Islands Creole, (here I stress this type of Creole) no one says: "*Us speak Creole,*" "*Him speak Creole;*" "*Her speak Creole;*" "*Us cum heh all deh time.*" Hence the use of the object pronoun in place of the subject pronoun is by no means universal in its application, and has its numerous restrictions.

Some Virgin Islanders insist that object pronouns are never used as subject in the Creole of the United States Virgin Islands and that this feature represents a linguistic trait seen elsewhere. But this apparent "resistance" illustrates a very important point: that oral elaboration is largely a subconscious act and most times we are not even aware of the way we speak because it is so embedded in our psyches. Many people who deny the usage described above do so honestly, truly believing that such morphological patterns are not present in the language. An example of this point of contention is the object pronoun "*me,*" about which many have argued is *never* used as the subject of a sentence in U.S. Virgin Islands Creole. Such a position is easily discounted with the following observation: The object "*me*" is used as a subject, even though it is generally reserved for negative constructions, and thus rarely heard in the affirmative: "*Me' ain goin'.*" "*Me'ain self-studyin' he.*" "*Me'ain know.*" "*Me'ain in da' wid dem.*" Sometimes, the pronunciation of the first two words glide to sound like: "*meen—ex. "Meen goin' wid dem.*" It would be very difficult for the uninitiated to know this rule of restriction except through practice and imitation.

The replacement of the object with the subject is more prevalent, but again would present a problem for the person outside of the speech community. In essence, when would one know when this substitution is allowed? The best answer is to acknowledge that there is that tacit consent directly related to constant usage and application—the cultural affinity. Consider the following sentences in Virgin Islands Creole: "*Ah tell ha Ah carn' do it.*" But also accepted: "A*h don' tell she Ah carn do it;*" "*Ah gon gi 'e piece ah mey min[d]*" and also the sentence presented earlier in this discussion, "*Me'ain self studyin he.*" "*I don' wid he.*" The popular phrase, "*arl ah we,*" (referenced later in the entries) represents yet another example of how the subject so often replaces the object ("*we*" in place of "*us*") in our language. These are some clear examples of how some subject pronouns are often used very freely in the objective case, in a rather "normalized" fashion.

Often underlining the sentences themselves is an emphatic tone, without which the sentence may seem unnatural. The statement, *"Ah gon call 'e tomorrow"* does not seem to fit the natural profile of Virgin Islands language; however, said with the proper cadence, in the right context and emphasis it represents a very typical Virgin Islands utterance. Consider the scenario in which someone told you: *"Boy, Jerry tarkin' 'bout yoh family."* Your possible reaction: *"Wait 'til (ah) Ah see 'e tomorrow."* Another example would illustrate how very interesting these patterns are. For example, a popular expression which emphasizes endearment and fondness is: *"Look (See) she fo' me, no."* *"Yestaday Ah see he fo' you")*. As a generalization, we can say that *"she"* and *"he,"* often reserved as subjects of the sentence in the English language, are very elastic in Virgin Islands Creole, and as seen here can be used objectively; hence, the frequent consternation experienced by critics of the Creole language and the very notion of its existence. Similar usage can be seen with the subject pronoun *"we,"* but it would be uncommon to hear a speaker of Virgin Islands Creole using *"I"* or *"dey"* (they) in the objective case.

The sentences *"Heen self studyin' we"* and *"We ain self studyin' he/ she"* if they were English sentences would be in clear violation of the morphological and syntactic rules. But, in fact, such sentences incarnate and epitomize the fundamental structure of our language. On the other hand, *"He gon gi' it toh I"* is not an expression generally heard in the language. The exception would be that those who are Rastafarians may very well used this grammatical structure (*"He gon gi' it toh "I-man"*). Similarly, *"we gon help "dey"* is an expression that would never be heard in Virgin Islands Creole. In essence, then, there is much flexibility in the subject/object interplay; and the limitations are tacitly known and adhered to by the speakers of Virgin Islands Creole. These structural tendencies would present a constant challenge to those on the outside of this particular language community, that like all language communities operate on the tacit adherence to cultural and traditional agreements and allegiances. In large part, to the uninitiated the rules may seem far too arbitrary and inconsistent. In the mind of the speaker of Virgin Islands Creole, however, the grammatical regulations are clear and rigidly set.

SUPPRESSION OF THE PREPOSITIONS TOH (TO)/FO'(FOR)/AT/IN/OF AND APOCOPATED (SHORTENED) PREPOSITIONS

A popular construction in U.S. Virgin Islands Creole is that formed from the suppression of several special propositions, *to, for, at, in,* and *of.* The consistent pattern of the employment of these prepositions as unique entities in our speech speaks to the fact that Virgin Islands Creole truly has its firm grammatical structure. Certainly it all points to a long history steep in traditions and customs. The statement, *"She toh deh movies"* would turn heads in the United States. Not that the communication would necessarily be totally lost, but that the sentence structurally would be illogical to the speaker of English. Virgin Islanders hear this statement, and without hesitancy know that it means —*"She is at the movies."* Later this feature will be examined as it relates to the substitution of one proposition with another. There is no translation necessary in the example stated above because the statement immediately registers, hence cognitively there is no struggle. The person outside of the community of languages, however, might have to make a conscious effort as that individual tries to decipher meaning. More on this feature later.

In the following pages I will supply examples of how these prepositions function within sentences. In addition to this, I will also look at the suppression of *"to/toh"* and how this suppression functions in Virgin Islands Creole. *Chart XI* offers examples from Virgin Islands Creole, followed by what would be the corresponding forms in English. Under the category "Standard English," in addition to highlighting the preposition "to" the linking verb is underlined to indicate its omission in Virgin Islands Creole:

XI. EXAMPLES OF THE SUPPRESSION OF THE PREPOSITION *"TOH (TO)"*	
USVI CREOLE	**STANDARD ENGLISH**
"She goin' New York."	*{She is going to New York.}*
"We comin' town late."	*{We are going to town late.}*
"Ah gon go soon."	*{I am going to go soon.}*
"Lydia gon do it today."	*{Lydia is going to do it today.}*
"Dey goin' back States next' week"	*{They are going back to the U.S. next week}*
"Si' down close meh"	*{Sit close to me.}*

Such common expressions confirm their prevalence in daily usage. It is important to know that Virgin Islanders are not only aware of the English expressions in parentheses, but that we also use them. The truth here is that frequently islanders move between languages (switching) hence, it is never considered unusual to hear the "standard" English versions. The one thing that would provoke a negative reaction would be if the speaker of Virgin Islands Creole, changed his or her tone or inflection when uttering the expressions in parentheses. That is, the speaker tries to emulate the accent and enunciation of a U.S. mainlander (see definition of *"mainlan"* in the entries). If the individual speaking Creole is suspected of doing this, then it would not be unusual to hear the term "yankin'," used as a criticism against what many would considered pretentiousness. (The word **"yankin' "** is defined later in this book, in the section under **WORDS, EXPRESSIONS…**).

Embracing the expressions under the column **USVI** *Creole* (Chart XI) would be tantamount to embracing our culture, and thus ourselves. Yet, the challenge is always how to do this while simultaneously "correcting" our students, and our community in general when they express themselves. The problem does not necessarily have to be an unsurmountable one, even though it may at times seem to be. If a child says *"Ah goin' town now,"* and receive a verbal reprimand (such as *"Stop speaking like that!"*; *"Learn to speak properly."*), then the child may well feel as if he or she is guilty of some unpardonable violation. The solution would be to explain to the child that we do have more than one way of expressing ourselves, an allusion to our bilingualism—part of the cultural wealth mentioned earlier. A discussion on when it is most "appropriate" to speak in a certain way may be most timely and fruitful. I assume that we would all agree that lecturing to an audience from Boston using Virgin Islands Creole may well be symbolically impactful and culturally affirmative; nonetheless, if no one understands you, your time may have well been wasted. But how do we initiate a conversation on "appropriateness", on applicability if we ourselves reject the notion of a legitimate Virgin Islands Creole Language? Therein lies a major dilemma.

In addition to the suppression of *"toh (to),"* the preposition *"fo'* (*"for"*) also is frequently suppressed. In addition, the preposition *"at"* is often eliminated in many constructions in our Creole. Both features ("fo' / "at") are represented in *Chart XII* presented below:

XII. EXAMPLES OF THE SUPPRESSION OF THE PREPOSITIONS "FOR" AND "AT"	
USVI Creole	**Standard English**
"Ah was lookin' food."	*{"I was looking for food."}*
"Warren was out de beggin' money."	*{"Warren was out there begging for money."}*
"Yoh need toh look wok."	*{"You need to look for work."}*
"Look he, no."	*{"Look at him."}*
"Stop starin' me, no."	*{"Stop staring at me."}*
"He home right now."	*{"He is at home right now."}*
"Benji de' home."	*{"Benji is at home."}*
"Dey don airport."	*{"They are already at the airport."}*

As mentioned earlier, the preposition "at" in *some cases* can also be replaced by "toh," a special feature of Virgin Islands Creole; however, *Chart XII* above emphasizes the omission of the prepositions "at" and "for," an enduring trait in our speech. An expression such as *"He aways out de lookin' trouble"* is typically heard. No one would argue that the sentence would not be understood if the preposition "for" were included, but it would also sound very contrived. Similarly, the statement, *"Da guirl lookin' mango"* is a sentence that would not capture the essence of the creolized thought were the preposition ("*for*") included. Of course, also frequently heard in these sentences are "fo' mango," "fo trouble," etc.

Just like the previous prepositions discussed, there are cases in which the preposition "*in*" is omitted in Virgin Islands Creole. Again, even though we are speaking of limited usage, we are still referring to a very identifiable component of the speech patterns of the United States Virgin Islands. *Chart XIII* below shows some *possible* elaborations that would demonstrate how this particular suppression functions. This is a feature that is commonly heard, and I stress that the speaker is *not* committing an error. The reason for this is simple—the Creole sentence has its own structure and syntax, and the speaker is preceding from the premise of the Creole, and not translating from English to Creole:

XIII. EXAMPLES OF THE SUPPRESSION OF THE PREPOSITION "*IN*"	
USVI CREOLE	**STANDARD ENGLISH**
"*Dey live Tortola.*"	{They live in Tortola.}
"*He wokin' Sin Thomas today*". "*Tomorrow he wokin' Sin John.*"	{He *is* working in St. Thomas today.} {Tomorrow he *is* working in St. John.}
"Ah *stayin' Grove Place tonight.*"	{I *am* staying in Grove Place tonight.}
"*Lydia St. Croix.*"	{Lydia *is* in St. Croix.}

For the individual not familiar with Virgin Islands Creole it is important to note that in all cases the reference is to a geographical space. If we tried to substitute other locations the utterances would be unintelligible. In this regard, we can say that every speaker of Virgin Islands Creole knows that it **is not** permitted to say: "*Dey live ah big house*" to mean "*Dey live in ah big house.*" Similarly, the expression, "*She deh yard*" to mean "*She is in the yard*" would be unrecognizable. Consider the question that might possibly generate the last entry in *Chart XIII* above: "*Wey Lydia? Ah ain* **see** *ha' in ah larng time.*" Response: "*Lydia St. Croix.*" (*Lydia is in St. Croix*). Not only is the preposition not used in this example, but the linking verb "*to be*" is not part of the construction.

Finally, the English preposition "of" is often replaced in U.S. Virgin

Islands Creole, substituting the Creole word *"ah."* Below in *Chart XIV* are various examples of sentences that demonstrate this Creolized prepositions:

XIV. EXAMPLES OF PREPOSITION "OF" TO 'AH'	
Sentence in English	**Sentence in USVI Creole**
All of them	*"Arl ah dem"*
All of you	*"Arl ah you/*yoh"
All of us	*"Arl ah we"*
Some of them	*"Some ah dem"*
Which one of these do you want?	*"Wich one ah dese yoh wan'?"*
Carol is thinking of all kinds of things.	*"Carol tinkin' ah arl kin' ah ting."*

In the case of the phrase *"all you,"* the preposition is eliminated, as we have also seen with respect to the other prepositions mentioned earlier (*"to," "for," "at," "in"*).

SUBSTITUTION OF PREPOSITION "AT" WITH THE PREPOSITION "TOH"

In Virgin Islands Creole there is the rare replacement of the preposition "at" with "toh (to)" in special situations. The individual not too familiar with the language might deduce that this type of substitution is pervasive, but it is not. The substitution, "toh" in place of "at" in general is a limited feature, in the sense that one cannot categorically replace "at" with "toh" in a formulaic manner. No one would say, for example, *"Ah goin' beach toh 3 o'clock"* to mean "at 3 o'clock." Neither should the two prepositions be considered interchangeable in any form. This notwithstanding, within its limited domain, in very specific contexts, we see this replacement. The examples given in *Chart XV* demonstrate how the substitution or replacement functions:

XV. SUBSTITUTION OF PREPOSITION "AT" WITH THE PREPOSITION "TOH"	
Janet: *"Austin don garn?"*	Sammy: *"Yea, he toh deh airport aready."*
John: *"Wey deh party gon be?"*	Cheryl: *"Toh mey sista' Carmen house."*
June: *"Wey Ellie dem?"*	Hubert: "Man, *Dey don toh deh house larng time."*

It is important to note that this is not the only situation where one preposition is used in place of another. On rare occasions *"in"* is used instead of "on" as in the following example: *"Who pu' dem ting in deh flo'*? However, the question, *"Who pu' dem ting in deh table*?" would *not be a* correct Creole expression, nor would the question, "*Who leave dem ting __in the ground?__*"— Where the preposition "in" is being used instead of "on."

Another popular feature of our Creole is to shorten some prepositions by generally suppressing the first syllable. Here again is an interesting paradox where the rule is that there is not a specific rule—except that everyone knows exactly when to use these forms. Below in *Chart XVI* are some common prepositions that fall in this category:

XVI. EXAMPLES OF SHORTENED PREPOSITIONS	
Preposition	**Sentence in USVI Creole**
Unless—less	(*Doan come* **'less** *you have deh ting.*)
Until-til	(Wait **'til** lata.')
Against—genz'	(Pu' it **'genz'** deh wall.)
Around- roun	(*he live* **'roun'** *deh fiel.*)
Across-crass	(*pu'it* **crass** *deh bed.*)
About-bout	(*Stop tarkin'* **'bout** *people.*)
Among—mong	(*Doan pu'it* **mong'** *deh good clothes.*)

Some of the apocopation that are **not** allowed: **below, behind, over, toward.**

ADJECTIVES AND ADVERBS USAGE

The doubling of an adjective often serves as the replacement of an adverb. For example, the statement *"It is a very big house"* is frequently rendered as *"It is a big big house."* Also, *"She is a nice nice woman;" "Man, she duz drive a pretty pretty car."* Functionally, in each grammatical structure the first adjective serves as an adverb, a strange kind of alliance. Its force as an adverb is clearly more powerful than that of the *"standard"* and traditional English adverb *"very"* that often is incapable of capturing the desired emphasis of the speaker of Virgin Islands Creole. Again, this is not to suggest that the doubling of the adjectives is not used anywhere else, but in the Virgin Islands the usage is truly extensive. Nor is there any inference being made in this discussion that people never use the "actual" adverbs as intensifiers. The truth is, however, as a child growing up in the Virgin Islands I do not recall the pervasive usage of the adverbs such as *very*, or *extremely*. I am sure that others may have a different experience; for example those children who may have been better prepared with respect to language usage; however, I would still contend that young children tended and continue to opt for the repetition of the adjective.

In the linguistic sphere of children the use of such adverbs as "very" or "extremely" was and in fact continues to be uncommon in Creole. However, the infrequent use of these adverbs did not in any way diminish the oral articulation and the conveyance of ideas, for in fact the creative spirit forged, more than compensated for the infrequency of adverbs such as "very" and "extremely." Adults and children alike use the adjectives in succession, but whereas adults also use regular adverbs (ex. *very*) to intensify their utterance, children

82

tend to adhere more to the doubling of the adjectives. For example, everyone speaking in Virgin Islands Creole would say *"Yestaday Ah eat ah sweet sweet mango."* The adult may very well employ an adverb in this case, *"a very sweet mango."* The likelihood of a child doing the same is greatly reduced in proportion to the child's age. In essence, the younger the child, the more improbable that he/she would veer from the creolized pattern of the repetition of the adjectives.

The English suffix, "ly", generally suggests the use of an adverb. For the most part the speaker of Virgin Islands Creole avoids this adverbial formation, opting instead for the word in its adjectival form, but *functioning as an adverb*. Consider the following English sentences and their counterparts in Virgin Islands Creole (*Chart XVII*):

XVII. ENGLISH ADVERBS WITH SUFFIX "LY"	
Standard English	USVI Creole
They were walking *slowly*.	Dey wuz walkin' *slow*.
She was *beautifully* dressed.	She wuz dress' *beautiful*
Sara speaks *clearly*.	Sara duz speak *clear*
Run *quickly*.	Run *quick*.

In addition to the doubling feature and the suppression of "ly", the words *"good"* and *"well"* are frequently used as adverbs to modify an adjective. This will be discussed more extensively in the entries given in the section, **WORDS, EXPRESSIONS, MAXIMS, PROVERBS—A VIRGIN ISLANDS CULTURAL LEXICON.** But in generally, expressions such as *"good smart"* mean that the individual is "very smart."

There are occasions when the word "well" may be substituted for "good." As will be discussed later, however, these two renditions (*"good"* and *"well"*) are not always necessarily interchangeable. In fact, even though the adverb "very" is a close translation of the adjective "good" in the expression, "good tall," such a translation would not work if the phrase were "<u>well</u> happy." In other words, the translation of the sentence *"You <u>well</u> happy,"* to mean *"you are very happy,"* would miss the essence of the Creole sentence which is imbued with irony or sarcasm (this is addressed further in the particular entries). The speaker in fact is rather curious or even suspicious of the person's "apparent" or "seeming" happiness; hence it would be an inaccurate translation or interpretation with the employment of the adverb "very." Such an adverb would miss the sarcastic or ironic undertone of the statement, "*You well happy.*"

PAST TENSE

One of the grammatical structures that create the most negative frustration and angst from the antagonists of the notion of a Virgin Islands language is the use of the past tense. But the cultural consternation is not the only issue here; there is also an issue relating to the complicated grammatical structure and the challenge for anyone not familiar with our Creole language. The biggest challenge is that most often the present functions in the capacity as a simple past, a construction that for the language outsider (the person unfamiliar with the language) could present rather ambiguous and often confusing situations. The fact is that the interpretation is totally driven by the context, and hence within the community of articulators of the language there is hardly ever any ambiguity or ambivalence.

Members of this community of language would know exactly the exceptions to the rule of past tense formation. This is a case where acquisition is linked primarily to practical usage. For example, in Virgin Islands Creole one might say, *"Ah <u>see</u> 'im yestaday in town,"* or *"We <u>eat</u> some good food las' nite."* *"Man, yestaday we tark 'bout arl kin-ah ting."* In these cases the infinitive verbs "to see," "to eat" and "to talk" are kept in the present indicative in spite of the past moment. The statement, *"Mammie, Ah don <u>do</u> deh dishes aready"* is a clear reference to the past. *"Do,"* typically a present tense verb, is functioning as a legitimate past tense. To express the past negative, in the Creole of the U.S. Virgin Islands *"ain"* and *"dain"* can be used:

"I (Ah) <u>ain' do</u> notin' <u>toh</u> 'im." or *"I (Ah) <u>dain do</u> notin' toh 'im."*

"He <u>ain' see</u> meh, bu' Ah was de." Also, *"He <u>dain see</u> meh, bu' Ah was de."*

It is worth noting that the verb "ain" is a verb that can be used both in the present or past tense, with the context being the major determinant for meaning. For example, *"Me <u>ain know</u> wey 'e garn"* refers to the present moment. Meanwhile, the sentence *"I <u>ain</u> see him yesterday"* represents the past.

It must be pointed out that there are notable exceptions to the rule for the formulation of the simple present: specifically, the three infinitives *"to be," "to go,"* and *"to have."* For example, when referring to the past no one would ever say in Virgin Islands Creole: *"Yestaday, we **go** toh deh movies."* Neither would anyone say, *"Yestaday she **is** here,"* nor *"las' week she **have** ah lat ah money."* These sentences would not resonate, and any member of the shared community of languages would immediately recognize their inadmissibility. And this is true even though with the adverb *yestaday* in place, or the expression "las' week," the context would be clear. The violators of the rule will only likely be those who are unaware of the tacit linguistic tradition.

The fact that the use of the present tense of *to be, to have*, and *to go*, is disallowed as markers of the past, flies in the face of logic since we readily accept all other verbs without qualification. So even though this may seem rather arbitrary—(the acceptance of one set of verbs and the rejection of another), the application itself is anything but arbitrary. Those who speak the language, subconsciously subscribe to the linguistic norms and communication, and proceed without obstruction. Some critics of Virgin Islands speech, however, see present tense utterances being substituted for the past tense as among the most heretical of violations of the "standard English" creed. In their view, it is among the most emblematic manifestations of the lack of education and of the insular nature that characterizes our unwillingness to change what is wrong. The thought of the present tense as an accepted grammatical form does not sit well with these opponents of Virgin Islands Creole. *Chart XVIII* provides a representative summary of the simple past tense:

XVIII. FORMATION OF PAST TENSE IN VIRGIN ISLANDS CREOLE	
Some Examples of Verbs conjugated in the present to talk about a PRESENT action	Some Examples of Verbs conjugated in the present to talk about a *PAST* action
Ah see 'im eveyday.	*Yestaday Ah see 'im in town.*

We speak toh dem arl deh time.	We speak toh dem las' night.
Dey live in Cuba.	Dey live in Cuba fo' ah year.
Notable Exceptions "**to be**," "**to go**," "**to have**"	
Some Examples of Verbs conjugated in the present to talk about a PRESENT action	**Past Tense Conjugation**
Elena is mey frien'.	Elena was mey frien'.
We go chuch evey Sunday.	We went chuch las' Sunday.
Dey have ah truck.	Dey had ah truck.
The _Present_ Tense of These Three Verbs Can Never Be Used For The Past	

What happens in the case of English interrogatives in using the formula for the past tense: <*Did you...?*> ; "*Did he...?*> etc. The fact of the matter is that in *United States Virgin Islands Creole* the verb "*did*" does not really exist. Creole speakers would simply keep the principal verb in the present tense, the word "*did*" would be ignored. Of course, the rules governing the exceptions for "*to be*," "*to go*," and "*to have*" will still be in place. In *Chart XIX* below, observe the questions in English and their contrast with those in Virgin Islands Creole:

XIX. PAST TENSE WITH "DID"	
Standard English	**USVI Creole**
Did you bring the books?	Yoh bring deh books dem?
Did Leroy cook the food already?	Leroy (don) cook deh food aready?
Did Lisa buy a house last year?	Lisa buy ah house las' yea'?
Did they go to the movies?	Dey went/garn movies*?

PRESENT PERFECT

The English present perfect (*"I have seen it already"* etc.) provides a very interesting grammatical component for speakers of Virgin Islands Creole. The rules are somewhat complex, and there are many renditions of this tense. To highlight the marked differences from "standard" English I will supply several illustrations. We can refer to the example given for the present perfect above. In this case the person speaking Creole is very likely to say: *"Ah don see it aready,"* or with a slight variation: *"I don see it aready."* The statement *"We have already written the letter,"* would be most typically rendered as *"We write deh letta' aready."* Also rendering the same sense is the expression: *"We don' write deh letta' aready."* Once again, then, the present can serve as a substitute. But what happens with the three verbs given as exceptions in the simple past (*"to go," "to be," "to have"*)?

Consider the English sentence *"They have already gone."* In the creolized version of this sentence, the present tense of "to go" *cannot* be used; instead the creolized past participle is necessary: *"Dey don garn"* or *"Dey aready garn."* In much the same way, the past participle of "to be" must be used in the present perfect construction; the simple present is not admissible: *"We have been there."* In our U.S.V.I Creole this would be translated as *"We bin de"* or *"We been de."* (See list of entries later with the words "**bin**" and "**been**"). The verb "to have" follows the same pattern when used in the present perfect. English sentence: *"They have had that before."* Creole version: *"Dey ha' had dat befo'."*

PLUPERFECT (PAST PERFECT)

As a contrast to the present perfect, in U.S.V.I. Creole the pluperfect is always constructed with the use of the word "*ah*" or "*ha.*" Consider the following two expressions: A) "*They had already seen the movie when I came home.*" B) *We had already eaten before she arrived.*" The sentence in (*A*) would be translated as "*Dey ha' aready (don) <u>see</u> the movie wen Ah come home.*" The other sentence (*B*) would be rendered as "*We ha' aready (don) <u>**eat**</u> befo' she arrive'.*" In these sentences, the present tense form of the verbs are used in place of the English past participles (*seen* and *eaten*, respectively). Also, of course, the simple present is also used for the past moment (*come / arrive*) as explained in the earlier section under **Past Tense**. However, as with the case of the ***Past Tense*** and ***Present Perfec***t, if the verb is "to go," "to be" or "to have" the use of the present tense is not permitted. The English sentence, "*She had already <u>gone</u> when we came,*" would very likely be rendered as "*She ha (ah) aready (don) <u>garn</u> wen we come.* In essence, in U.S.V.I. Creole, it is not permitted to say "*Elroy ha' **go** wid dem.*" In our language the speaker would employ either "***garn***" or "***went***," as part of a creolized expression with no resonance in English. The same argument must be made for "*to have*" and "*to be.*"

HYPOTHETICAL CASES / SHOULD HAVE / COULD HAVE / MIGHT

Hypothetical cases create constructions that vary significantly from their English counterparts. Let us consider the sentence, *"If I knew his name, I would talk to him."* In Virgin Islands Creole this would be translated as *"If Ah know he name, Ah wo' tark toh' im."* Note the present tense usage of *"to know,"* typical of the usage with most verbs in this type of hypothetical constructions. Once again, however, as in the case of the simple past tense, the use of the present tense verbs *"to be," "to go,"* and *"to have"* is prohibited in U.S.V.I. Creole in this situation. Hence the utterance, *"If Ah have money, Ah wo' buy it"* does not convey accurately the idea of the English sentence, *"If I had money, I would buy it."* In the same vein, if the verb is *"to be,"* it would not be acceptable to employ the present tense, *"If he is mey frien,' I wo' tark to 'im."* (The "standard" English form, *"If he were my friend, I would talk to him."*). These types of contrary-to-fact sentences do not admit the present tense application of the verbs listed as exceptions.

Hypothetical cases that are irrevocable would present additional challenges for the person unfamiliar with U.S.V.I. Creole. Let us consider the sentence, *"If she had seen us, she would have been mad."* In Creole one can say, *"If she ah see us, she would ah be mad."* The present tense "see" is permitted functioning in effect as a past participle. The English past participle "been" becomes *"be"* in Creole. If the past participle in English is "had," then the Creole speaker maintains that tense. In English one would say, for example, *"If she had had my number, she would have called me."* In Creole, the second *"had,"* the past participle, must remain as part of the construction: *"If she ah had mey numba, she would ah call meh."*

A look at sentences of probability ("might have") and hypothetical sentences employing the constructions "should have" and "could have" points to the unusual nature of these verbal structures. Two verbs that we have cited as exceptions (*"to be"*; *"to go"*) assume different forms with these expressions. A few examples would suffice: The English statement *"I wish that you could have been there"* might be transcribed in Creole as *"Meson, Ah wish you coudah_be de,"* a transcription that totally ignores the rules of English grammar. The Creole sentence, *"Ah might ah go wid dem, if Ah ha' know,"* (also, an alternate form, *"Ah might ah garn wid dem, if Ah ha' know,"*) is a translation of the English statement, *"I might have gone with them if I had known."* Finally, the sentence *"Leroy should have gone to the bank"* is rendered as *"Leroy shoudah go toh deh bank."* Chart XX summarizes this maze of grammatical structures.

XX. SUMMARY OF PRESENT PERFECT, PLUPERFECT & HYPOTHETICAL PROBABILITY	
Standard English	**USVI Creole**
Juan has written the letter.	*Juan (don) write deh letta.*
We had seen them.	*We ha' see dem.*
If I knew him, I would talk to him.	*If Ah know 'im, Ah wo' tark toh 'im.*
I should have gone with her.	*Ah shoudah go wid ha.* * *Ah shoudah garn wid ha.*
They could have had the money.	*Dey coudah had deh money.** *Dey coudah have deh money.*
That might have been his car.	*Dat might ah be' he ca'.** *Dat might ah bin (been) he ca'.*

*Note that the verbs, "to go," and "to have" can be kept in their present tense forms, quite a contrast with its use in the simple past discussed earlier. As an option, they can also be expressed in the participial form. *"To be,"* on the other hand, can be rendered in participial form, but not in the present. Instead, the other option is that *"To be"* may be in the same form as that which is used for the imperative—though clearly not a command.

THE POSSESSIVE

The possessive is generally used by substituting a subject pronoun. As we will see, however, this is not permissible in all cases of the subject pronouns. Nonetheless, the feature is a common one that merits a discussion. Note the following statements: "*Dat is he mudda.*" "*Mr. Richard is dey fadda.*" (In this case, the father of several people— *their*); "*Ah believe dat's she mudda.*" In all of these cases the subject pronoun functions as the possessive, however, this not a universally standard rule. For example, the following expressions would be unacceptable: "*Dat's I friend*" or "*Dat's we house.*" "*Dat's you books*" (Note, however, that the plural "*ah you*" is allowed, as mentioned below). These expressions, using "*I*," "*we*," or "*you*" are not part of the structure of the possessive adjectives in Virgin Islands Creole.

To further complicate this, the object pronouns are not used as the possessive in Virgin Islands Creole, except with the word "yoh." ["*yoh*" can function as both subject and object.]; hence, it would be highly unusual to hear "*Dat's me ca'.*" This is rendered as "*dat's mey ca'.*" The second person singular possessive is rendered by the word: "yoh "—*Dat's yoh business.*" To express the second person plural possessive the expression, "*ah you*" or "*ah yoh*" is used: "*Dat's ah you/yoh business.*" In general, the subject pronoun "we" is not used as a possessive in Virgin Islands Creole. Virgin Islanders would never say "*we book*", "*we ca'* " as the first person plural possessive etc. but instead employ the conventional English possessive "our" as the possessive to represent the collective plural in the first person. For the uninitiated this can be extremely confusing. There are really two types of possessives; one used as adjective and the other used as a pronoun. *Chart XXI provides* the information on the possessive adjectives, while *Chart*

XXII focuses on the possessive pronouns. Both Charts provide the forms first in "Standard English" then in USVI Creole.

XXI. EXAMPLES OF THE POSSESSIVE ADJECTIVES	
Standard English	**USVI Creole**
my	*mey*
your	*yoh*
his	*he*
her	*she/ha*
our	*our*
your	*ah you/ah yoh*
their	*dey*

It is interesting to observe that the creolized sentence, *"He name Roger"* actually combines two major features of Virgin Islands Creole that we have discussed here. One is the possessive adjective as exhibited in *Chart XXI* immediately above, and the other is the suppression of the linking verb, *"to be,"* presented in the section under **"Verbal Suppression.** So that, *"He name Roger"* is translated *"His name is Roger."* (See more discussion in particular entries given later.)

XXII. EXAMPLES OF THE POSSESSIVE PRONOUNS	
Standard English	**USVI Creole**
mine	*Mines/Mine own/My own* *"Dat's mine own."*
yours	*Your own/Yours own* *"Dat truck is yours own?"*
his	*Hees own* *"Dis TV is hees own."*
hers	*Her own/Hers own* *"Deh book is hers own."*
ours	*Our/Ours own* *"Dis truck is our own."*

yours	*Ah you/Yoh own* *"Da' boat is ah you own?"*
theirs	*Dere own/Deres own* *"Da house is deres own."* *Dem own*

In the *Chart XXII* above when there are several options, I give one illustrative sentence, however, in each case any one of the other options may be substituted. An example is the statement, *"Dat's mines"* which conveys the same meaning as *"Dat's mine own."* The expressions listed under the USVI Creole column are all unique and are not allowed in English.

REFLEXIVE PRONOUNS

These are *generally* formed by the combination of the subject pronouns and the word "*self.*" As in many cases in Virgin Islands Creole the speaker code switches with frequency, for example between "*sheself*" and "*herself.*" These reflexive pronouns "*meyself,*" "*yohself,*" "*sheself,*" "*heself,*" "*deyself,*" and "*ah you/yoh self*" are commonly used and represent an important grammatical component of our Creole. The main variation from English can be readily observed in the *Chart XXIII* below:

XXIII. REFLEXIVE PRONOUNS IN V.I. CREOLE	
Meyself	*Leave it. Ah gon do it meyself.*
Yohself	*Yoh goin' by yohself?*
Heself	*He fix it heself.*
Sheself/Haself	*Ah say she gon do it sheself.*
Ah you self	*Do it ah yoh self.*
Ourself*	*We gon do it ourself.*
Deyself	*Dey wan' toh do dat deyself.*

*At first glance this may appear to be the same as in "Standard English." But the word does not appear in English. In fact the combination *our + self* would be a grammatical impossibility since "our" suggests plurality; yet "our*self* is an expression that flourishes in Virgin Islands Creole.

DEMONSTRATIVES ADJECTIVES
AND PRONOUNS

The demonstratives adjectives and pronouns in English are localized in United States Virgin Islands Creole and follow their unique pathways in the language. The numerous and varied expressions used are truly reflective of the creativity and richness of our speech patterns. In U.S.V.I. Creole words such as "*Dis*" and "*Dat*" and at times "*Dem*" are often used as replacements for the English demonstratives "*this*," "*that*," and "*those*" respectively. These are our most conventional substitutes. It must be pointed out, however, that these are not the only expressions with respect to the demonstratives. In point of fact, there are several other expressions that highlight the hyperbolic nature of our Creole. Those are the ones in which "*de*" accompanies the more conventional demonstrative and makes the sentence much more emphatic. I will supply some examples to demonstrate how this works because this is one of those situations in which those outside of the community would struggle to grasp the meaning completely. It is not at all unusual to hear in USVI Creole "*Dat de*" or "*Da de*," or "*Dem de*"- - compound constructions with no counterpart in English. Consider the following sentences in which the demonstrative is represented in various manners:

1. "*Dat (Da) man is mey frien'.*" This is used as a regular demonstrative adjective. "*That man is my friend.*"
2. "*Dis book is yours own.*" Another regular demonstrative adjective which means that "*This book is yours.*"
3. "*Dat de (Da de-) is wa Ah doan like.*"—In this case the demonstrative in English would be simply "that." It is clearly a

96

neuter demonstrative that is referring more to a situation than to something tangible. An example of this would be if someone did something objectionable, the individual who expresses his or her disapproval might say: *"Da de is wa Ah doan like wid he, meson."* English would very likely use an expression such as *"That is (or That's) what I don't like."*

4. *"Dem is his own."* There are several aspects about this sentences (or other similar ones) that should call our attention to the unique and duplicitous nature of U.S. Virgin Islands Creole. The use of the word "dem" always sparks a longstanding discussion in our community (United States Virgin Islands), as to how pervasive is its usage. Interestingly, the sentence above (*"Dem is his own."*) could mean both *"Those are his"* and *"These are his."* Unlike other areas in our West Indies, in U.S. Virgin Islands parlance "Dem" is used in place of the subject pronoun, "they," in limited situations. For example, the sentence *"Dem comin' lata' "* would not be a likely utterance in U.S. Virgin Islands Creole. Even though it is used at times for emphasis. By contrast, however, the question, *"Who dem is?"* is not only an admissible question, but a popular one as well. At the same time, the question, *"Wey dem garn?"* is generally not used in the vernacular. Evidence of the subtleties in the language, there are other expressions that are similar, but that are interpreted ever so slightly differently, as is seen in #5 below.

5. *"Dem de crazy."* In English, the closest that we can come to a translation of this sentence is to say "Those/These [people] are crazy." *"De"* is added to our conventional demonstrative giving the sentence its very unique structure. The truth is that there is no possible substitution in English that would adequately convey the meaning intended here. The word "there" would not make sense. And if we try to replace the expression with "over there," not only will this not capture the meaning, but may also give an erroneous one.

In the examples in both #3 and #5 it is clear that the important feature of these sentences is that they are emphatic. As stated previously these are alternative expressions (instead of the regular demonstratives, #1, #2, #4) that are very popular and represent an even further distancing from the "standard" English utterances. How the demonstratives are used is no doubt challenging for the person not too familiar with United States Virgin Islands Creole. In the chart following (*XXIV*) there is a brief summary compilation of sentences (with the word "*dem*") that highlights the contrast between admissible expressions and others. Though the expressions in both columns are structurally similar, those in the second group are not typically heard in the Creole of the United States Virgin Islands. The chart includes not only the use of "dem" as a demonstrative and possessive, but also as the subject of the sentence.

| XXIV. SAMPLE COMPARATIVE VIEW OF "DEM" ||
ADMISSIBLE IN USVI CREOLE	UNCOMMON IN USVI CREOLE
Dem is ours	*Wey dem garn?*
Dem de crazy	*Why dem do it?*
Who dem is, man?	*Dem gon leave soon.*
Dem boy comin' big.	*Call meh wen dem reach.*
Who dem fa'?	*Wa' dem name is?*
Who dem tryin' toh fool?	*Dat's dem sista.*

It is important to emphasize here the choice of words used in *Chart XXIV*, that is, "UNCOMMON," not "wrong." In fact, in the second column, given certain stress of the word "*dem*," and intonation, it may be possible to hear some of the expressions. However, they would not be as common place as those expressions in the first column. Moreover, even if the expressions signified in the second column were used locally, there would not be a scintilla of ambiguity or ambivalence with respect to their comprehension.

FORMULATION OF QUESTIONS

A feature of the Creole of the U.S. Virgin Islands that stands out is the syntax when questions are formulated with such interrogative words as *"when," "why," "who," " how," "where."* The main aspect of the structure is that the subject/verb inversion typically used in English is not as common in Virgin Islands. In our Creole the tendency is to maintain the subject/verb construct used in the typical declarative sentence. Hence, affirmative statements such as *"They are eating," "The girl is a student,"* and *"Those books are difficult"* would all maintain the same order of the words if they were formulated as questions in USVI Creole. The *Chart XXV* below provides a few examples of the interrogatives and how they generally function:

XXV. SUBJECT/VERB ORDER WITH INTERROGATIVES	
Standard English	**USVI Creole**
Where is he?	*Wey he is?*
Where is Phil now?	*Wey Phil is now?*
How old is she?	*How ole she is?*
Who is that woman?	*Who da woman is?*
When can they go?	*Wen dey cou go?*
Why did you go?	*Why you/yoh went?*
Are those books difficult?	*Dem books difficult?*

Many questions have a creolized form that is a total fissure from the "standard" English. For example, questions, —i.e. *"Wa' yoh lookin' ah meh fa'?"* or *"Wa he tarkin so fa'?"*—go against the grain in English, ending with a preposition, and also suppressing the linking verb.

There is no question that we need to take a closer look at how U.S.V.I. Creole is structured in order to truly begin to appreciate the fact that there are not only numerous features that are rigidly fixed but that the speakers adhere to these "rules" of pronunciation with uncanny regularity. I hope that our awareness of these "regulations" in our Creole helps to dispel the myth of it simply being a ragged sampling of English. The discussions of topics such as the present, the past, possessives, reflexives and others are essential for our attaining a much better understanding of the language that we speak, and in some cases the language that we resist speaking. When we combine our grasp of the syntax and morphology with an intimate sense of maxims, adages, beliefs, and cultural philosophy, we take ourselves one step closer to claiming our Creole— as vibrant, durable, sustainable and, above all, worthy of being uplifted, deserving of being viewed on the level of any other mode of speech.

The section that follows, a dictionary of sort, examines several Creole words, phrases, expressions, and maxims, and aphorisms. It is my hope that the reader will be able to connect what has been presented in the grammar and pronunciation sections with the definitions and descriptions provided in the Section that follows. Taken as a whole, the pronunciation and grammatical rules embedded in our Creole, combined with the multiple words, expressions, and sounds, affirm the unique nature of our language. In my view, a work that only stresses particular words and expressions would not do justice to the variety and complexity of United States Virgin Islands Creole.

WORDS, EXPRESSIONS, MAXIMS, PROVERBS—A VIRGIN ISLANDS CULTURAL LEXICON

Many of the words and expressions heard in the contemporary settings of United States Virgin Islands have been around for centuries. But, as is expected many others are recent or relatively recent utterances that glided into the local context through contact with the United States and other regions. Others have resulted naturally from changing social and economic realities. The entries of words and expressions in this section represent a fusion of the new sociological realities and fading or gradually fading tendencies. The alphabetization system adhered to here depends on whether the emphasis is on a particular word or on the expression in its entirety. For example the phrase, *"He maybe geh ah jumbie an' he"* emphasizes the once well-known expression, and does not focus on the meaning of the word *jumbie*. Hence the alphabetization is based on the first word of the expression and not on the letter *"j"* of *jumbie."* As much as possible I try **not to** emphasize words or expressions that are typical or common in American speech, except if the pronunciation, inflection, or intonation of the expressions renders distinctly unique nuances of meanings in our islands. In essence, the entries provided here are not only about words, but even more importantly, about the ways in which our words—no matter their origin—are articulated in the Virgin Islands social context.

In these entries I will use the expression *"Wey de…. Garn"* to recall things that have disappeared from our area, or are now barely referenced. The expressions *"by deh"* or *"down by deh"* will be used to refer to Virgin Islands landmarks, some of which might be still functional, but none with the same practical usage as in the 20th century (probably up to the 1960's). For many who are new to the community of speakers of the Creole of the United States Virgin Islands many of the words and phrases may sound patently foreign. The individual may have been born in the Virgin Islands but this in and of itself does not guarantee familiarity with particular expressions. Moreover, the person might in fact be very familiar with a word or phrase but have no idea about the origin, nor the context.

It is obvious that accounting for the etymology of all entries here would be too extensive. But such an impracticality does not deter me from this exploration that speaks to my own sentimentality and sense of connection to the islands' linguistic legacy. As can be expected, the words and phrases included here cannot sufficiently capture the inflection, intonation, and subtle nuances of an oral utterance. For this reason, at times I created hypothetical situations in order to ensure that the functionality of the entry is clear. Most importantly, the inclusion of words and expressions does not in any way infer that some are not heard elsewhere. But, while some words or phrases may be recognizable as common English usage, their Creolized particularities set them apart from routine, "standard" English utterances.

In addition, the point has been made earlier with respect to Virgin Islands Creole and other Caribbean and West Indian Creole languages, their intersectionality and their divergence. In point of fact, in so much of the West Indies there are shared traditions and customs, which include overlapping language components. Even *though* the author acknowledges commonalities among the various Creoles languages, there is also the fact that the expressions presented here are very endemic to the United States Virgin Islands, imbued as it were, in the cultural fabric of the three American islands. Although we can talk about "speaking like a West Indian," in a kind of paradoxical inversion we would not be able to define clearly what that means. There are general markers that signal West Indian or Caribbean speech patterns. Within this context, United States Virgin Islands Creole has a character that clearly identifies it as the language of a few small Caribbean territories under U.S. domain. The variety of words and expressions in the vocabulary section attests to the extensive linguistic tapestry that not only marks our speech, but also our interpretation of our world.

Finally, in some cases, in order to highlight a particular entry I find it necessary to separate it from others in the same category. Two examples of this are the following entries: "**bun**" (food in a pot that is burnt, but edible) and "**bun**" to run to exhaustion. Similarly, "**ciarn**" and "**ciarn be**" are presented as two distinctively different expressions. Rather that include "**ciarn be**" as part of the discussion emanating from the word, "**ciarn**," I included that construction as an entry with its own unique inference. Add to this list the word "**ah**" and its many usages.

The words "**meson**," "**self**," "**ting**" require extensive explication because they are employed in multiple ways. If the word "**meson**" is considered a typical Virgin Islands word with its endless combinations, then "**ting**" and its many combinations is not far behind as a staple in the language. The same holds true for "**self**." The frequency of their usage, combined with the multiple creative spins of these words, makes them signature indicators of Virgin Islands Creole. Finally, the list of entries are not only reflective of our mode of speech, but equally important signals markers of the social and cultural inclinations of the U.S.V.I. community.

WORDS, EXPRESSIONS, EXPLICATIONS

Ack/Ackin'—The word is used to refer to how someone is behaving. The replacement of the "t" with the "k" makes it a creolized word, in fact a very popular one: *"Yoh aways ackin' silly." "She duz ack so stuiepid."*

Ackin' like yoh jus' see ah jumbie—Your behavior is strange. This is an expression deeply rooted in Virgin Islands culture. No one can honestly say that he/she does *not kn*ow about the jumbie; paradoxically, however, no one can honestly say that he/she *knows* what a jumbie really is. In essence, everyone knows what it is, but if you ask, no one will be able to tell you. This is an expression that has fallen in disuse. Younger residents of the islands may have vague ideas about this, but may have never ever heard such an expression that was once prevalent. In the United States one might hear *"…as if he saw a ghost."*

Acks—To inquire. *"Ah jus' wan' toh acks 'im someting."* Also: *"Stop acksin' meh so much questions."*

Acks meh no question, Ah tell yoh no lie—Simply put, don't seek information from me for which I know I do not possess the answer. A fading adage.

Again—Nothing unusual about the word, just its unique usage in context. It is often used for confirmation and affirmation, often the reaction of someone responding to a comment made by another person; a gesture of agreement, as exemplified in the following example: Jackie: *"He tall, eh?"* Clinton responds: *"Again!"*

Ah—In the Creole of the United States Virgin Islands this one word has several interpretations depending on the context of the sentence. It can function as an indefinite article, *"a." "Dey have ah book."* In addition to this, the same word is heard in reference to the personal object pronoun "*her*": "*Give it toh ah.*" "*Doan tell ah notin'.*" Also, as seen under the section on **Prepositions** given earlier, it can replace "**of.**" "*He geh 5 ah dem.*"

Ah—Used in place of the preposition "at." See the section, PRONUNCIATION: A NOTE ON SUPPRESSION OF CONSONANTS "g", "d", "t" and "r" IN SELECTED POSITIONS. "*Who i'tis ah deh do'?*" "*Wa yoh lookin' ah me fa?*"

Ah—In its function as a personal subject pronoun ("**I**") this word is quite peculiar, and the person not too familiar with this Creole usage has to be careful. For example, one can say, "*Ah doan know 'im.*" In that sentence, "Ah" is used in place of "**I**." However, this Creolized subject pronoun can never be used as part of a compound subject. It is not permitted to say, "*Pauline an' Ah.*" Nor for that matter, "*Jerry, Tony, Shirley and Ah, goin' town lata.*" Also, it cannot be used to answer a question such as: "*Who ah (at) deh do'?*" The responder cannot say "*Ah,*" to mean "I" in this context. Furthermore, the English expression, "I myself" cannot be rendered in U.S.V.I. Creole as "*Ah meyself.*"

Ah—In certain contexts it is used emphatically to express negation, in a construction that implies "*any.*" In the following cases it stresses the lack of something or the denial of it.

"*Me ain goin' **ah place**. Ah geh wok toh do in deh house.*"

"*Juniah, yoh ain' goin' **ah way** tonight. Geh in yoh bed.*"

"*Dey ain geh **ah ting** toh do.*"

"*Ah doan have **ah cent**.*"

Chart XXVI presents a synopsis of the functioning of this versatile word:

XXVI. SUMMARY OF MULTIPLE USAGES OF "AH" AND EXAMPLES
1ST PERSON PERSONAL SUBJECT PRONOUN
Ah live Sin Croix. (I)
PREPOSITION
Mos' ah dem garn. (of)
3RD PERSONAL OBJECT PRONOUN
Call ah tomorrow, man. (her)

ARTICLE
Marlene geh <u>ah</u> house. (*a*)
ADJECTIVE
Me ain goin' <u>ah</u> place. (any)

Ah ain—I am not. "*Ah ain goin wid dem.*" See later entry "**Arn.**"

Ah call—Apart from the entry immediately preceding, this is such a popular expression that it deserves to stand by itself. This means "no reason, or "no purpose." "*Yoh <u>ain'</u> ha' ah call goin' de in deh fus place.*" Also, "*Yoh (<u>dain</u>) ha' ah call (no call) goin' de in deh fus place.*" In other words, you did not belong there. No one gave you the permission. You are in violation of some rule, implicit or explicit—very often a family ideology, or simple common sense.

("*Wa call yoh had goin' town an' not tellin' me?*" Also, "*Wa' call yoh geh' tarkin toh da fellow?*")

Ah cause—Very similar to the previous entry—"no reason;" "no right." "*Yoh ain' ha' ah <u>cause</u> (no cause) goin' de in deh fus place.*"

Ah Donno Wa—An expression used to refer to someone in a negative manner. Supposedly the speaker is at a loss for words in describing the person; however, the Creole expression makes it clear that it is not complimentary. "*Man Ah see 'im yestaday. He look like Ah Donno Wa.*" No doubt this is more telling than filling in the blanks! It is as if the phrase were the name of someone; for that reason it is expressed here using capital letters. This is really a unique expression in the Creole of the United States Virgin Islands. Of course, the other meaning, "I don't know what" is also a translation of this common phrase, for example, "*Ah donna wa she wan' from meh.*"

Ah goin' deh bay toh swim—Long ago uttered often by Pearson Garden and Polyberg children in St. Thomas, and of course by those who "*live on deh Bayside*" (the present site of St. Thomas' Federal Court). Unfortunately because of changing environmental factors no one "*duz go toh deh bay toh swim.*" It is an example of an expression that has disappeared because of the many economic, social, and indeed political changes in our islands. It certainly merits being mentioned, if not for any other reason, for sheer nostalgia.

Ah goin' heh (A variation of this is, *"I"* instead of *"Ah"*)—A way of ending a conversation, or if a person is leaving to go elsewhere. A good example of the richness and creativity of our language. This is an expression that would only be understood by those who are part of the shared community of the language. To signal the end of a conversation, for example, Mello tells Shirlene: *"Hi meson, I (Ah) goin' heh."* (Also see later entry *"garn." "I garn heh."*). Also, *"Ah (I) garn dis way."*

Ah goin' toh hat mey pat—A creative metaphoric expression meaning *"I am going to cook."* As children when we heard that expression, we were all smiles knowing that our mothers were getting reading to feed us. Nowadays, it is still heard occasionally but not anywhere close to the frequency of yesteryear when the use of the *"deh coal pat"* was the principal means used to prepare meals. It took a while for the coal to reach the required temperature for cooking, or for the pot to become hot, but the results always justified the wait!!

Ah ha tingy-wap—Language reserved exclusively for children when they observed something wrong that another child had done. It would be highly irregular to hear an adult speaking in this manner. It generally suggested that someone was going to be in trouble for his or her behavior Example: A child, Calvin, breaks his mother's glass. Another child, Lando, responds: *"Ah ha tingy-wap."* (This could be followed by, *"look wa yoh do."*). In the innocent, ludic world of children, in decades past this was frequently followed by *"Mammy suck ah lolli-pop.!!"* This is an expression in virtual disuse.

Ah lie—This is an interjection often used when the speaker is immediately aware of an error in his or her oral utterance. The person has misspoken. Manuel: *"Coreen call me an' say she comin' Monday; no,* Ah lie, *she say Tuesday."* This self-correcting interjection is not heard with the same frequency as when I was a boy, but it is undeniable that it is still used and universally understood. It is important for those unfamiliar with the language to understand, that the reference is not really to *"a lie,"* per se, but rather to an inadvertent utterance on the speaker's part.

Ah man—Interesting expression with an inference to the "third person," but in effect the reference is to the first person. For example, Julio is sitting in a chair. His friend remarks, *"Wa wrang wid yoh?"* To which Julio responds, *"Ah man carn take ah lil break?"* It must be noted that girls and women also used this expression in the context shown here. Even though the reference is to a "man" the translation is really, "<u>a person</u>." Hence, the meaning in

"Standard" English "Can't I take a break?" Also, generically it can mean, "no one", or "anyone.": "*Not ah man doan call meh lata.*"

Ah mine (ah yours etc.)—This stressed possessive is a very popular construction which when translated —"of mine"—into English would be considered generally awkward. Consider the following usage: "*Dat daughta ah mine doan listen atarl.*" [This is about MY daughter, not someone else's]. Even though the phrase, "*my daughter*" would be alluding to the same referent, it lacks the emphatic power of "**ah mine.**"

Ah tell (telling') yoh—An interjection, or introduction to a declaration; also a confirmation, a sign of approval. "*Ah tell yoh dat ting was heavy!*" In this sentence, "*Ah tell yoh*" IS NOT a creolized version of "*I told you.*" It is part of the story-telling formula, or someone relaying news. The speaker inflects his/her voice emphasizing the word "*heavy*" as if asking a question. Also: Jamie: "*Da' food taste good, meson.*" Ellie: "*Ah tell (tellin') yoh!*"

Or consider the following: Someone comes to visit Miss Maggie, and says: "*Ah goin' states tomarro'.*" Miss Maggie responds: "*Ah tell you!*" The general meaning, is that it is good to hear. Sometimes the expression is rendered without even a word spoken by the other individual. Example: Janet who is very well-dressed comes to visit Miss Maggie. Miss Maggie looks at her admiringly and remarks: "*Ah tell yoh!*" *(Ah tellin' yoh!")*, a sign of approval of how she looks, a kind of complimentary reaction.

Ah ting call—This is an expression used in a special, and limited way in United States Virgin Islands Creole. This entry emphasizes the entire phrase and not any particular word in the phrase. If the speaker of Creole says, "*Boy, Jerry hate ah ting call wok,*" the suggestion would be that the individual refuses to work, even if in fact that person has the opportunity to do so. This is one of many colorful Virgin Islands expressions that stresses a situation in a unique manner. To say "*Jerry hates to work*" would not capture the force of the criticism. The main image that this phrase conjures is of a person who finds any excuse not to work—laziness being among the possibilities for criticism.

Ah yoh—Both second person plural *subject* and *object* pronoun. The general meaning is "*All of you.*" "*Ah yoh live Sin John?*" Contrast this with the object pronoun: "*Ah don tell ah yoh.*" In some sections of St. Croix the pronunciation may vary with the last word. This is in no way universal in

St. Croix, a much bigger island than the other two. In fact, even among the writer's extensive Crucian family there is much variation. But as is always the case, there is no misunderstanding or ambiguity when this is uttered on any one of our islands. Notice that this can also be used as a possessive (see grammar section discussed earlier): "*Dis ah yoh money?*" In other words, *does this money belong to you (plural)?*—a reference to a specifically identified group.

Ah you—Used as second person plural *subject* and *object* pronoun, but this expression is also used as a possessive adjective, meaning "your" (plural) (consult previous sections on possessives and pronouns). This phrase is uttered in all of the United States Virgin Islands. When it is used, the principal translations are "you" (plural) or "your." Example: "*Ah you neva' home wen Ah go toh ah you house.*" The distinction between this entry and "ah *yoh*" is one of pronunciation.

Ah yoh man or **Ah you man**— In a general sense, this is the equivalent of "you guys," or "you men." "*Ah you (yoh) man goin' town?*" Admittedly, it is not used by all segments of the population, but is certainly understood by all; particularly popular among younger residents. It is really a kind of modified plural for "**Deh man**"—an expression the plural for which is really "**Deh man dem.**" (See "**Deh man**" in later entry).

Ahback—In the past; ago. Consider the following conversation between two neighbors: Doreen: "*Joycie, wen las' yoh see yoh cousin Mae?*" Joycie: "*Some time ahback. Ah doan even remba.*" The time frame is very imprecise, and as such only the context of the conversation will guarantee coherency.

Ain' easy—The inference is to an unusual characteristic or behavior of a person. In some ways it may suggest that this is an individual with whom it is difficult to get along. But it can also be a light-hearted comment about a person. Consider the following: "*Man, Ah hea' yoh jus' buy anodda ca'. Boy yoh ain' easy atarl.*" The speaker, in a jovial manner, is indicating that the person has done very well. This is only one of many contexts in which this expression can be used. It is, for example, used to highlight the exploits of someone: Lester: "*Dey tell me Katie divorce las' week an' geh married two days afta'.*" Jean: "*Wa Ah hearin'? Man, she ain' easy.*"

Ain good in he/she/yoh head—This may refer to a mental health issue or to someone who is not acting right; is doing things that he or she should not do. *"He doin' arl kin ah strange tings. Ah tell yoh da' man ain good in 'e head."* In many cases the phrase is presented as a criticism of a person, and is not given as some kind of gratuitous platitude about the individual. There are times, however, in which the speaker might employ this phrase in a more light-hearted manner, often about a person who might be humorous, for example *"someone who like toh tark stuiepiness." "He cou' tark some nonsense, yoh hea'. He ain' good in 'e head atarl."*

Ain' no true (ain' true)—That is a lie. *"Wa he sayin' ain no true. He cou' lie, yoh hea'."* (Also, **tain true**; see discussion later on the word "**tain.**")

Ain' no use—-The individual may not be helping his family, or not very helpful to his friends. Consider the following: *"Yoh wan' us toh call Joseph?"* Ans: *"No, he ain' no use toh nobardy."* One of my mother's favorite admonition to her children was, *"Doan be wid nobardy who ain' gon be no use toh yoh."* When it is truly dismissive, it is common to hear: "He / She ain' *ah bit* ah use." The converse is also popular in our islands when someone employs the phrase in a complimentary way; the person is beneficial to others: *"Da young lady is ah use toh ha mudda."*

Ain' self—Not even. *"Ain' self time toh eat an' yoh don hungry."*

Airoplane— From the word "a<u>e</u>roplane." Was once the preferred word. Now in virtual disuse, except occasionally still heard among very young children. *"Pan Am geh some big airoplanes, meson"* would be a commonly uttered statement in decades past.

All you—This is a variation of *"ah yoh/ah you,"* a derivative of "**all of you.**" *"All you need toh behave all you self."* The difference is that this is mainly used as a subject of the sentence, not so much as a possessive, even though it is occasionally used as a possessive. The question, *"Dis all you own?"* is certainly not universally used, but can be heard, especially from more senior citizens of our Virgin Islands community.

Amon'—Almond. Even though we are not out of almond trees, because of rampant and often indiscriminate construction developments many of the trees have disappeared. Climbing *"amon' trees"* was a pastime enjoyed by all children. *"Pick deh amon' an' poung' dem out."* Did anyone ever speak of buying *"Almond* Joy?—probably, not, but *"Amon' Joy,"* YES!

An' dem (dem an' so; dem so)—And others, usually associates of each other. *"Lois an' dem done heh."* There are other combinations to this construction, slightly different but capturing the same basic idea: *"Man, Ah hea' Ruben an'dem so was toh deh party."* Also: *"Ruben dem an' so."*

An' so—And so forth; etc., and others. *"We was jus' de eatin', tarkin' an' so."* (also drinking, laughing, etc.). In some situations, similar to **"an dem"**: *"Pauline an' so was de."*

An' ting (also, **an' ting so**)—And so on, and so forth. It is not really a specific designation of anything, but presents no confusion in conversation, precisely because it is part of the story-telling formula. *"Dey ca' arl mashup an' ting."*

Anti man—A derisive expression used to refer to a gay man. It has its roots in homophobia. It is important to note that there is no "antiwoman." Literally, the prefix *(anti)* naturally indicates "against." Such a designation is negative and rightfully rejected by many in our community. Apart from the abrasive underlying ideology, it is a long standing Virgin Islands expression.

Aready—Already. *"He garn aready."* Not to be confused with **"Ah ready:"** *"Ah ready toh go now"* ("I am ready to go.").

Arl <u>ah</u> we—The phrase suggests "All of us." *"Arl ah we went movies."* As discussed under the section on pronouns, in U.S.V.I. Creole the subject **"we"** is often used instead of the object of the preposition **"us."** Also see the earlier discussion of the word **"ah"** used in place of the preposition **"of."**

Arl deh time— The idea is, "meanwhile," "while," "in the meantime." Even though this popular expression seems quite standard ("All of the time"), its usage is not. In fact, the way that Virgin Islanders use this expression goes contrary to the idea inherent in the phrase, especially because of the adjective "all." It is not surprising that this could lead to misinterpretation by the listener who is not familiar with the language. Consider the following exchange between Albert and Colville: Albert: *"Ah gon fix dis ting lata."* Colville: *"Lemme hol' on toh it arl deh time, no."* Colville is not requesting to keep the item for ever, but just to possess it while it is not in use.

Jackie to Claudette: *"Ah gon iron mey clothes, bu' tark toh meh arl deh time."*

But also in some contexts it could mean *"always."* *"She duz tell 'im arl deh time toh behave heself."* In this case, the syntax, the position of the expression in the sentence, is crucial to the interpretation. For example, if the phrase, *arl deh time,* were positioned at the end, then the sentence *"She duz tell 'im toh behave heself arl deh time"* <u>could</u> also mean *"She tells him to always behave himself."* The second meaning would be radically different.

The phrase also indicates that something was happening for a protracted period, constantly: *"Ah was callin' <u>yoh arl deh time</u>. Wey yoh was, man?"*

Arl dis time so—The popular phrase is often used to refer to a future moment that is expected to approximate the time frame at the time that the speaker expresses the idea. Ex. Elaine is planning a trip to Clifornia. Her comment: *"Arl dis time so tomarro', Ah gon be in deh plane."* The expression means "at this time tomorrow." The individual is thinking about the future trip and is trying to imagine where she would be at a given time.

Arl in—Used often to characterize a person's demeanor, generally it refers to exaggerated behavior: *"He come in deh house arl in ah flustarashun."* (See this word in later entry.)

Arl time—Always. *"Ah arl time tell yoh toh lisen."* A frequent expression of my dear mother, Marjorie Asta Stevens.

Arm Ting Dem— (*Note*: I have capitalized the initial letters to represent the allusion to specific people). Used when the speaker is unsure of a name or names of a person, persons, or a family. Often the speaker seeks assistance from the listener to identify the individual(s). *"Ah believe he live down de by Arm Ting Dem, man."* Often the listener would respond *"Yoh mean...?"* What is frequently common is that the listener knows exactly to whom the speaker is referring, without even hearing the name!!

Arn—A contraction formed from "**Ah+ain**," the equivalence of *"I am not."* It expresses the same sentiment as *"Ah ain."* (See earlier entry). *"Arn goin' now. Ah geh tings toh do."* The expression "**Ah ain**" is also popular, often used for emphasis: *"Yoh hea' Ah say aready, Ah ain doin' it."*

Aways—Always. *"We aways eat in deh marnin'."*

Awright—This one has a double meaning. Daphne: *"How yoh mudda?"* Liston: *"She Awright,"* meaning that she is fine. But contrast this with the following utterance: *"Janice **aw**right; she doan listen toh nobardy."* Meaning let her have her way. In this case, much stress is placed on the first syllable, and the idea is that we are not going to pay attention to her. She will do what she wants to do. Charlene: *"Clarence say he 'ain wan' no food."* Carolyn: *"He awright, meson; Ah know I gon eat."* *"Dey awright wid* *dey foolishness."* See later entry of the expression, "**cou' stay de.**" They express very similar sentiments.

Ba—A kiss on the cheek. This word was frequently used in conversation with children. It has disappeared. It is even questionable if most people born in the seventies have ever even heard the word. My memory of the usage centers mainly in the 1950's and perhaps part of the sixties, but undoubtedly in the 50's or before. *"Give meh ah lil ba befo' yoh go."*

Baba- Refers to a baby. It was not unusual for the name "Baba" to become an affectionate pet name for children.

Back—Used as "repeat." *"Open it back. Ah wan' toh see it."* The argument is not that this word is not used in "standard" English. In fact, consider the expression: *"Bring back the car before noon."* This is the "standard" usage of the word, to return something. In U.S. Virgin Islands Creole, however, the emphasis is on repetition, and in fact its usage is redundant. The expression, *"Do it back again, man,"* typifies the type of hyperbole emblematic of our speech. This last sentence simple means "Do it again." "Repeat it."

Back Back—Reverse; this is an expression generally used for driving. *"Ah carn' back back good"*—can't reverse well. A child at play in St. John, St. Croix, St. Thomas: *"Ah gon back back deh ca'."* (simulation). Not as frequently heard, however, the majority of Virgin Islanders would understand what the person is saying if the individual said: *"Ah cou' drive, bu' Ah still carn' back back good."*

Back chat /tark—An uninvited verbal reaction and challenge to an adult's words or action. Consider a serious moral and cultural violation. Note the following example: Parent: *"Juniah, stap makin' noise in deh house."* Juniah: *"Bu' tain me alone…"* Parent: *"Yoh betta' stap givin' meh back chat befo' Ah give yoh some blows."*

Back ova'—To repeat; a typical emphatic Creole expression, very similar to previous entry with "back." *"Play it back ova. Ah wan toh hea' it one mo' time."*

Backside—Rear end. But in U.S.V.I. Creole this word most times is used to admonish, castigate, or in general react negatively to someone or about someone. Parent to children: *"Ah you betta' geh ah yoh backside in heh now."* This is a culturally prohibited language for children. It is certainly not a word to be uttered by anyone in a church setting! It would also be most inappropriate to use such language in the presence of an elder resident.

Coreen to Janet: *"Ah ain' gon eat deh food yoh cook'."* Janet: *"Dat's yoh backside. Ah know I don eat."* Interestingly, even though "**Ah**" and "**I**" are generally thought of as equivalent, the previous sentence would lose its essence if Janet said, *"Ah know **Ah** don eat"*—again this speaks to the subtle twists in our Creole.

Bad—This common English word has an interesting function in United States Virgin Islands Creole. The peculiarity is that we are familiar with the word as an adjective, but in the Virgin Islands we employ it with equal frequency as an adverb. The sentence *"He ignorant bad"* would have as a rough interpretation that he is a" very ignorant person." Similarly, *"Ah like it bad"* indicates that *"I really like it."* These expressions are prevalent in the Virgin Islands and are used to express the degree of something. The commentary may be complimentary or critical. It is interesting to note that both "*bad*" and its opposite "*good*" are still in vogue as intensifiers. See "*good*" in a later entry in this section. There is no relationship whatsoever between this usage and such Americanized expressions such as: *"That is a bad ride."* This is not to suggest that no Virgin Islander ever utters such an expression, but it is not universally used, and in general is heard among the younger generations of United States Virgin Islanders. I do not consider such expression in any way a part of Virgin Islands or West Indian Creole languages. In my view, anyone who says, *"That is a bad movie"* to mean a "good movie" is speaking something other than United States Virgin Islands Creole.

Bad man—An expression with double meaning, depending on the context and the stress. For example, consider the statement *"He tink he is ah bad man."* The sentence does not necessarily suggest morally bad, but a bully; the intonation will determine the meaning. In the expression "he is a *bad* man," emphasis is on the adjective (morally repugnant); in the entry here, *"He tink he is a bad **man**,"* the voice drops and "man" is stressed. Someone might say: *"Boy, stap ackin' like ah bad man, nobardy ain' 'fraid ah yoh."*

Bad-minded—Willful, somewhat selfish, and inconsiderate. In St. Thomas and St. John the stress in pronunciation of the word "bad' is extended in this expression; the vowel "*a*" is longer in pronunciation than in St. Croix. *"She so bad minded. She doan care wa happen toh people."* Not only might the individual be seen as self-centered, but the inference may also be that he or she has an evil inclination.

Bade yoh skin—The expression took root during the days of "badin' pan," when a shower stall was not even a known concept in our islands. *"Boy, go bade yoh skin now. Use deh badin' pan outside."*

Badin' pan (Bard pan)—A cylindrical container once used especially to bathe babies and other small children. *"Geh in deh badin' pan an' bade yoh skin."* An expression obviously lost to modernization, but popular during the first six decades or so of the last century.

Bagup—The person is not allowed to leave the house, for example to play with other children. This was a constant source of teasing among children in the 1950's. *"Tony carn come out deh house, he bagup."* *"He geh bagup."* Often this expression was used to tease, or make fun of an individual. No longer universally uttered or even recognized in our islands. The expression was not reserved exclusively for children by any means.

Bamaku—(also heard at times **bamanku**). An expression used to refer to a man who people believe has swollen testicles due to a strain from lifting heavy objects, thus such utterances as: *"Meson, pu' down da ting, yoh wanna ah bamaku?"* or *"Da ting heavy, yoh know, i'gon gai yoh ah bamaku."* I have never heard an adequate medical explanation for this condition, but whether or not it is based on science, or pseudoscience, the expression survives, and the science becomes secondary, or even unimportant. It is very likely that the word was passed down from Western African. Fortunately, the word continues to be used by young people, or at least they are quite familiar with the word. It is not at all unusual to hear this word referring to females.

Bamboshay—To dance; also a popular place where dances were held in St. Thomas. Some older folk in St. Thomas might still be heard saying *"down by Bamboshay,"* or *"down by wey Bamboshay was."* So popular was the particular dwelling. This was never a word used as a substitute for dance in general conversations; however, in reference to Carnival it was commonly heard: *"Jump in deh tramp, an' bamboshay."* The expression would still be intelligible for most people in the United States Virgin Islands, even though there is no question that its popularity has dwindled significantly.

Bamboula dance—A popular Virgin Islands dance, a cultural gift from our West African ancestors, specifically Ghana. There were always a series of bamboula dancers in our islands, and they were seen regularly. This is no longer the case. However, I must applaud those who have been making an earnest effort to revive the tradition. The energetic, heart-felt dances that highlight our African connection were popular during the last century on our three islands. The word "bamboula" itself refers to a type of drum, primarily from western Africa. It is a word that has not survived in our islands as an independent word used in a context apart from "dance." I want to see the revival of this dance and tradition.

Barn wid ah card—"*He barn wid ah card.*" According to popular belief, this meant, for example, that the person was capable of seeing spirits, jumbies. This is another expression that was once heard regularly. I suspect that some people may very well still believe that there are such omens, but choose to suppress their beliefs because of antagonistic cultural pressures: "*Ah yoh believe in too much stuieppiness.*" "*Dem is ole' time nonsense.*" In a rapidly advancing technological age, there is a tendency to distance oneself from cultural norms, and beliefs. Too often, allegiance to some cultural tenets brands us as "backwards," "uninformed," or "ignorant." There is no question that this places limitations in the minds of some people; that is, it increases their resistance to showing evidence of their acceptance of certain local beliefs.

Barna—Refers to one's anatomy, the person's "rear end." This word has not seen its last days. Even though it is no longer heard in daily conversations, it is likely universally understood. It has always been a word perceived as inappropriate in certain situations. Certainly children still are prohibited from uttering this word. Undoubtedly, it would be considered disrespectful to use such a word in churches, or speaking to an elder. It is restrictively colloquial.

Barney— Like the **word barna** (in entry above) this is used in reference to one's anatomy. It is a colloquialism referring to the rear end. The socio-linguistic taboo associated with the use of the word is essentially the same as that of the noun "Barna" cited earlier.

Barra—A popular nickname for the barracuda. "*It geh mo' barra in deh sea.*" As children swimming in the sea and in the bays, we saw the "*barra*" fairly frequently. The word is still recognizable among people familiar with the sea and fishing. I suspect that in context the individual would understand, for example, the expression: *"It geh barra in da' wata."*

Bassin—Was the word once used when referring to Christiansted.

Bateau—The word is French, meaning boat; in the 1950's and most of the 60's everyone was familiar with the bateau. It was a simple "boat" but had to be constructed well in order to stay afloat. Many adolescents were quite professional in manufacturing their product. The bateaus were used to travel far distance in the bays or oceans. Galvanize and tar were the principal materials used. Most unfortunately, the skills involved in constructing the bateau are very likely lost forever.

Batney Bay—Really the Creolized version of **Botany Bay**—located at St. Thomas' West End. As children most of us had only heard of that site, but never went there because of lack of transportation. We always referred to it when trying to conceptualize far distances, for example, *"From heh toh Batney Bay."* It is interesting and ironic how we used an unfamiliar referent to concretize a vague notion of distance. The fact is, though, we were aware that the bay was quite a distance from where most of us lived. In 2015 in a conversation with a St. Thomian who has lived in New York for over 40 years, I was surprised to hear her reference distance in New York in a most unconventional manner. Commenting on the fact that some cousins lived upstate New York and she in Queens, she remarked: *"Dey live fa' fa' from meh, like from heh toh Batney Bay."* This was a totally subconscious utterance. I am sure that to this day she is not aware that she used a local referent to concretize distance in New York City. I was quite intrigued to hear this, as it was clearly so ingrained in her sub conscience.

Bawlin' out—Screaming out, making noise, calling in a loud voice. *"Stop bawlin' out in mey head; Ah sleepy."* Also, *"Jerome say he foot hu'tin' 'im bad. He in de bawlin' out wid deh pain."* The expression can also be used in place of speaking loudly, screaming. Lyra: *"Guirl, yoh ain' hea' meh bawlin' out yoh name?* Emeline: *"I ain hea' ah ting."*

Bayie— A common pet name used in several families to refer to a boy. (See its opposite "**Guirly**" later). *"Yoh know 'im, man, he name Patrick bu' dey duz call 'im Bayie."*

Beastily— In the 50's and 60's this word was often heard when speaking about boys who were considered to be physically strong, tough. Charles laments: *"Bernard beastily, meson."* This sort of expression is now extinct. Hardly anyone in contemporary United States Virgin Islands would understand the usage, even in context.

Becausen—Because. Still heard frequently. *"She do it becausen he was mad wid 'im."*

Beel—Once uses to reference a car, based on the generic word, "automobile."

Beel tire—A reference to the tire of an automobile. The reference is to the 1950's and 60's. But it was also used to refer to a kind of make-shift toy that children possessed. They frequently rolled the tires in the streets as part of "play," a rare sight these days, for many reasons including safety. At times the tire was put in motion by the palm of the hand, or often by a wooden paddle, or wire hanger. Just another example of the creativity of the children, who lacked the economic means to own many toys, but found ways of compensating.

Been—(often heard "**Bin**") Can be used to mean "was" / "were." Also used to generate the present perfect ("has been" or "have been") or pluperfect perfect ("had been"). (Refer to the earlier discussion on the **Present Perfect / Pluperfect**). Examples of these usages: *"Man, Ah been (bin) de so much time." "She been (bin) heh earlier." "Ah wish yoh been (bin) heh wid we."*

Beg she (he) pardon—This expression suggests that the person is being "full of himself/herself." *"She gon do wa she wan,' meson. Ah geh toh beg she pardon."* In essence, her behavior or attitude is just too objectionable for me to handle.

Behin'—Rear end, used in a variety of contexts, usually as a rebuke, examples: *"he lazy behin;'"*

"He stuiepid behin'," *"rude behin',"* equivalent to *"Yoh rude self."*

Behin' God face—The perception that you live very far away from the main hub of the island. *"Dey live behin' God ["Gard"] face."* The "G-<u>a</u>-r-d" is included to highlight the greater emphasis of the "a' vowel in St. Thomas/St. John. An expression used a lot in St. Croix back in the 50's and 60's, and is still heard on all our islands. As a young boy I spent most of my summers between Grove Place, La Vallee, and Frederiksted St. Croix; sometimes friends from other areas of the island would tell us: *"Ah yoh live behin' God face."* We of course felt that we were in some of the best places that God has created.

Belly bawlin—This is an expression used to indicate that a person is hungry. "*Man, mey belly heh bawlin'. Ah starvin.*"

Benye—This is a delicacy consisting of banana combined with flour. No longer very popular except for its rare appearances at some food or agricultural fair.

Big people— Adults. "*Boy, move from heh. Yoan see big people tarkin'?*"

Big ting—Speaks to a person's important standing, for example in a church. "*Yes, she is ah big ting in ha chuch.*"

Bigitive—Refers to the arrogance of an individual, a criticism of how the individual views herself or herself. The person considers himself or herself to be better than his peers. "*He so bigitive he even doan tark toh he own family.*"

Bine' up—The inability to go to the bathroom. "*If yoh eat da' green mango e' gon bine yoh up.*" This was a popular expression, but like several other expressions in this collection, is heard far less now than in previous decades. Familiarity with the local culture guided Virgin Islanders as they made determinations about food, fruits conducive to regularity. See also "**cark up**" in later entry.

Birt' Papah—A birth certificate; official document. "*Ah plan toh take out ah passport. Dey say Ah need mey birt' papah.*" It is surprising to see how well this expression has survived in spite of all the population shifts. No question everyone in the Virgin Islands knows what a "Birth Certificate" is, however, most would still opt for the local phrase.

Bit ah— None; any. "*He ain geh ah bit ah sense.*" This could be interpreted in two ways. One is a literal interpretation ("He is a silly person."), but the other could refer to the fact that the person is funny, someone "*who tark stuiepiness.*" In the second case it is more of an endearing commentary. This is an expression used often as a kind of qualifier or quantifier. It is very common to hear. "*Doan min' he; he ain geh ah bit ah money.*" It is used in even more "unconventional" ways as in the following: Roy: "*Ah geh ah house in St. Croix.*" Doris, responding to that comment, tells a friend: "*Doan min' 'e; he ain geh ah bit ah house.*" Doris' statement is clear, that Roy does <u>not</u> have a house. This can only make sense in context. See the earlier entry "**Ah.**"

Bite yoh finga'—The prevalent superstition was that if you pointed to a graveyard or a grave site, in order to protect yourself you had to bite your finger. *"Yoh jus' point toh dat graveyard; yoh betta' bite yoh finga."* I suspect that this belief has all but disappeared. In the days when children walked long distances they often walked by or through grave sites and such conversations were prevalent. Cultural conventions and beliefs often dictate actions. Children were very careful to avoid pointing to grave sites, and if they did, there was always the opportunity to rectify the error!

Bitin' yoh (he/she etc.) tongue—This is an expression that is never used as a compliment, but rather as a criticism, serious or not. It specifically refers to someone who is perceived as *"tryin' to tark"* like an American. A prominent expression is: *"Bitin' 'e tongue like ah Yankee."* However, in the Virgin Islands community, the expression *"bitin' 'e tongue"* is self-sufficient. It is never necessary to use the simile, *"like...ah Yankee."* It is very often only used for emphasis. It is a saying that is still very much alive.

Bittah bush—Folk medicine. Mother to children in the early and mid-20th century: *"Ah yoh line up toh drink deh bittah bush toh clean out ah yoh inside"* (a regular practice during the early part of the last century). Children would "drink" "bittah bush" to help them stay healthy—avoiding infections, stomach ailments etc. It was always both curative and preventive medicine. Our mothers were not wrong about the natural products that they chose, as evidenced by the multibillion dollar consumer market that now incorporates many of the aloes, roots, and plants that were common in our islands. It speaks to the genius of those women who had a profound understanding of the islands' natural resources. While there may be no statistics to support the claim, there is no question in the minds of Virgin Islanders that many of us were cured of ailments (or spared certain illnesses) by using the products of nature.

Bittahs—Alcohol. *"Dat man like he bittahs; he always drunk."*

Bitto—Alcohol. *"Man, he drunk again? He duz drink too much bitto."*

Blackout—In the Virgin Islands when lights are out island-wide; the local expression for power outage on a large scale. *"We had blackout again las' night. We cou'n see ah ting."*

Blockin—This was a popular term used mainly by young people to indicate that another person was interfering with his/her opportunity to talk to someone amorously. *"Man, Ah was tryin' toh chat wid Dora, an' ha' sista' keep sittin' by ha. Ah cou'n' talk. Da guirl aways blockin'."* As was often the case, this expression was often used tongue in cheek, with no malice intended.

Bolanjay—The Creole word used in place of eggplant. This is a word that is now primarily heard among the older members of the Virgin Islands community. There was a point in time, however, when it was used with regularity—especially, during early or mid-20th century. In fact, it was the word most commonly heard when referring to eggplant. It is clear that the English word "eggplant" has now become the prevailing word used to describe this vegetable.

Bonkonko—A swelling specifically on one's forehead. The word is automatically associated with the head. Hence, one cannot *"geh ah bonkonko"* on his/her hand. Those who are part of the language community are innately aware of this tacit linguistic rule, as they are of many others that govern our Creole. Generally speaking, residents would still recognize this word. It is clear, however, that it is uttered far less these days. For me, it is one of those words that has always been intimately associated with the culture of the U.S. Virgin Islands.

Bony—Meaning slim, thin. *"Boy, he bony; he need toh eat some fungi."* Again, here is a word that is used universally in the English language. However, the manner in which it is used in Virgin Islands Creole is very unique. *"Da bony ting"* is often an expression used to refer to someone who is notably thin. Consider the following typical description: *"Yoh know 'im, man; he bony bad."*

Boo boo—Never used in the Virgin Islands as it is used in the song made popular by the great Calypsonian Lord Melody or by the great singer and social activist Harry Belafonte: *"Mama, Look ah Boo Boo De."* In the Virgin Islands this referred to soft particulars blown to and fro by the wind. This is a term that has not survived. *"Yoh have ah boo boo on yoh clothes"* was one of the more popular expressions that is now virtually lost.

Boo boo—This was often used as a reference to a person who was seen as being somewhat silly, very similar to "moo-moo" in a later entry. *"What ah boo boo! He doan understan' ting."*

Boot up—To try to encourage a person to do something, usually when they are not so inclined to do so. A lost expression is: *"Boot' kill' Lincoln, bu' he ain' gon kill me."* Not many of us knew that we were referring to John Wilkes Booth, the notorious assassin of Lincoln in 1865 at the Ford's

Theatre in D.C. The exact connection to the historic event is vague, but the clear inference is that someone planted the idea in Booth's head. As is so typical in our islands, Virgin Islanders have co-opted the historical data, creolizing it.

Bostick—A multi-purpose stick; can also be used to show who is in charge. "*He was bein' rude 'til mommy bus'im one bostick.*" Also, frequently with reference to baseball. For example when a team was not playing especially well: "*Boy dey geh some bostick. Dey lose 10 toh notin'.*"

Bot in—To collide. This can refer to a physical collision, for example - "*Deh cars dem bot in.*" But the expression also can refer to an unexpected meeting of people. As an example, —"*Yoh know who Ah (I) bot' in toh yestaday?*" (Sometimes, "*I*" in place of "*Ah*" for emphasis). Still a popular expression on all islands.

Bot up—To collide. Similar to the previous expression. "*He was drivin' too fas' an' bot up toh ah tree.*"

'Bout—About. "*Yoh ain' know ah ting 'bout me.*" "*Ah hea' dey wuz tarkin' 'bout arl kin ah problem. Le' dem tark.*" (See grammatical discussion on prepositions.)

Bowels—This refers to an upset stomach resulting in diarrhea. "*He geh deh bowels.*" Once a popular expression, now in disuse.

Boy—A popular interjection, (like "man"); used by both male and female. Ana speaking with her friend Pauline: "*Boy, da(t) ting was heavy.*" Pauline: "*Yea, man.*" Claudette speaking to her daughter: "*Boy, wa' wrang wid yoh meson? Stop makin' noise.*" The word essentially functions generically. It is interesting to note how the previous sentence employs both "boy" and "meson" for emphasis.

Bragadam—Supposedly an onomatopoeic sound; the result of a fall. "*He was runnin' fas', arl of ah sudden, 'bragadam', he fall down.*" Still heard, especially among older residents.

Bring up—To vomit. "*But Lizzy, if yoh keep eatin' so much yoh gon bring up.*" There can be no past tense for this, except the use of the same tense verb to represent the past. No one would say, "*Yestaday Lizzy eat so much dat she* brought *up.*"

Bring up—One of the many expressions on the list of collision vocabulary in the Creole of the USVI. "*Drivin' like a wile man, he bring up in ah wall.*"

Bring yohself—To go, to come, always in the form of a command, usually said in a very assertive manner. *"Tell dat guirl toh bring haself heh right now."*

Brok'—Interesting word, almost sounds like the past tense of the word "to break." What makes this so unique is that it can be used as part of the future tense construction: *"If yoh keep jumpin' on deh bed, yoh gon brok' it."* Often it is in the form of a warning. *"Careful so yoh doan' brok deh ting."* The future tense construction is the most common. But we also hear: *"We aways brok up into small groups."* It is also used to form the present participle. Consider the unusual construction: *"She aways <u>brokin'</u> up ting in deh house."*

Brok' foot—There are two particularly interesting characteristics about this expression that make it compulsory to present it as a separate entry—rather than explaining it under the previous entry. In the first place, the use of "brok" as an adjective goes against any grain in the English language. In addition, in Virgin Islands parlance "foot" may in fact be a reference to a leg. The statement, *"He brok' he foot yestaday tryin' toh skate,"* could very well be an ambiguous comment. In other words, *"He geh ah brok' foot,"* but does the speaker really mean *"foot?"* It is most likely that the reference is to the person's leg. Most of the people who we know that have had a *"brok' foot"* have been those with broken legs. In much the same way, if we said *"Suzy fall down an' brok her han',"* the great likelihood is that Suzy now has a broken *arm.* There is little question that in most people's mind the news that someone *"geh ah brok foot"* immediately conjures up images of a damaged LEG.

Bruds—Once frequently uses to refer to one's brother-in law. Not heard these days. *"Dat's mey bruds, we duz geh along real good."* Also said jokingly if a person was "cotin' " (courting) someone's sister. *"Give meh some money, man. Yoh know Ah is yoh bruds."*

Bu'—A non-translatable expression in U.S.V.I. Creole that is often used as a kind of preface, or introduction to a statement. Example: *"<u>Bu</u> wa wrang wid dem atarl?*

Bu' ah you/yoh—Frequently used to introduce a thought, a comment. Like the previous entry this expression cannot be translated. *"<u>Bu' ah you</u> see deh devil fo' meh."* (The expression, *"see deh devil fo' meh"* is addressed later.)

Bu' how—Roughly translated as "That." *"She say bu' how she carn sleep."*

Bu'…..notin'- –Just where to place this expression was itself a challenge. An emphatic parental interjection. In the parent's mind the child should already have complied with a particular directive. A hypothetical dialogue between parent and child will help to explain the circumstances under which this is used. It normally occurs when a child is trying to explain an action, or lack of it. Parent: *"Yoh ain do yoh homewok."* Child responds, attempting to explain: *"Bu' mommy (daddy)…."* Parent (interrupting): *"Bu' mommy, notin!"* In conversation between parent and child, it was never really debatable as to who was in control.

Buck— To consume a fruit before it is ripe. *"Ah know dis suga' apple ain' ripe, but Ah gon buck it."* This is an expression gasping for air, as less and less young people are familiar with it. The difference is primarily because children of past decades had more access to fruit trees and liberally picked and tested fruits.

Buddy—As stated in the introduction to this book, words or expression heard in the United States are included in the entries if their usage is different. This is one of the words used regularly, very much like "man." Wilma: *"Yoh goin' sleep now?* Shirlene: *"Yea buddy, I sleepy."* Jimmy: *"I tired, meson."* Jackie: *"Me too, buddy."* Also heard as an exclamation: Karen: *"Alfred geh ah lot ah cars, eh?"* Doris' response: *"Buddy!"* A rough American expression would be "absolutely!" Another example: Tara says *"Man, it so hot."* Tricia responds in agreement, exclaiming: *"Buddy!"* (See **Pappy** in later entry.)

Buh—An expression of denial. Consider the following dialogue: *"James geh ah lot ah money."* Response to this assertion: *"Buh!"* means "not true." Another example: *"I cou' lif' dis heavy ting."* Response: *"Buh!"* This means that the listener does not believe what the person is saying, or is simply denying the claim. More the language of children.

Bum bum—Rear end, this repetition of the word is generally heard among children, or adults speaking to children. It is not very common to hear adults using this expression among themselves. In fact, it would be highly unusual.

Bumin' chow—*"He garn bumin' chow;"* begging for food (also was a nickname of a popular St. Thomian back in the 50's). This was not said in a complimentary fashion.

Bump up—To cause to swell. Naturally the word, "bump" is commonly used in English; however, its usage in the Virgin Islands is markedly different. *"Meson, she bus' meh one lick, bump up mey eye."* Also, *"deh jackspania bite 'im on he lip an' bump it up."* Later in the entries there is a discussion on the use of "up" as a suffix; the emphasis, however, is more on the word "to bump" because of its unique creolized usage. It is used in place of swollen: *"Mey face arl bump up."*

Bun—The part of the meal (rice for example, cereal) that sticks to the bottom of the pot. It was a favorite of many: *"I wan' deh bun."* (See also "**deh pat**"). Interestingly, in Puerto Rico the rice that sticks to the bottom of the pot (called the *pegao,* from the word *"pegado," "stuck") is also highly sort after.* No family wanted to waste anything—especially food. Therefore, if a part of the food was inadvertently burnt, families did not have the luxury to discard it. Ironically, this "overcooked" portion of the dish became a cherished part of the cuisine!!

Bun'—-Run to the point of exhaustion. The individual is out of gas. *"He wuz runnin' an' geh bun'. He had toh sit down fo' ah wile."*

Bun' arf—Almost hit something or someone, or almost collided. *"Da' fella' bun' meh arf' wid' he bicycle; Ah tell yoh he almos' knack meh down."* This interesting expression has endured, even though there is no doubt that it is not used with the same frequency as in the past generations, for example, that of the 50's and 60's.

Bun' up—To burn; burnt; *"he han' arl bun' up."* As another example of this usage:

"Ah hope yoh know wa' you doin' so yoh doan bun' up deh fish."

"Man. I carn eat dis ting; it arl bun' up."

Buryin' Groun'—Cemetery. *"Down de by deh Buryin' Groun'"* is a phrase that is losing its legitimacy because of the many other grave sites that have been constructed over the last thirty or forty years on our islands. The use of the expression is disappearing because of a natural result of population expansion, and unfortunately, an increased mortality rate. It is still used among a small group of older residents.

Bus arf—To leave or to leave rapidly; to "break apart." *"Partna', Ah gon bus arf now. Ah geh toh go toh wok."* An utterance that is still popular, but interestingly used differently by young residents. A young individual may use it to indicate that he or she is leaving. The other use is the equivalence to "leave quickly." *"We wuz so scared we bus arf runnin'."*

To break apart: *"Deh ting wasn' arn good. Dat's why it bus' arf."*

Bus down—Literally, to throw down; figuratively, to indulge. *"Take up dem ting from de befo' it bus yoh down."* Often used with reference to a physical struggle: *"Two ah dem was rastlin' an' Timmy bus 'im down."* Used also to refer to food, especially if the speaker is expressing delight in the meal. *"Yestaday we bus down some fish an' fungi. Da ting was good, yoh hea'!"*

Bus' im ah clout— In a general sense, the word "clout" refers to a "strike," "a blow" anywhere. In Virgin Islands Creole, however, when the word is used in this expression the blow is always understood to be exclusively to the head. *"Meson move from heh wid yoh nonsense befo' Ah bus yoh ah clout."* Some variation are **"Hit 'im ah (one) clout," "Give 'im ah (one) clout."** No one would say: *"She clout meh in mey arm."* It would be self-sufficient for someone to exclaim, *"Ah bus 'im ah clout."* To the listener the message is automatically registered.

Bus' im (ha) (ah) (he) ah lick'—Hit someone. The implication is that the person was hit with some force. The statement, *"Alvin hit 'im"* versus *"Alvin bus' im ah lick"* expresses the same basic truth, however, the second statement stresses the impact of the blow. An alternative could be *"He bus' 'im <u>one</u> lick."*

Bus' im ah nogle—The use of a marble to hit a person on their knuckles for losing in the alternate marble game called "*t(h)ree hole*" (See reference to this game under marble). Needless to say, this was a painful aspect of play. This is an expression that has been in disuse for several decades now simply because the marble game itself, "*T(h)ree hole*," once a popular pastime, has vanished.

Bus' meh—To tell; to relate something. *"He bus' meh ah lie."* Also used as part of the storytelling formula, *"an' she bus' meh."* Maybe from our Akan ancestry or other confluences of African cultures, the Virgin Islands are a storytelling community. Consider the difference between two distinct scenarios, one American and the other Virgin Islands/West Indian: *"Excuse me, sir could you tell me how to get to the mall?"* **American response** : *"Yes, drive about 2.5 miles until you get to the intersection of routes 15 and 17, then proceed another 1.8 miles, at which times you would... etc."* **Virgin Islands Response**: *"Drive, keep drivin' 'till yoh see ah big mango tree, close toh way Arm Ting dem live. Ah tink dey some family ah mine, yoh know. Anyway, drive drive, yoh 'gon see ah big big rock stone. Ah believe Wa' He Name dem* *live…* etc." Notice that in the Virgin Islands there is always an opportunity to tell a story—we can call them intercalated stories, again a testament to the richness of our linguistic culture, and our penchant for the narrative.

Bus' meh da again—Repeat that. Usually the listener is enamored by the conversation; a lighthearted reaction, a part of the storytelling formula of teller-listener. With this line the listener shows that she/he is very engrossed in the story. The particular line, nuance, transition or climax was so compelling that I want to hear it again. This is no time to stop *"givin' deh melee!"* *"Bus' meh da again; dat's some real melee."* But it can also mean: *"I can't believe what you are telling me."*

Bus' toe—A severe cut on one's toe. Interestingly enough the word cannot be used to describe something similar with one's arm. Those who are part of the community of the language know this, and no one would say: *"He geh' ah bus han'."* Even though one can have a *"bus finga'."* It is also possible to have a *"bus' lip,"* or a *"bus' mout'."* However, in island parlance you cannot have *"ah bus' neck."* The popularity of the expression *"bus' toe"* was due to the fact that during the 50's and earlier children played without shoes resulting in the very common occurrence of injuries to the toe. It would be logical to surmise that current usage is less prevalent than in the early part of the 20th century; still though, it is heard fairly regularly.

Bus-up—Serious cuts, or when speaking of things as fruits, it refers to substantial opening. *"He eye arl bus-up an' ting. He betta go hospital."* *"Man dis mango arl bus-up. Ah carn eat dis ting."*

By—Used often in a special way in place of the preposition "at." Consider the following exchange: Phillip tells Robert: *"Yoh know 'im, man, he duz be down by Normandy Bar."* In our Creole the expression could be ambiguous. The person can be found inside the bar, or simply nearby. *"Meet meh by Judy dem."* The inference is that I will be in Judy's house, not just necessarily in the vicinity.

By fadda'—We have the same father, but not the same mother. *"Dat's mey sista by fadda."* It needs to be made clear that in general, in the Virgin Islands we make no distinction as far as siblings are concerned. As a general rule, we do not think in terms of *"half-brother/ half-sister."* We have various types of extended families and as a general rule embrace that reality. However, sometimes someone might be curious enough to ask or comment on the issue. For example, Harry in his conversation with Lance: "*I didn't know Karen wuz yoh sista.*" Lance's response: "*Yes, she is mey sista' by fadda'.*"

By mudda—Certainly not heard with the same frequency as the previous entry. The socio-cultural explanations for this are too deep to discuss here. But clearly, the mother is the default parent!

Ca—Once used frequently in place of "because." "*Ah do it ca Ah wan toh hea' wa he gon say.*"

Cacaroach—Cockroach, extra syllable added, in addition to a vowel switch, "o" to "a." "*Man, dis place full ah cacaroach.*"

Cackin' up—Generally to put up one's foot, to sit in a relaxing, carefree manner. "*Stop cackin' up yoh foot in deh chai', an' si' down propaly.*" Or "*Yoh cackin' up like yoh ain' geh notin' toh do.*" Still a fairly popular Virgin Islands expression. The expression was primarily gendered, focusing more on girls, than on boys, a clear inference of how patriarchy works in our society. As can be surmised, the commentary was generally presented as a criticism, and never complimentary.

Calabash—This make-shift utensil used for cooking at one point was very popular in our culinary history. Obviously replaced and displaced by the high tech computational ranges now. But, no fungi tasted better than that cooked in my Granny's and Aunt Miriam's calabash in Grove Place or my aunt, Vivian Acoy's, in La Vallee, St. Croix, two places (along with Frederiksted) where I spent a substantial part of my boyhood.

Callaloo fo' ole years—Special dish generally reserved for consumption on December 31. It is a signature Virgin Islands dish that continues to be cherished by the community. Fortunately, this Virgin Islands expression survives as vibrantly as ever. Even though the dish can be prepared during any period of the year, its association is generally with "*ole years*" (see description of this phrase in a later entry).

Callin' yoh, callin' yoh— Our language is known for its repetitive (emphatic) nature. This is an expression that captures that feature. When someone says, "*Man, Ah keep callin' yoh, callin' yoh, arl deh time,*" it does not necessarily mean that this is done on a regularly basis, the speaker may simply be saying that she **was** trying to contact you yesterday. Notice the hyperbolic structure, not only is the participle repeated (callin'), but the phrase '*arl deh time*' is added to give the statement an even more added emphasis. (See the entry, "**arl deh time**," given earlier).

Careless—Another example of a word typically used in English, but with a unique ring in its usage in Virgin Islands Creole. In "standard" English no one would say: "*She/ He is too careless*" referencing the manner in which a person is dressed. In U.S.V.I. Creole, however, such an utterance is common as a critique or criticism of how a person carries himself or herself. "*Man, she duz dress too careless.*"

Cark up—Inability to go to the bathroom. "*Ah eat ah bunch ah kenips, now ah arl cark up.*" (See "**bine up**" in an earlier entry). The word is the Creole variant of "*cork.*" When we think of this item plugging up a bottle, it is easy to see what our creative articulators were thinking with this expression.

Carn/Ciarn—-The contraction for "cannot." "*Ah carn go wid yoh, man. Ah too busy.*" **Ciarn**" is a variation." "*He ciarn swim.*" The expressions are interchangeable, with no real distinction, apart from pronunciation.

Carn/Ciarn be—It is important to include this as a fixed expression. The meaning is quite dissimilar to the previous usage of "**carn/ciarn**," meaning not "possible." Here the idea is more like the person does not desire, or "it looks like/ does not look like"; "it is unlikely that." "*Chuch startin' soon, an' only now you gettin' up. Yoh carn/ciarn be wan' toh go.*" ("It does not look like you want to go."). "*He drivin' so slow, he carn/ciarn be wan' toh reach early.*" These constructions have no equivalence in English. The sentence, "*He carn/ciarn be went,*" deserves special attention because no amount of deciphering can make it sensible to the person not familiar with the language. Example: "*She doan understan' dis; she carn/ciarn be went toh school.*" (Meaning, "she probably did not"). Even more unusual is the phrase, "*He carn/ciarn be use' toh visit he family.*" The idea of joining the verb "carn" with two other verbs is very unusual. Other examples are: "*I carn/ciarn be know 'im.*" "*Yoh carn/ciarn be hea' wa ah say.*" "*Doreen carn/ ciarn be like da boy ah tarl, deh way she treat 'im.*"

Carn deh fish an' putit (pu'it) in deh ceilin'—It was a normal sight to see fish well salted and hanging from the ceiling. Because of the lack of refrigeration this was done to preserve the food. The fish lay next to the corn pork and banana or plantain. Clearly this is something not seen at all today. If we were to do this today, we would be looked at with scorn and disgust. We would immediately be branded as "unsophisticated," maybe even "backwards."

Carn (Ciarn) done—This is still a popular expression used to highlight an excessive quantity. *"Toh deh party dey ha' food carn done."* It is not even necessary to have a complete sentence. For example, if one goes to an event, sees a lot of food and remarks: *"Food carn (*ciarn*) done!"* If you are a new comer to the language, it is important to note that the relative, "that" is not admissible in this construction. In other words, the statement *"food that carn done"* would not be admissible Virgin Islands Creole. The idea would still be understood, however, the structure of the sentence would be antithetical to the creolized expression. Also, in the opening *"Toh deh party,"* we use, the preposition *"toh"* in place of *"at."* For a more in depth discussion on this grammatical feature, see the earlier section on **Prepositions**.

Carn hide—An express used to indicate that a familial relationship is undeniable. *"Jacob carn hide atarl. He look jus' like he fadda."*

Carn see yoh atarl—Here is one of those expressions that at first glance might seem typical, until we truly analyze its uniqueness. Within the context used here the individual is not speaking about his or her inability to see someone (for example because of poor sight). Here the speaker is really saying: *"I don't ever see you. Where have you been?"* This phrase is generally used in a congenial manner because it is clear that the speaker would not mind seeing the person more often. *"Man, Ah carn see yoh atarl. Look like yoh hidin' from meh."*

Carto *(cardboard)*—I know that this word has not disappeared from our language, but there is no question that it is used less. But the reason behind this is not so hard to understand. Children at play in the 1950's, for example, used pieces of cardboard to sit on, on to slide on (in gutters in Savan, for example). In fact, children used the "carto" to sit on in often dusty yards as they listen to stories. The *"carto"* has simply been displaced by the various computational gadgets used for games. Who still says when playing: *"Cova' it wid a lil' piece ah carto"*? —Admittedly some people, but the numbers are scarce, and dwindling. It is most probable that this word came from the word "carton."

Caryin' arn—Acting unruly, disturbing the peace. *"Ah hea' he wuz down de caryin' arn."* But it can also indicate that one is enjoying herself or himself. *"Man, Ah hea' toh deh party yoh wuz caryin' arn. Dat's good yoh enjoy yo'self so much"* (For example, dancing a lot).

Catta—Typically a piece of cloth on one's head used for transporting water or particular goods, such as coal. We know that this was a popular headgear used by the women in the 19th century. The use of the word, "catta," conjures up memory of Queen Coziah, the undisputed leader of the 1892 Coal Workers Strike in St. Thomas. For me, the catta symbolizes the exploitative labor and the immeasurable contribution of the women coal workers. And of course the tireless sacrifices of Virgin Islands women in general.

'Cause—Short for "because." *"Ah eat it 'cause Ah was hungry."*

'Causen—Sometimes replaces "because." Language associated with children.

Chabo—From Spanish CHAVO. *"Ah 'ain geh no chabo."* Most people would still know the meaning, but less use this expression today than in the 50's and 60's. Interestingly enough, when people in our islands say this word, it is clear that they are saying cha<u>b</u>o. In Spanish, there is absolutely no phonetic distinction between the "v" and the "b." They represent the same sound, even though it is important to stress that the significance of a word would change. In the Virgin Islands, however, the "*b*" in "chabo" is pronounced with more force that the "v" in the word "chavo."

Cha'in'—With a top, a toy hardly seen these days. This was a game in which the opponents had as their objective the destruction of the other individual's toy. *"Let's play cha'in."*

Charlotte Amalia—Historically important. Even though we continue to see the words *"Charlotte Amalie,"* the original designation was "Charlotte Amalia." Some St. Thomians insist that it is essential to keep the original pronunciation of the capital city, "**Charlotte Amalia,**" for the preservation of the historical integrity. Hence the statement, "**Charlotte Amalia** *is deh capital of deh United States Virgin Islands,*" is uttered by some with an unmistakable purpose.

Chat down—To engage a person in extensive conversation: *"Man, he had meh well chat down yestaday, tellin' meh arl kina ting."*

Chile—Child. *"Dat's mey chile."*

Chook—Got stuck, probably with something sharp. It is also a noun. *"Ah geh chook from deh kasha."* *"Deh nail chook meh;"* this last expression, quite common in the 40's, 50's, and 60's is not so prevalent today; many children of the early part of last century played outside without shoes or "rubbers" (sneakers) hence their encounters with nails!!!! The word also was used frequently in reference to vaccination, especially done in the 50's when children were required to take numerous shots because of prevalent diseases—polio, infantile paralysis, measles etc. The statement, *"Ah gon take yoh to deh docta toh geh yoh chook"* or *"chool chook"* was quite common.

Chuch out—This means the case is close; that is the end. *"Yoh betta' do dis ting now, or else Ah tell yoh, chuch out."*

Chuck him/her arf—Hit/push. Generally the person who "chucks off" the other is understood to be the initiator of the conflict. This expression was more prevalent among children who were often in groups, and challenging each other was the norm. *"He chuck me arf fus'; dat's why Ah hit 'im."*

Ciard—Card. The word also refers to a person who is being unfaithful to a partner. *"Ah hea' he ciardin' ha."* In the English context this means, *"I heard that he is being unfaithful to her."*

Ciart water *(cart)*—In St. Croix we often brought water using horse and cart; later the expression simply meant to carry. Naturally, it is an expression well known in all of our islands. One distinction is the fact that in St. Croix the horse and cart were used with much more frequency when transporting water.

Ciat bile—This was said when someone gives something to another person then ask for it back. *"Yoh gon geh ah ciat bile 'cause yoh gimme dis ting yestaday, now yoh wan' tit back."* The frequency of this usage has been lessened, although we know that the expression is still heard in our islands.

Clean cope— The English word, "cope" is never heard in our islands as a NOUN outside of this given expression. Long ago there was also a reference to *"he copey."* It refers to a cleanly shaven head. Even though this is an expression not heard with the same regularity as during previous decades, it is still heard in a limited way. (See also *"goby"* in a later entry.)

Clean fo'get—This is an expression used in place of "completely forgot." It is generally used as a past tense, even though it is possible to be used as a present. The combination "clean+forget" is a unique combination with no substitute. *"Man, Ah clean fo'get to tell 'im dat yestaday."*

Clear skin—A reference to a person's skin color, not dark; in the view of the particular observer, a light complexioned individual. *"Yoh know ha', man. She tarl an' clear skin."* A person who is considered "white" is never referred to as "clear;" instead it is a designation reserved for others who are considered "nonwhite."

Clout 'im up—See earlier entry, "**Bus 'im ah clout.**" The two expressions connote more or less the same meaning. The difference lies in the fact that the present entry suggests a more aggressive act.

Coal Goose—A reference to the iron used for clothes. "*Deh goose don' hat (hot)*." Here is an example of how "modernization" totally displaces language. Very few people today would have a clue of what "*Coal Goose*" means. Those who make an effort to keep words and expressions alive may have used the words enough that they exist at a level of familiarity in the minds of those with younger family members. Some residents still say "*iron goose*," to refer to the device used for ironing clothes. I knew some residents who held on to the word "goose" well into their later years of life.

Coal pat—Apparatus used for cooking in earlier decades, in the absence of the stove. Many residents have held on to this valuable "cooking range," as a backup for when "current go arf!!!"

No bread, no food ever tasted so good using this apparatus!!!

Coc'nut—*Coconut.* Under some circumstances (always in a lighthearted manner) this is used to refer to the head. The second "*o*" was customarily swallowed up. "*Ball come, hit'im right in 'e coc'nut.*" "*He head hard like ah coc'nut.*"

Coc'nut jelly—This is the expression used instead of "coconut meat."

Coco pelao—(Pelao, from "pelado," peeled, from "pelar" to peel)— Literally this means "*a peeled coconut*" but in actuality also refers to a *cleanly shaven head*, an expression borrowed from Puerto Rico. It is important to note that this interpretive meaning is unfamiliar in Spain and many other regions where Spanish is spoken. In other words, a Spaniard would obviously know the literal meaning, and of course comprehend the expression in context; however, very likely would not use it in connection to a person's cleanly shaven head. Our usage of this expression is directly related to our proximity to Puerto Rico, and our long history of inter-island relationships, both familial and commercial. (See "*clean cope*," earlier entry).

Cocoa tea—*Ah gon drink mey "cocoa tea.*" It is important to note that the word "tea" does not mean that this is in fact a type of "tea." I suppose that today one would say "hot chocolate." The fact is that the word "tea" is used as a frequent and, fortunately, still popular generic noun covering a wide range of drinks, uniquely West Indian and Virgin Islands—"bush tea" etc. This has to be somewhat confusing for those not familiar with this expression, which still survives.

Cocobay an tap ('pon top) ah yaws —In many places " *'pon tap*" is used instead of "*an tap*." The literal idea here is that one illness was already present and is now compounded by another sickness (leprosy). The application is that there was trouble and now on top of that, there is now more trouble. Things are just getting worse. We might consider this an expression that has virtually vanished in the sense that it is no longer heard. As would be expected, however, there is still familiarity among older Virgin Islanders. A fairly comparable American English expression is: "*To add insult to injury*."

Comado—The mother of one's godchild (from the Spanish, *comadre*). The word, however, became popular referring to close familial relationships, friendship among families. This was considered a very serious relationship. Another one of those words that is primarily recognized and utilized by an older generation of Virgin Islanders. After that particular generation is gone, it is logical to surmise that this word will disappear from our vocabulary. The prospect of that happening is unbelievable when I think of the social significance of the word and its popularity at one point: "*Yes, Ah know ha', dat's mey comado*."

Come—In some contexts this can mean "to become." "*Judy, study hard, yoh cou' come ah doctor*." "*Man, Ah see yoh son las week; he come so tarl*." "*Ah yoh keep workin'; ah yoh gon come something one ah dese days*."

Come—Actually part of the formula for storytelling, as in: "*He come tellin' meh nonsense….*"

"*Doan come tellin' meh notin' 'bout he*." "*She aways comin' wid her stuppidness cussin'*."

Also common is the combination, "*come bu'*." "*He come bu' I mash' up he ting;'*" "*She come bu' she suckin' up she teet at me*." Still a very popular Virgin Islands saying. It is clear that the speaker does not appreciate the other person's action or attitude. The same form is used for the past tense: "*Yestaday, dey come bu' I trouble dem*."

Come bet—An expression used to affirm a person's prediction about some issue. The speaker is certain that something is going to result in a specific manner. "*Leon gon call meh today. Come bet he gon beg fo' money*."

The speaker has no doubt that Leon is going to do what she expects—"*beg fo' money.*"

Come down/Comin' down—This refers exclusively to the declining physical condition of a person. "*Ah see Mr. Sanford heh deh odda day. He really comin' down.*"

"*We see Dolly las' week. She come down ah lot.*"

Come from way yoh (she/he) come from—Action or commentary is not appreciated. This is an expression that establishes quite firmly the disapproval felt by the speaker. The phrase (and other similar ones) also highlights the fact that it is just not words themselves that are powerful in our culture, but their unique usage. The words are clearly recognizable as English words, but their utilization is uniquely ours. "*She come from way she come from tellin' we wa toh do.*" It is important to stress that this does not necessarily have anything to do with geography. The expression is simply alluding to the fact that the individual has no right, no authority to tell us what to do.

Come go—This oxymoron means "Let us leave." "*Ah you come go, no, I hungry.*" Here we see an unusual alliance of words in our Creole: "come"; "go" and "no." It all seems rather contradictory, but of course is not!

Comin'—In certain contexts in U.S. Creole this can mean "*going.*" The stress here is "in certain contexts." "*Ah comin' toh yoh house lata'.*" In fact, even if there is a clear awareness that the listener is not at home this expression is used. "*Ah comin' toh yoh house even tho Ah know yoh ain home.*" (See also "*How yoh comin'*" in later entry.).

Comin' toh come—Used to indicate that something is improving, a person is making steps in the right direction with a project, for example. Thomas is building a house and is asked how the process is going: "*It comin' to come, man.*" In other words, the project (the situation) is not yet at the point that the person desires. It could also be used in reference to a person's health: "*How yoh foot, Miss Mary?*" Ans: "*It comin' toh come. Each day ah lil' betta'.*"

Compado—The father of one's godchild (from the Spanish, *compadre*). Very much like the case for "comado," this may refer to close ties among families. This relationship was a much honored one in our Virgin Islands community. It represented a serious commitment to family stability and the establishment of unbreakable bonds of friendship. Without doubt older residents still know and occasionally use this term. It is no longer universally used in Virgin Islands vernacular.

Confusion—Here is a word that all would consider a "standard" English word but one that is used in a very unique way in our Virgin Islands Creole. For example, one might hear *"Yoh carn depen' on Ruben atarl; he's ah bunch ah confusion."* This may suggest that no one has any idea what the person is doing. *"Ah ain askin' ha notin'. She is jus' ah bunch ah confusion."* Maybe she causes problems, rumors, gossip, or simply talks too much. The use of the word *"bunch"* creates another one of a kind Creole construction.

Continental—An expression used to refer to Americans from the United States mainland. The word stems from the expression: *"continental United States."* This distinguishes the individual from the "local" resident.

Cook' food—In this case the word "cook" is <u>not</u> a verb, but an adjective. This was an expression frequently used to refer to prepared food, rather than canned food or uncooked food items (like fresh meat). The key here is the stressing of the words in pronunciation. Not heard today. *"Ah feel like eatin' some good cook' food right now."*

Cookshap—Today this would be called a restaurant. *"We went toh deh cookshap toh eat."* It is no longer common to hear this expression in the Virgin Islands, even though it may very well reside in the heads of those of us intimately familiar with it: *"Meet meh de by Mamá Cookshap."* This was a popular place to eat in Savan (St. Thomas) in the 1950's.

Cool/Coola—In this context it refers to an individual who is acting tough. *"Alex tink he so bad, somebardy gon cool 'im."* // or, *"Alex gon meet he coola."* The translation of this particular sentence is that the person *"will meet his match,"* someone who can rival his aggression. The cultural inference is that no matter how tough you believe that you are, there is always another individual that is even meaner. It is the philosophy of communal justice.

Coolin' out—Relaxing, taking it easy. *"Ah jus' de coolin' out, man 'cause Ah ain geh notin' toh do."* This expression should not be confused with the American English usage; for example, "I am cool" or "He is cool," reminiscent of the 1960's. In the Virgin Islands the idea of "coolin out" or "coolin it," signals a moment of relaxation. *"Man, we jus' heh coolin' out 'til time toh go back toh wok."* One of the unique features of this expression and similar ones is their flexibility without change of meaning. For example, the person could be "*heh' coolin out*" or "*de coolin' out*" and would be conveying exactly the same message.

Coopin'—Looking at someone in a suspicious or investigative way. "*Me an' Rosy wuz de tarkin' toh each odder, an' he wuz de coopin', tinkin' Ah like ha.*" The expression does not have to refer to a specific moment, and in fact could be more symbolic. Very often this is a lighthearted exchange among friends. Consider the following: "*Man, Ah hea' arl kin' ah ting' 'bout yoh; Ah coopin' yoh, yoh know.*"

Copetal—A variation of "*copey;*" not heard today, again one of the words once used almost exclusively by children. "*He geh hit right in 'e copetal. Dat's why 'e cryin' so much.*"

Copey—A person's head (see also "**goby**"). "*He geh hit right in 'e copey.*" In the Virgin Islands there are so many colloquial ways to refer to one's head, some of which are still recognizable, but naturally are virtually lost in everyday usage.

Cou'—Used in place of "can." "*Emma cou' swim good, meson.*" Interestingly, this form does not have a negative in the present tense. If we wanted to negate the sentence above, we would say: "*Emma carn/ciarn swim.*" The negative of *cou*, is reserved for the past tense: "*He coun / cou'in go wid us yestaday 'cause 'e was sick.*"

Cou' do—This will suffice; maybe it is not the ideal, but it will serve the purpose. Austin: "*Glen, yoh gon use dat pen?*" Glen: "*No man, dis pencil cou do.*" (See **Dis gon do** and **Make it do**.)

Cou' pass—Something is not exceptional, just ok. This is often in response to a previous question or statement: Speaker I: "*Meson, Jay hansome, eh?*" Speaker II: "*He cou' pass.*"

Cou' pu down/ cou' trow down—Used to indicate excess. Example: "*He cou' pu' down ah rum.*" In other words, that individual drinks too much. (Used also for food; a person seen as gluttonous). "*Harry cou' trow down some food. He geh toh stop eatin' so much.*" Again, another testament to the Virgin Islands hyperbolic style of oral delivery.

Cou' stay de—The expression suggests that the listener is taking a contrary road. You do what you want; I will not follow your lead. Consider the following: Robert brags: "*Later I goin' out toh ah party.*" Edwin's reaction: "*You cou' stay de, I goin' right in mey bed.*" Another example:

Tony says: "*Charles, dis man wuz givin' Wayne 50 dollars, an' he 'ain take it.*" Charles' reaction: "*He cou' stay de, Ah woudda take it.*" Similarly to the word "**awright**" in an earlier entry.

Coun' (also rendered as "**coun'in**)—This is the contraction for "**could + not.**" "*Ah coun' (cou'in) go wid dem las' night 'cause Ah wuz too tired.*"

Country—A rather vague word used specifically in St. Thomas to refer to the area roughly east of Donoe Gut. With exaggerated expansionism, modernization, and shifting demographics what was "country" looks more now like a city. Nonetheless, residents have continued to use this word, with unique expressions such as: "*Dey live country.*" "*I goin' country.*" "*It rainin' country.*" Old familiar expressions, such as "*He is ah countryman*" no longer resonates in St. Thomas.

Couple—One of the unique aspects of our language is the way that we "bend and twist" words moving them away from their original meanings. Of course, this expression can have a literal meaning, but it can stray very far from the generally accepted notion. Note the following examples: "*Ah have couple fish dat Ah gon fry lata'.*" Very often the person could in fact be referring to 10 pounds of fish. "*Ah give 'im couple dollars.*" This could well refer to $200. Two important features associated with this construction: 1) The "ah" (="a") is often omitted 2) the preposition "ah" (="of") is generally omitted. ("*She give "im ah couple ah dollars.*")

Couple cent—A general reference to money. Example: "*Yestaday Ah give 'im couple cent 'cause he was hungry.*"

Coxin—A game using a *locus'* seed attached to a string. The idea is to destroy the other person's "seed." This was a popular children's game, now extinct. It is not surprising that the game has vanished when we consider that the fruit itself is such a rarity. If the fruit is no longer easily accessible, then it follows that the game will lose its major source. (See the later section on this fruit.).

Crab foot an' hangers—Refers to one's illegible penmanship. If you were ever told this about your writing, it meant that your handwriting was a real disaster. "*Boy, wa da' is you jus' write? It look like crab foot an' hangers.*" Admittedly, this writer himself has often had his penmanship described in this manner!

Crappo—This is a frog; in addition to this fact, it also refers to a left-hander. The expression was never used complimentarily. The expression said among young children was, "*She/he is a left-handed crappo.*" It is interesting how culturally being right-handed can constitute the norm, the default. As a result, the left-hander was seen as "different." The reality is that such broad generalizations have no basis of scientific support.

Crazo—A variant of the word "crazy" used often in a lighthearted manner. "*Doan pay da crazo no min'.*"

Crazy MAN/WOMAN—In the Virgin Islands context this is an expression used often to refer to a person's behavior, or how the person might be perceived stylistically. "*He come in heh yestaday makin' ah bunch ah noise, ackin like ah crazy MAN.*" In pronunciation, the emphasis is on the last word. Also, "*Wen Ah pu' arn dat bright color dress, Ah ha' look jus' like ah crazy WOMAN.*" // "*Dis marnin' Ah ha so much toh do Ah was jus' like ah crazy WOMAN.*"

Crazy people wok—An action that makes no sense; seems irrational; can refer to behavior or a decision that seems strange or unpredictable. "*Dat's crazy people wok!*"

Crazy Wall—An unfortunate expression used in the 50's and 60's to refer to the facility where mental patients were kept in St. Thomas. The word was a slippage from the word, "Ward." Even though not *universally* used in the island, many people did speak of the "crazy wall." Fortunately, such structures have disappeared as facilities for the mentally ill.

Crookidy—*Not straight.* In our language this type of creativity is common. "*Look at dat line, it so crookidy. Do it ova'.*" "*Bu' look how 'e walkin' so crookidy, like he drunk.*"

Crucian maufé (St. Croix)—This is a dish with which even *some* Crucians themselves are not familiar these days. It is one of the tastiest dishes that include a variety of healthy foods. This dish needs to become once again a staple of St. Croix and hence, Virgin Islands cuisine. It was a very popular Virgin Islands culinary treat, perfected in St. Croix. These days many islanders would readily say that they have never even heard the word *maufé*. To be sure, one of our expressions that needs rescuing!

Crucianrican—Term used to highlight a Crucian's Puerto Rican heritage.

Cruz—St. Croix

Cucu—Human or animal feces. It is also used as a verb. It was and still is expected that children would use this word rather that words that are considered socially unacceptable, in essence, linguistic taboos. In fact, in the very religious Virgin Islands tradition many words are considered "curse words." Those who wish to avoid "cussin'," both adults and children, will use this word. I have never met an adult who would permit a child to use expletive expressions to refer to this refuse.

Come roun' de patishun— (The typical wood house had a divider-"partition")—Sometimes someone visiting a house would be asked to *"come roun' de patishun"* in order to be seen. With modernized housing with their fortified concrete walls this last century notion is lost forever.

Current Arf—Commonly used to refer to electricity, the loss of electrical power. *"Deh current arf again."*

Current garn—See above

Cuss arf—Curse someone out in a most emphatic way. *"Mabel had meh well cuss arf."* This expression highlights the fact that Mabel was very forceful in her reaction. The expression is one that I predict will be around for a very long time.

Cuss (cussin') bad wud—-The expression used in the Virgin Islands to refer to the *uncivil* act of using obscene language. *"He ain geh no respec', always up an' down cussin' bad wud."*

"She duz cuss too much bad wud."

Cut-arf—This expression in U.S. Virgin Islands Creole can be used as a NOUN in a special circumstance—with respect to utility agencies. It is an expression understood by all: *"Meson, WAPA jus' sen' meh ah cut-arf."* *"Yestaday we geh ah cut-arf from cable."* There is no need to follow this statement with the word "bill." It is clear that the speaker is alluding to the possibility of service being temporarily suspended.

Cuss mey mudda—This is such a cultural taboo that it is worth some space here. Perhaps the single worst thing that a person can do is insult someone else's mother. From this, one should not infer that it is acceptable to curse another's person's father, but just that the socio-cultural dynamics are different. For the uninitiated, this does not necessarily mean speaking directly to the individual's mother. Most times it refers to a statement by an antagonist who verbally slanders the person's mother. There have been countless physical confrontations as a result of this major cultural violation. Such strong reaction to a major cultural infraction is not very likely to change, and I hope it never does.

Cuttin' eye (variation, "cuttin' up yoh eye")- —Watching someone with some scorn, somewhat aggressively. *"Yoh tink Ah ain see yoh cuttin' mey eye."* A child making this gesture to a parent was truly asking for trouble! (See also *"suckin' teet"* in a later entry). There are several gestures that were, and in many ways, still are tacitly prohibited in Virgin Islands culture, especially if children are performing them: *"Suckin' yoh teet'"* (A sound associated with language and not that easy to reproduce if you are outside of the language community), *"cutin' eye," "pushin' out yoh mout,"* and *"skinnin' up yoh face."*

Da/Dat—That. *"Da(t) one is mine." "Da(t) is wa Ah been tellin' yoh."*

Da de—That. It might be referring to something specific, for example, a plate of food: *"Da de is mine. Ah yoh doan touch it."* Often though, it refers to a situation, a kind of neuter construction: *"Look no, da de is wa Ah doan like wid dem."*

Da one de—General meaning, "that one there," however, this phrase can be generated even if the object of the conversation is not in the immediate surrounding. Take for example that in a conversation between Jerry and Tina, Jerry mentions the name Bobby. Tina might respond: *"Da one de crazy, meson. I leavin' he alone."* Tina is alluding to Bobby. Also, as in the previous entry, the speaker can use the expression to reference a situation. If someone just explained an unusual situation to me, I might respond: *"Ey, da one de geh me garn. Ah ain understan' it."* (da one de=the situation)

Da ting—Used at times to refer to someone in a negative manner, or in lighthearted way. *"Da ting crazy, yoh hea'."*

Da wa make—That is the reason. *"Yoh was actin' so rude yestaday. Da wa make she ain' wan' toh see toh."* This is an expression that still is heard frequently. It has been around for a long time, and seems destined to be around for much longer.

Dain—Did not/are not. This is a contraction formed from did+not=didn't or from *dey+ain*. From that, the local expression glided into a different word. Like numerous other Creole words, this has taken on a life of its own. *"But mommy, I dain do it. Tis Melvin." "We dain go toh deh sho 'cause we <u>dain have</u> no money."* The last part of this sentence can be altered: *"…'cause we <u>ain had</u>…"* (Later in the entries see commentary on the word *"Sho."*). *"Dain home now"* [Meaning: "No, they <u>are not</u> home now."]

Dain (didn') foget 'im/her/she/he—Still a popular and special Virgin Islands Creole expression used to relay a response to someone's unacceptable comments, or action. Generally, the speaker is relating how he or she responded to the other person's comments or actions: *"He cum in deh house cussin' an' carryin' arn; well meson Ah dain' foget' im."* In other words, the person was *"put in he place."* The speaker has no qualms with reporting how he/she handled the situation; the American expression, *"I gave him a piece of my mind"* comes close in equivalence. There is a feature of this construction that is particularly emblematic of Virgin Islands Creole: the personal pronouns (him, her etc.) are variable; they can be both subjective and objective. (*"….dain foget 'im"; "dain foget he"*). *Please see earlier section,* THE PRESENT TENSE AND PERSONAL SUBJECT AND OBJECT PRONOUNS. The idea of someone "not forgetting" another may seem like a nonsensical or at best paradoxical construction to those unfamiliar with Virgin Islands Creole, but this is a well-entrenched notion in the language: *"Wen she see meh deh next day, she dain foget meh atarl."* (For example, *"She cuss meh out"*).

Darbin' in—When two people are not speaking to each other, the one that decides to make a truce (to speak to the other first) was said to be *"darbin' in."* Not heard these days. This was primarily the vocabulary of children. *"She see meh yestaday an' cum' darbin' into meh."* Interestingly, the expression was heard primarily among girls. The reason for this is unclear; I will leave this for the socio-linguists to decipher. The idea was that no one wanted to be the first to resume conversation with the other person, possibly a sign of capitulation and weakness.

Darn—A contraction that can have several translations: 1) "That is not." *"Darn wa Ah sayin'."* 2) "That was not." *"Darn wa she give meh yesterday."* 3) "That does not." *"Darn tase bad atarl."*

Dats yoh (he/she) business—-You can do whatever you want, but this is not meant as encouraging words, quite the contrary. Consider the following: Phillip: *"Ah goin' away an' Ah ain gon tell nobardy wen Ah leave."* Ray: *"Dat's yoh business. Ah doan care wa' yoh do."*

Dats you?—In addition to being a question, *"Is that you?"* this is also used as a type of greeting especially when people have not seen each other for some time. Consider Pete and Frankie seeing each other after a year. Pete: *"Dats you, meson?" Ah ain' see yoh in ah larng time."*

De—The/there. *"Pu' de ting ova' de." "Dat man de is mey cousin."*

De by Barracks Yard—There are sometimes references by older people to this landmark of gone-by days located in the area of the Federal Building in St. Thomas.

De by Logan Chuch'—Was and as to the date of this writing, still is one of Savan's and St. Thomas' major landmarks.

De by Red Ball— *Store, a landmark in Savan.* I cannot imagine anyone in the 1950's or 60's not purchasing something from Red Ball, with its variety of goods, folksy attitude, a paragon of Virgin Islands traditions.

De De—Ok, *"I am ok, nothing much happening."* "(Ah) *I jus' de de."* Even as a child regularly visiting St. Croix this was my most cherished expressions. A variation of this is *"I jus' de ya"* used in St. Croix. In St. Croix there are numerous variations depending on the section of the island that the individual lives. In the St. Thomas / St. John district is more common to hear, *"I jus' de."*

De home—At home. This is a popular expression used in St. Croix. Contrast this with **"Dey home,"** in a later entry. *"He de home."*

De ya—Here, a unique expression heard primarily in St. Croix. *"We de ya."*

Dead— The numerous constructions that can result from this one word makes it a very interesting entry. Its natural feature is as an adjective: *"He dead."* However, it can also be used as a verb: *"He dead las' year."* (See the section on **VERBAL SUPPRESSION**). *"If he keep dis up, he gon dead."* Even the present participle is admitted in some constructions. It is not uncommon to hear for example, *"Every time Ah look people jus' deadin' arl deh time."*

Deady—Adjective and adverb; the person exhibits no energy; or a place was quite boring. It is an expression used to describe the personality of an individual perceived to be apathetic or passive. The following are some typical examples: *"He doan tark atarl; man, he so deady;"* or *"He duz ack so deady;"* also, *"Wid he deady self."* Still a prevalent expression. *"We went dance las' night. Da ting was so deady."* Also, *"I will neva' live de. Da place too deady fo' me, meson."*

Deh—This refers to the definite article, "THE." *"Deh woman come from Sin John."*

Deh belly—Stomachache. The person really feels like going to the bathroom. *"Ah geh deh belly."* This expression is uttered by children and adults alike, even though it is most likely to be heard among children. It expresses the fact that the individual has an upset stomach, but the suggestion is that a visit to the bathroom is imminent.

Deh box—As legend has it, a mysterious box showed up on St. Thomas' waterfront and no one knew the origin of it, even though everyone could tell you about it—one of the great paradoxes of Virgin Islands lore. The "box" has remained ingrained in island mythology.

Deh cow foot woman—Part of Virgin Islands folklore, this mythical animal-human was "seen" throughout the Virgin Islands in the early sixties. There are still vague references to her. She ranks alongside the Green Face Man and The Box as part of Virgin Islands mythology. Any poll of Virgin Islanders would yield different descriptions of this Virgin Islands character, not surprising since this was always subject to the imagination. No one quite knows the origin of this mythological figure, but the discussions surrounding her were quite frequent, and very animated. I would argue, however, that children in the 1950's were more fearful of the Green Face Man than the fear exhibited by the 60's and 70's children with respect to the Cowfoot Woman.

Deh devel beatin' he wife wid ah hambone—Once a popular expression said if it was raining while the sun was shining. Nowadays it is still heard but with less frequency. The origin of this is lost somewhere through generations of language evolution.

Deh devil is ah busy man—All kinds of unpleasant things can happen if you don't stay busy. There is a suggestion that idleness fosters an atmosphere for problems. The devil plans his strategy and tactics against the "idle soul" who has no defense against the satanic onslaught on inactivity. Often it is an expression uttered after receiving some kind of negative news: Louis: *"Deh chiren dem pu' paint arl ova deh clothes Ah jus' wash."* Karen: *"Deh devil is ah busy man, yoh hea.' Dem chiren too idle."*

Deh fiel—In St. Thomas this is a specific reference to Lionel Roberts Stadium. *"Deh parade gon en' up en' deh fiel."* This can have no other meaning than the event will end up in the Lionel Roberts Stadium. Yet, I have no doubt that a number of St. Thomas residents would be unfamiliar with the term. The good news is that it is still used and understood by numerous residents.

Deh Green Face Man—One of Virgin Islands mythical protagonists. It is believed that this mysterious figure roamed the islands scaring people out of their wits. Like the Cow Foot Woman and "deh Jumbie," no one ever saw him, but has at least one family member that has claimed that he or she did. One of the Virgin Islands most endearing legends. As far as anyone knows, this legendary figure never hurt anyone, nor ever even tried to do so. He was under constant pursuit by the police.

Deh head of deh pave' street—One of the first paved roads on St. Thomas. The site refers to the most eastern point of Narre Gide (close to the Memorial Moravian Church). This is an expression probably now used only by older island residents on St. Thomas. There is still, however, much familiarity with the expression, in contrast to references to "Barracks Yard," "Fish Wharf", and other places in St. Thomas virtually unknown these days. Most young islanders would not know the area being referenced, even though it is also true that a small number would have an idea gleaned from family and friends.

Deh heh—I am ok. Jakie: *"Teddy, how yoh comin'?* Teddy: *"Meson, I jus' de heh."*

Deh man—Actually an expression that substitutes for "you," or "yoh" masculine; of course it is also simply and literally, "man." *"Ah gon tark toh deh man lata.' "* This could be interpreted as *"I will talk to you later."* This of course is a departure from the other meaning—an allusion to another individual. As is typical of the emphatic nature of the language, even though the personal pronoun "you" may already appear in the sentence, the expression ("**deh man**") can be still used. *"Yoh wrang, deh man."*

Deh man, awright, oh wa? –This greeting merits its own entry. As a child growing up in the U.S. Virgin Islands I never heard this expression. Now, several generations later, it is fairly prevalent, though not universally used nor accepted in our islands. But it is understood by everyone. Sometimes someone might simply use the greeting, *"Yea, deh man"* as a way of saying hello to a male. Many older residents will never consider using such an expression. Unquestionably, though, the expression, *"yoh awright"* is used frequently by speakers of Virgin Islands Creole, both young and old. The plural, in addressing more than one male is, *"Deh man dem awright, oh wa?* Or *"Ah you/yoh man awright, oh wa?* (See "**Ah you**

(yoh) man" in earlier entry.) These are examples of changing patterns of speech.

Deh Markit—The stress is always on the last syllable. This is not a reference to the modern supermarkets, but refers to the historical site- **"Unda deh Bongolo."** When people said, *"Meet meh by deh markit,"* this was universally understood on St. Thomas. It is still used and understood by most residents, and certainly by the majority of long-term St. Thomas residents.

Deh pat—Refers to the food that is burnt and sticking to the bottom. Some popular expressions were: *"I wan' deh pat." "Save deh pat fo' meh." "Gimme deh pat."* This expression has not survived. (See also "**Bun**")

Deh (De) Rock—An affectionate reference to St. Thomas, also **Rock City.**

Deh time yoh look—(or also simply **"time yoh look).** An expression that speaks to the fact that time does not stand still. When this expression is used in the general sense, only the personal pronoun "you" is allowed. *"Yoh movin' so slow. (Deh) time yoh look 'tis 8:00 o'clock."*

Dem—This is a word of multiple functions. It can be the object of a sentence, demonstrative adjective or pronoun, suffix for pluralization or even the subject of a sentence. While "dem" is not generally used as a subject in U.S. Virgin Islands Creole, there are sufficient cases where it is. There are notable examples of subjective usage, especially when used for emphasis: *"Meson, **dem** duz do wa' dey wan'."* It is important to recognize that in such a construction, the second part of the sentence uses *"dey"* and never *"dem."* Variation, *"Dem de duz do wa' dey wan'." "Dem de crazy."* Yet another feature of this versatile Creole word is its use in combination with another subject or subjects: *"Wen Ah went toh deh party Marilyn an' dem was de."* The vagueness of the word *"dem"* in this context makes it extremely unique in that there always appears to be some tacit agreement between speaker and listener as to what *"dem"* really means.

The following chart outlines the versatility of *"Dem,"* a demonstrative, (much more on this later), but also a multifaceted word. Even though it is not prevalent as a possessive pronoun in U.S. Virgin Islands Creole, the word can also be used in that way, in a very limited sense: *"Dat's dem own."* (*That's theirs.*) At the same time, no one would say *"Dem shoes"* to mean *"their shoes,"* nor *"dem business"* to mean *"their business."*

XXVII. SUMMARY OF MULTIPLE USAGES OF "DEM" AND EXAMPLES
SUBJECT OF SENTENCE
"Dem is too much."
"Who dem is?"
OBJECT OF THE SENTENCE
"Give it toh dem."
DEMONSTRATIVE ADJECTIVE
"Dem tings belong toh you?"
DEMONSTRATIVE PRONOUN
"Meson, dem is mine!"
SUFFIX FOR PLURALIZATION
"Deh bed dem."
"James an' dem garn movies."

Dem Bay Side *Boys/Guirls*—In the fifties and sixties we young boys in the Pearson Garden, Polyberg, 'Roun' de fiel' and others admired the boys from this area for their great swimming skills. This is an important entry for me because that entire area "Bayside" was part of the heart of St. Thomas.

Dem man—The word "**dem**" was addressed separately in these entries. It is, however, essential to include the entry "**Dem man**" as a separate category because, besides its literal interpretation it has a unique generic usage when employed by younger residents. As an example, if referring to a government agency an individual might say: *"Meson, dem man doan know wa dey doin."* Here the speaker is not necessarily thinking about gender, even though implicit in the generalization is that ideology. In the example given above "**Dem man**" can be interpreted as "those people working there."

Dem so—*Not* to be confused with the expression "**an dem so.**" Virgin Islanders can sift through the ambiguity of this expression which, depending on context, could mean one of the following: 1) They are "<u>very</u>" 2) Those people. Consider the statement: *"Dem so 'fraid ah guana."* This could mean "They are *very* afraid...." or simply "Those people are afraid..." The connotation can be radically different meaning "those kind of people." *"Me doan tark toh dem so." "Dem so duz ack funny."*

Dereckly—An expression that contradicts the true meaning of the word "directly." *"Ah comin' dereckly."* In this case, the person is asking you to wait, for example, until he/she has completed a task. It is purely contradictory. Proof of this inversion is the following hypothetical conversation: *"James, come here."* James' **Response**: *"Ah comin' dereckly, man, Ah have toh finish sometin'."* It is clear that the person will not go "directly," but will follow his or her own dictates. No one thinks of the actual implication of the English word, "directly" when employing the Creole word.

Dese one(s)—These items here. *"Wich ah dese one(s) is yoh's own?*

Dey—Refers to the subject *"they." "Dey gon come lata.'"*

Dey/(Dem)/ (Dem de) / (You)] ain geh notin' toh do—An expression that alludes to a situation that seems rather banal, or idle. Consider the following conversation between two friends: Bianca says *"Dey outside countin' deh ca' dem passin'."* Karla: *"Dem de ain geh notin toh do."*

A variation of this is *"Dey ain geh ah ting toh do."* See also the later entry *"Geh tit toh do."*

Dey garn poochin'—Looking for crabs to catch and later cook. *"Tonight we gon go poochin' toh try toh ketch some crabs."* Lost expression.

Dey had—This is used to indicate "there was" or "there were." *"Man, dey had ah lat ah people in town yestaday."* This is used often instead of *"it had."*

Dey home— A special expression that in our Creole has no parallel in English. As discussed in the earlier section on prepositions, the preposition "at" can be suppressed, and we know that the linking verb is also often eliminated in a sentence. This particular entry means *"They are at home."* Contrast this with the earlier entry, "**de home**." The pronunciation is identical in both *"Deh home"* and *"de home."*

Die arf—To die. There is often a sense of suddenness when the speaker utters these words. But the suddenness or surprise of one's death is not at all a prerequisite for the use of this expression. *"I know dat he wus sick, but he jus' die arf so."*

Dis (Dat) gon do—This expression means that a particular item or thing will serve a particular purpose. *"You have deh tool?"* Ans: *"No, but this rock gon do."* See also, "**cou do**" and **"make it do."**

Disgustin' / disgus'— this expression sometimes causes a lot of confusion for those who are not familiar with it, especially when speaking with people from mainland, United States. In this case the word *"disgustin"* is generally referring to an unruly child; or sometimes it refers to someone who is annoying, overbearing. *"Dat chile too disgustin'; he doan lisen toh nobardy."* We generally do not use this to mean "nasty." Used as a predicate adjective (*disgus'*) it means to be tired of something, or a situation. If for example someone is doing something that another finds objectionable you might very well hear: *"Ah disgus' ah he now wid he stuiepiness."* // *"Mr. Marcel so disgustin.' He duz complain 'bout eveyting."*

Do an' do—To persist with something, always with the idea that there will be some result, not always good, not always bad. *"Wilfred, yoh gon do an' do til yoh broke da ting. Pu' e' down."* *"Gena doan give up atarl. She duz do an' do til' she understan' someting."* The same expression is used for the past tense: *"Da guirl do an' do til' she fix da rajo."* There is no possibility of ever using "DID" to express this idea in the past, an indication of the phrase's unique nature.

Do/doin' bad; duz do bad—Even though the words may ring familiar for an English speaker, the usage certainly will not. This means to "cause problems," "to treat badly." *"Dis pain doin' meh bad."* *"Las' night dis pain do meh so bad."* *"Man, dis ting duz do meh bad"* (for example, an injury, sickness, etc.). But it is also heard in reference to individuals: *"Ah hea' she duz do ha' mudda' so bad,"* meaning that she does not treat her with respect.

Do fo' do ain' no obeah—I too can extract my revenge. A popular adage and maxim. Do not complain if what you do to someone is met with an equal response. In other words, you are not the only one who can act in a certain manner. You cannot refer to an act as "obeah," if it is reciprocated! One of my all-time favorite Virgin Islands proverbs. *"He complainin' 'bout wa she do toh 'im, but 'e forgettin' dat 'e do it fus. Well, do fo' do ain' no obeah."*

Do good, good duz atten' yoh—You will benefit from your benevolent ways. This clearly has its roots in the Bible. Many Virgin Islanders try to follow this mantra, a very special one heard regularly in our community. My mother stated this regularly.

Doan come + 'in'—An unusual expression is the adding of "in" to words that are not verbs. Only a hypothetical situation can help to illustrate how this unique Creole expression works. Jeremy after being rude, tries to speak to his mother: *"Bu', Mammie…"* His mother interrupts and says" *"Doan come mammie- in'* meh." In other words, don't try to change the topic….

A couple, Carl and Carmen, are engaged in a dispute: Carl pleads: *"But sweetheart…."* Carmen retorts: *"Doan come sweetheart-in…meh."* Whatever the word used, the speaker turns it into a participle. A one of a kind construction.

Doan go pantoom if yoh carn' swim good—This particular entry brings back fond memories. For those familiar with the area where the West Indian Company Dock is located in St. Thomas, the water was exceedingly deep. For young boys from various areas during the 1950's and 60's this was the swimming area with its rite of passage. It was, however, the virtual "backyard" for the "Housin' " boys. If you were able to swim there, your skill as a swimmer could never be denied. The thought of young people swimming there "unauthorized" and without the presence of life guards is now a daunting one, but this was a common occurrence. An expression that is now totally lost to industrialization and commercialization.

Doan han' meh no stuiepiness (foolishness)—The command must be seen in the context in which it is most popular in our islands. "I really don't want to hear what you have to say at this time." For example, Timmy tells his father: *"Ah jus' las' mey school book."* His parent retorts: *"Boy doan han' meh no stuiepiness."* In other words, you had better find that book.

Doan hea'—Apart from the conventional interpretation of this expression (i.e. a person's disability, for example), this is also used to refer to a person's stubbornness. *"Dat boy doan hea', he gon geh heself in trouble. Ah tired talk toh 'im."* This speaks to the individual's disobedience and failure to follow directions, or heed advice. It always suggests a refusal rather than an inability to do something. The person being criticized is making a conscious effort to be contrary.

Doan leh [specific time] meet you—It is a warning, usual by an adult to a child. You better return before the time stipulated. *"Look guirl, doan leh midnight meet yoh in town."*

Doan make meh laugh—This is an expression which on first sight might seem to be like a typical English utterance. But, it is not. In the Virgin Islands this is often said to express surprise, disapproval, or incredibility. Example: Jacob says: *"I gon be deh governa of dese isluns one day."* His friend responds: *"Boy, doan me meh laugh. Darn gon happen."*

Doan (duz) study—Here is another case where the saying seems like "standard" English (apart from the pronunciation). But in fact the application is rather unique. It means to pay attention to, or to ignore; care for, or not care for; to listen, or not: "*He doan study he po' mudda' atarl.*" This is an expression that has not lost its momentum in usage. It is heard with the same frequency as when used during past decades. "*He cum tarkin' craziness. Me ain' self sudyin' he.*" Also heard, "*One ting wid dem, dey **duz** study dey family.*" Another context is the following: Joan: "*Ah tarkin toh you an' yoh even ain self studyin' meh.*"

Doan pass me—The person always acknowledges me by either stopping to talk or at least saying hello. "*One ting wid she, she doan pass me wen she see me.*"

Doan worry—Used as rough equivalent of the American expression, "never mind." Consider the following scenario: Tyrie is calling Carl for help, but is eventually able to complete the task without Carl. Carl then asks if he needs help, to which Tyrie responds: "*Doan worry, man, Ah do it aready.*" Also, Lorna is calling her sister to help with something, but changes her mind and tells her sister: "*Doan worry.*"

Doh doh—Moo moo. Silly, a fool. "*Bu' look he, no. He actin' like ah real doh doh.*" Possibly an allusion to the now extinct Dodo bird.

Don—Used often in place of "already." Also, "finished." "*She don garn*"- - She has already left. There is also a redundancy so typical in our rich Creole utterance. "*She don finish.*" "*She don went aready.*" "*Jus' eat deh ting an' don.*" Here, the American expression "*do it and get it over with*" would be fairly comparable. "*Dey don wok, dey home now.*" "*Deh party don.*" "*I hungry bu' it look like arl deh food don.*" The command expression "*don it*" is equivalent to "finish it" in English. "*Don it now.*" In the Virgin Islands context this usage is very distinct. "*Don deh ting, people geh toh go.*"

Don wid 'e/she—Used to convey that the speaker has no interest in communicating with another individual, or continuing a relationship of some sort. This is a declaration of separation. At its most extreme, the speaker does not even want to hear the person's name: "*Doan tell me notin' bout' Jason, Ah don wid 'e.*"

Donin' mey, don yoh etc.—Indicates that someone is making you spend your money, and you are not happy about it. "*Yoh keep spenin' money on da boy. He gon don yoh.*" "*Yoh son donin' yoh. He gehtoh look ah job.*"

Donkey years—Used to generalize a period of time that is undefined, but always refer to a long but unspecified period of time. All depends on the interpretation of the speaker. *"Ah donno wen las' Ah see 'im. Tis donkey years."* The informed listener understands the expression without ambiguity, well aware of the speaker's point. As can be imagined, such an expression was more prevalent during the years when this animal was seen and used more regularly.

Donno— Don't know, not aware. *"Ah donno wey dey garn."*

[[Down de by Buckhole—Would not be a site known by new residents and in many cases not even people living in the islands for many years. **Down de by seventy-five carna'—These days one could probably go a few years without hearing this expression. **Down de by Silva' Dollar**— Would not be a site known by new residents and in many cases not even to people living in the islands for many years. **Down deh Road**—*"He live down deh road." "Ah sho yoh know dat family. Dey use toh live down deh road."* Some older residents in St. Thomas still use this expression to refer to areas west of the city, in the vicinity of the Western Cemetery. Because of the numerous changes in our islands over the last few decades this expression no longer resonates universally on St. Thomas, except of course when the conversation is among residents who date back to the 60's or earlier.]] **[[Some lost geographical expressions]].

Down house—Used when referring to something falling. *"She went up on deh ladda an befo' yoh know it, down house, she was on deh groun'."*

Down wet—Soaked. *"Boy, go take arf dem clothes, dey down wet."*

Draf—A cold. *"He ketch ah draf."* The person is sick; he has a cold. It can also be a reference to the outside moisture. For example, *"Ah you come in out dey draf."*

Drag yohself/ah you self—A command stated with urgency and insistence. *"Boy, drag yohself heh now." "Ah you drag ah yo'self heh now."* It is clear from the nature of the command that this is a directive given to children, and not typically to grown-ups. Still extremely popular in Virgin Islands parlance.

Drap down—An allusion to dying suddenly because of some extraordinary reason—hot sun, hunger etc. *"Ah so hungry Ah feel Ah gon drap down."*

Dress up/Dress ova' —Move in order to accommodate others. The person is being asked to "move over." *"Ah yoh, dress up ah lil bit. We need some mo' room heh."*

Drunka' dan rum—An indication of person's extreme level of intoxication. *"Jayson was staggerin' so much; boy, Ah tell yoh he was drunka dan rum."* Clearly a serious situation, however, the utterance can be given in a light hearted manner.

Dum bread—A Virgin Islands staple, very popular and used for a variety of occasions

Dumsy—- Unfortunately a negative characterization of an individual's abilities. Often heard with respect to academics ability. *"He carn add, he so dumsy."*

Dung guts—Oversized stomach; the stomach is being "headed *down*wards." *"He is ah dung guts man. He need toh exercise."*

Dut pan—Still a popular expression for garbage can. Years ago, the idea of sophisticated garbage cans used these days in the public sphere was absent. *"Man trow da ting in deh dut pan; it smell so bad."*

Dut truck—Synonym for "garbage truck." The expression is not as popular as it once was, but is still recognized and used by many. *"Pu' deh dut outside. Deh dut truck comin' roun' lata' today."*

Duttyin' up/Duttin' up—In the Virgin Islands most times this expression has absolutely nothing to do with dirt, even though we know that it is a derivative of that word. In fact, when it is used, it is normally confined to the house: *"Man, ah you stap duttyin up/ duttin' up deh place. Ah jus' clean it up."* It could be a reference to children putting toys out of place, or someone refusing to make a bed. The phrase emphasizes a general disorder, untidiness in the house, or elsewhere.

Duz/Duh'— An emphatic word used as an auxiliary to form the present tense. In other words, rather than sayin, *"Ah wok everyday,"* one might say *"Ah duz wok (duh' wok) everyday....."*; *"She duz wok." "Jayson duh wok wen he feel like."* There is much more about this under the section, **THE PRESENT TENSE AND PERSONAL SUBJECT AND OBJECT PRONOUNS.**

Duz be/ Duh'be—This construction deserves a place by itself, apart from the entry that precedes it because it really has no *direct* translation in English. However, there are approximations: *"are," "is," "am,"* but this is not always the case. Look at the following examples: Sheila: *"Meson, wey* *yoh duz be (duh'be) wen people lookin' fo' yoh?"//* Jimmy: *"I duz be (du'be) home."* It is often used in place of the simple present tense of a verb: *"Boy, dey duz be behavin' so rude sometimes."* (They behave rude). *"Felipe duz be playin' in deh park."* (*"Felipe plays in the park."*—however, the sentence can never mean: *"Felipe is playing in the park."*). Consider the following statement that captures the uniqueness of the utterance: *"Yoh know 'im, man; he duz be down by Normandy Bar."* Roughly, the speaker is saying that the person "can be found," "frequents," often goes to Normandy Bar.

Duz maka yoh/ Duz maka people—This is an expression that speaks to the embracing personality of a person. The individual is friendly, personable. It is always seen as highly complementary to use this expression that infers that the individual is not self-centered, nor "stuck up.": *"Ah really like ah; she duz maka yoh (or people) wen she meet yoh (or dem)."* To use an American expression, *"she is down to earth."* This is in sharp contrast to the entry given later: **Geh ah lat ah ting in ah ('im) [Geh too much ting in 'im (ah)]**— a reference to an overly proud individual.

Dyin' fo' want—Another ingrained hyperbole to express hunger. *"Tain geh ah bit ah food in dis house; Ah heh dyin' fo' want."* (See earlier discussion on when to pronounce the "t" in the word "want.").

Eatin' table—Dining table. This expression has virtually disappeared. Many decades ago almost everyone used the expression to refer to the table where the family ate. In typically small dwellings many years ago this was most likely a small table with 4 chairs; naturally, the situation varied according to the family's economic standing. The term itself was used regularly and was universally understood. I would suspect that today if I said, *"Put it on deh eatin' table,"* some people would wonder why I used such an expression, though they would likely understand through their application of logic.

Eh—Used as a kind of confirmation. *"He tall, eh?"; "She nice, eh?"* A close English proximity would be *"Isn't he?" "Right?"*

English Church—At one point this expression was sometimes used to refer to the Anglican Church. The expression has all but disappeared in our islands.

Eva'— Actually this is from the word "ever." In context it is "always." But in Virgin Islands Creole how this word is used in certain situations is markedly different to what one hears in utterances in English. The following sentences would have no resonance for an American visiting the U.S. Virgin Islands: *"Look no, yoh betta' shut yoh mout' cause yoh eva' tarkin' Melee."* // *"She eva' tellin' people ting 'bout me."*

Evey/Eveyone/Eveyting/Eveybody— Every etc. *"Eveyting good, man'."*

Evey single way—This stresses "every place." *"Ah duz take dis wid me evey single way Ah go."*

Fa' fa—To indicate in the speaker's mind what is a long distance; "very far." *"Cito dem live fa' fa' from we."*

Facen—To confront, to face. *"Ah gon facen dem tomarro' an' tell dem deh trut."*

Fakey—Unauthentic, a negative charactererization. One cannot confide in another because that person does not appear to be genuine: *"Ah doan talk to 'im dat much. He too fakey."*

Fallo' fashion Monkey darg—A reference to those who just like to imitate others. *"Jus' because he see me pu' on mey shoes, he pu' on his own. He is ah Fallo' fashion Monkey darg."* Hyperbole knows no end in our Creole. The merging of "monkey" and "dog" together in one phonic group indeed is an unlikely construction, but it is this type of combination that often characterizes our expressions.

Fan deh coal pat—This was done to foster the flames. Still used from time to time today, when there is no electricity and people are forced to use alternate *methods* of cooking. Also could have metaphorical significance. (i.e "fanning the flames"; causing problems).

Fara'—*Farther/further.* It is interesting to note that this word can be used to represent both "farther" and "further." Consider the following examples that illustrate how this word is used: *"Pu dat ting fara' away from deh stove befo' yoh geh bun."* Also, *"Ah only finish' two pages ah dis book. Yoh fara' along dan me."*

Fas—Rude. *"Da chile too fas'. He parens' dem need toh tark toh 'im."*

Fatty—Adjective used to describe a person's size. *"Yea, yoh know who he is. He's ah real fatty man."*

Fava'—To look like someone. *"He fava' he mother."* Was always more popular in St. Croix than on St. Thomas or St. John.

Feelin' up (also see "Touching up")—Unwarranted touch, or excessive or exaggerated touching. *"Stop feelin' me up. Ah doan like yoh."* *"Stop feelin' up deh pillow."*

Fiah one—Often used by individuals to refer to taking an alcoholic drink. No one would speak of "firin' one" if referring to a soft drink. *"Dey went toh ah rum shap toh fiah one."* (See **He garn deh <u>rum shap</u>** in later entry).

Fiahbun—A word that speaks to our great history and especially the action of Queen Mary and other queens in St. Croix who in 1878 rebuked the unfair labor laws and the suppressive contract laws.

Filapino—This refers to a kenip with a double seed. The typical kenip or genip was a single seed.

Flam/Flam in—To close with force. A clear variant of "slam." Nonetheless, a self-sufficient Creole word. *"Boy, Doan flam (in) deh do' like dat 'cause yoh gon mash it up."*

Flambo—Light prevalent in the 50's and earlier. *"We goin lookin' crab lata'. We need ah good flambo toh see dem crab."* Not heard in contemporary Virgin Islands vernacular.

Fling/ Fling down."—To throw, to toss, but also to throw with some force, such as, *"Da guirl so strong she fling 'im down."* *"Man, jus' fling de ting toh meh Ah gon ketch it."*

Flit—*"Flit"* was actually a brand name of a particular defoliant for flies and mosquitos, manufactured decades ago. Eventually in the United States Virgin Islands the word became more generic and was adopted as a verb to speak in general terms about the act of spraying; to spray insects, bugs mosquitos etc. It is the classic example of a metonym. *"Too much mosquito in heh; yoh have toh flit deh place."* // *"Befo' goin' toh sleep tonight we gon flit deh house toh keep out dem disgustin' mosquito."*

Flit truck—Expression at times used as a synonym for **Smoke truck** (later entry.)

Flouncin' up—Having an attitude as demonstrated through body language that is confrontational. *"She was standin' in front of ha aunt, jus' flouncin' up herself. She too rude."*

Flustarashun—To be in a frenzy, upset, agitated, excite. *"Wen she reach in deh house she was don in ah flustasrashun, screamin' an' makin' noise."* Often the word is modified by *"<u>arl in</u>."* *"Deh man come in heh <u>arl in</u> ah flustarashun."*

Fly into—To start a raucous. To physically, or verbally accost someone, often considered to be without provocation. *"Wen she see meh, she fly intoh me, widout sayin ah word."*

"Yvonne watchin' meh like she ready toh fly intoh meh."

Fo'—Used in place of the English preposition **"before."** *"Call meh 'fo yoh leave."*

Fo'—Used in place of preposition "for." *"Do it fo' mey, no."*

Fo'day marnin'—Very early in the morning, before the sun rises. The expression still survives, however its prevalence is not as it once was. *"Ah gon geh up fo'day marnin' toh look fish."*

Fo' days—Another versatile Virgin Islands expression used in multiple ways. It indicates a large quantity of something, or of people. Speaker 1: *"A lot of people went toh deh party?"* Speaker 2: *"Man, It had people de fo' days."* This is another situation in which the members of the linguistic community would know exactly what the limitations of this expression are. Still a popular expression.

Fo deh day—An expression that roughly translates to *"all day long."* *"Boy ah so hungry. I ain eat ah ting fo' deh day."*

Fo' purpose—Used to indicate a lack of excitement or enthusiasm toward something. Example: Mel: *"Lily, yoh like crab?"* Lily: *"Toh tell deh trut Ah doan eat it fo' purpose."*

Fo' real!//Fo real?—Right / or Is that a fact? Jimmy: *"Mey cousin' livin' St. John."*

Robby: *"Fo' real? Ah tink he was still in St. Croix."* Other example, as an affirmation: *"Amos duz act so outta place sometimes."* Response: *"Fo' real!"*

Fo' spite—Done willfully, to annoy or spite someone; with intention, also revenge. *"Sorry, Ah ain hit 'im fo spite."* Another use of the expression is as a kind of vengeance. *"Fo spite Ah gon mash up yoh cell phone."*

Fo' true//Fo true?—-Confirmation, agreement, surprise. Sally says: *"Dem chiren too outta place."* Troy responds: *"Fo' true!"* In St. Thomas, the expression **"Fo' trut!"** is also sometimes used as a substitute. Howie: *"Carl too lazy."* Joan responds: *"Fo' trut!"*

Also the expression of surprise: Charlo: *"Ah jus' buy ah new ca'."* Corey: *"Fo true?"*

Foge in **/ Fogin' in**—-Enter a paid function without authorization. *"We foge' in toh deh hass race, 'cause we ain' ha' no money."* Not a popular expression these days.

Force ripe—A reference to someone trying to act older than he or she is. *"He keep ackin' like ah man. He so force ripe."*

Forward an' outta place—This compound expression emphasizes the speaker's assessment of someone. The person is not only "forward;" his or her objectionable behavior extends well beyond that: *"He come wid he stuiepiness tellin; meh 'bout meh shoes. He forward an' outta place."*

Fraid— Afraid, scared. *"I fraid ah guana."* // *"Doan be fraid, jus' go an' do it."*

Fraidy—Afraid, scared. Interesting word that can function both as adjective and adverb. The following examples show how it can be used in each case. *"Jamal so fraidy. He duz run from eveyting."* // *"Camila is ah real fraidy ciat."* / *"Da man duz act so fraidy."*

Frako—A frozen beverage, a cousin of the Special. Years ago it was sold regularly in the streets, different flavors, different colors. On a hot Virgin Islands day, this was one of the remedies to quench one's thirst and to feel "cool."

Fraut—Foolishness, nonsense. *"Man, you always takin' ah bunch ah fraut."*

Free papah bun'—The period of free time that you had available has expired. This is often said to people whose vacation is finishing, for example, or children who have to return to school. *"Deh chiren dem goin' back school tomorro'. Dey free papah bun."*

Freebs—A reference to something that is free. *"Dat's ah freebs. We doan have toh pay ah cent."*

Fresh wata' Yankee—Reference to someone who after being in the United States for a short time is trying to change his/her speech to sound like an American. Most important is the fact that the person hopes that others believe him to be an American. Here is a clear indication of identity crisis. This is also the name of a very popular and productive Virgin Islands/New York organization.

Frig up—Used as an adjective, this refers to a person with an annoying, grating attitude. Often someone who might be intolerant, sorely, and unpredictable. Used as a verbal construction it refers to being bothered. The statement, *"He is ah frig-up man"* indicates that he is disagreeable individual. On the other hand *"Don't frig me up,"* means don't bother me, don't mess with me; don't upset me. As a noun, the context suggests an annoying individual. The statement, *"He is ah lil' frig"* in Virgin Islands Creole means that the person is annoying, a pest. An expression that will be around for a long time.

From marnin'—The expression is used to stress a protracted period of time. The speaker is conveying some level of frustration about a situation and the time expended without result. *"Tain from marnin' Ah tell she toh do da' ting, an' she ain' do it yet."* For the uninitiated, it is important to know that the time frame should not be taken literally. The speaker may be referring to something that has been going on for years.

From marnin'—There is yet another use of this expression to indicate a lack of knowledge about a particular situation, or just in general. *"He ain know notin' from marnin."*

Frowsy—Speaks of a negative appearance or smell. *"Dem clothes smell frowsy."* (smell bad). *"Man, yoh look so frowsy. Fix up yo'self."* Being told this was a real "put down."

Fry fish—Important inclusion of this expression, not only because of the verb "fry" in place of the adjective "fried," but because of the special place of this rich cuisine in Virgin Islands culture.

Fry in yoh own fat—You will be the cause of your own demise. Your actions will contribute to be your downfall. *"Keep it up. Yoh gon fry in yoh own fat."*

Full—In our context here it refers to a fruit at the verge of become ripe.

Full mout—An indication that a young person is overstepping his or her bounds in the way he or she addresses an older person. *"Imagine, Donna cum callin' meh full mout,' usin' mey fus name, like Ah is some kina ah frien' ah hers."*

Full up—Fill. *"Deh bucket don full up."* As a verb: *"Full up de bucket wid wata."*

Full up—Once was a popular term used to refer to a woman who was pregnant. Sometimes the inference was negative. Not an expression heard these days.

Fungi- A staple food popular in both the United States and British Virgin Islands; basic ingredients of cornmeal, butter, and okra. Generally eaten with fish, but people have their own combinations. You cannot claim of having lived in these islands if you never heard that word, or worst, never tasted that delicious dish!

Fungi ban'—a local band that preserves traditional music with the most basic of instruments that have been passed down from generations. *"Da fungi ban cou' play some real Quelbe music."*

Fus- First. *"Deh fus ting Ah wan' toh do is sleep."* See the section under **A NOTE ON SUPPRESSION OF CONSONANTS.**

Fussy- This is beyond being dissatisfied with something. The individual is seen as somewhat testy and exaggerating a situation to an extent not necessary: *"Yoh always complainin'. Yoh too fussy, man."*

Ga—To have, to possess, to get. This is often used in place of "**geh**," in a later entry. *"Ah ga toh leave now."* *"Me ain ga' ah ting toh do."* *"Mr. Curry ga ah latta money."*

Gade—The Danish word for streets in the Danish West Indies. A carry-over from the Danes. No one uses the word, except in mailing addresses. There are only a few cases where residents actually use the "official" street names, generally residents revert to local NAMES—- "Mainstreet," "Backstreet," "Goat Street," etc.

Gallery—A word used in the early part of last century to refer to a porch. It has fallen in disuse these days, though not at all extinct. *"Ah you stap playin' in deh house. Go out on deh gallery toh play."* As a resident of the Pearl M. Pearson Gardens Housing Project in my youth, this was a frequent exhortation. These days it is more common to hear the word "porch."

Garm (variations; "**Garmy**"; "**Gardy**")—Euphemism for "God" to avoid blasphemy, violating the Third Commandment— *"takin' deh lawd name in vain."* Still heard with much frequency. Also the expression is used to express sympathy. *"Oh garm' man, tis ah sin."* (You feel sorry for someone in a bad situation). Prevalent is the exclamation: *"Oh garm! Ah forget toh….."* *"Oh garm, Ah wuz suppose toh call mey mudda"* etc. *"Oh garm, watta lie!!"*

Garn—Went; left; leaving; past; also used as a past participle. *"Wey dem boys garn?"* *"Dem boys garn town."* *"Bu' wey he garn atarl? He was jus' heh."* But even though the verb *"garn"* can be used in place of *"went,"* such a substitution is not possible in all situations. For example, the following statement is not admissible in U.S.V.I. Creole: *"Dey garn movies yestaday."* Instead, the appropriate utterance would be: *"Dey went movies yestaday."* Other popular expressions with this verb are: *"I garn, meson."* *"Ah garn."* *"Ah garn heh,"* used at times to signal that a person is leaving, not that the person has already left. Also still popular, *"I garn dis way. (See earlier entry: "Ah goin' heh.")."* *"Ah garn dis side."*

Garn as "past" — *"Sunday garn we all went toh chuch."* (Last Sunday)

Garn back—As an expression this deserves its own space, apart from the previous entry. The phrase means "to return." "*Wen Ah garn back, eveybardy don sleep.*"

Garn 'bout yoh (he) business—You are out doing what you want. Sometimes this is said with much sarcasm. "*Ah carn find him atarl, Ah guess he don garn 'bout he business.*" "*Look no, go 'bout yoh business from heh.*" Also a popular expression as part of the storytelling formula, "*He garn 'bout he business tellin' people wa' he ain know.*" In other words, he had the audacity to do something like that.

Garn' Mandahl *(alternately,* "**He in Mandahl**"*)*—A home for boys was located in this estate. This expression was used to tell where some boys were housed. It is interesting to note that boys were sent there sometimes for not going to school and often for reasons that were not at all criminal. The truth is, in general these were NOT "bad" boys. It was just that our society chose what it considered the most convenient resolution in dealing with social issues. When we consider the types of social entanglements that young people are in now, we are forced to ask ourselves whether it was justified to institutionalize most of those boys. Ironically enough, even after the juvenile facility was opened in St. Croix, people in St. Thomas continued to say "*He garn Mandahl in St. Croix.*" An interesting twist!

Garn roun' deh rocks—Expression often used when searching for whelks. This was a popular activity many years ago. It is still done, but clearly with less frequency. The term itself is not used as often in part because of the changing socio-economic situations on our islands. "*We goin' roun' deh rocks lookin fo' wilks.*"

Garn states—This is an expression often used when referring to someone who has moved or is visiting the United States mainland. Speaker 1: "*Ah ain see Dora in years.*" Speaker 2: "*Man, she garn states larng time.*"

Garn tellin'— This introductory really is a past tense that refers to what the person "did." "*She/he garn tellin' dem stuiepidnes 'bout meh.*" This is one of the many markers that people used and still frequently use to relate a situation.

Garpin' *(variation giarpin)*—Used often to refer to someone who, instead of begging, is watching someone else very intently because they want something that individual is eating. "*She hungry. Look how she de garpin' (giarpin').*"

Gatoh—Have to; an obligation. *"Ah gatoh pay deh bill today."*

Geh—To have; (to possess); to arrive; to get, as in to retrieve; also used to express obligation. *"He geh ah lot ah money."* *"Lisa geh home late las' night."* *"She geh ah big house."* *"We geh toh go toh he house today."* If someone tries to equate this to the word "get" in English, it will not necessarily function. In pure creative spirit we also have the participle that may be used. Only an intimate familiarity with the language would allow the speaker to know those selected situations. *"Ah gehin' ah headache listenin' toh yoh."* *"She gehin' arl kin' ah trouble wid ha' son."* Of course, the participle "gehin" also has another connotation, "becoming." *"Da boy gehin' big, meson."* Finally: *"Geh me dat papah ova de."*

Geh ah foot/ han' etc.—An expression used to indicate an injury or physical limitation. The listener knows immediately that the speaker is referring to some particular ailment with respect to the foot, hand etc: Ralph: *"Why she ain come?"* William: *"Man, she geh ah neck de troublin' ha."*

Geh ah lat ah ting in ha/ah ('im) [Geh too much ting in 'im (ha/ ah)]—This is usually a criticism of someone who appears rather arrogant, vainly proud, overly self-centered. *"Boy, she geh ah lat ah ting in ah, yoh see ah de."*

Geh back—To return. *"Laverne gon geh back tonight."* Also, *"Wen ah gon geh back de money ah give yoh?"*

Geh chap—Refers to a cut specifically in the head. *"He fall down an' geh chap wen he hit 'e head."*

Geh comb—An expressive used often in sports to indicate that a person did not earn any points. *"Da boy geh comb, he ain score one basket in deh game."* Also, *"He went dance, an' nobardy ain dance wid 'im. He geh comb."* Not currently a popular expression.

Geh in (Geh back in)—To enter (or reenter) into a relationship, not necessarily romantic. A person might simply be making an effort to become closer to someone else. It often suggests a special effort. *"Man, I tryin' to geh in wid she, but Ah ain geh no luck."*

"He nack me arf; now ah tryin' toh geh back in."

Geh pulls—Having connections; inside contacts; influence. Still an expression that is heard, but again, the frequency does not compare to the earlier years of the 1950's and 1960's. *"He geh pulls wid dat official."*

Geh tit toh do (you/he/etc.)—The inference is that the person is wasting time. The implicit thought is: *"Don't you have anything better to do?* Of course in our Creole we find a colorful way to express this. Consider the following conversation. Doris to her brother: *"Wa' yoh doin', Claytie?"* Claytie: *"Ah heh tryin toh fix dis ole shoe."* Doris: *"Boy, you geh tit toh do."* Doris' response does not express an obligation. In no way is she telling her brother that he must perform the task, or that he needs to do so. It is, though, a clear suggestion that he could be doing something more worthwhile.

Geh toh call—A very popular expression used to express familial relationships. For example, the relationship between two people. *"Yes, Ah know 'im. Ah tink he geh toh call Mr. Thomas, uncle."* Often times in our language relationships are expressed in hyperbolic terms. This expression has not lost its relevancy over the last decades. To the individual unfamiliar with the speech it can easily be very confusing: *"I geh toh call he gran' fatha' uncle."* The person trying to decipher such an expression may feel very lost. Yet to the speaker of Virgin Islands Creole the unraveling of this statement would be largely rudimentary. In the sentence included here, we are second cousins. Another popular option is: *"I 'pose toh call he gran' fadda' uncle."* See later entry with respect to *"pose."*

Geh yoh (him etc.) garn—Yet another interesting Virgin Islands expression. It suggests that someone or something has the upper hand, control over you. *"Da guirl look like she geh yoh garn."* // *"Da boy look like he geh ha garn."* One possibility is that the person may be so much in love that he or she is figuratively "under the spell of the other person." The expression suggests that someone is gaining an advantage over another. It is, for example, used in sports. *"Dey had us garn, but we come back an' win."* (They were winning initially, but we eventually overcame them.)

Gehin—Becoming. *"Da chile gehin' so big."*

Gehin' down—A person is declining physically or mentally. *"Po ting; he really gehin' down. Da sickness doin' im bad."* Unlike "**come down**" the expression *"get' down"* is not admissible.

Gi' blows/ (some good blows)—Apart from the generally expected meaning of such a phrase in English, in U.S.V.I. Creole this specifically can refer to corporal discipline and is an expression that is still frequently used. When used in context, it is well understood by the speech community. Parent: *"He was de playin' man. Lemme tell yoh, Ah gi 'e some good blows."*

Gi' yoh sometin' toh cry fa'—A parent uses this expression when disciplining a child and feels like the child is crying unnecessarily, sometimes suspected to be pretending. The parent threatens to "beat," discipline, the child even more, prefacing the action with the following: "*Yoh betta stap cryin' befo' ah gi' yoh sometin' toh cry fa.*"

Giang—A gang. "*Wa wrang wid he bu' he wan' toh join ah giang?*" In addition to this, however, there is a usage that has no parallel in English: "*Da is ah giang ah stuiepiness.*" Also the expression, "*Yoh tarkin' ah giang ah stuiepiness*" has no equivalence in English.

Gimmie (gi' meh)—Give me. "*Gimmie deh pen now. Ah wan' toh write sometin.*" "*Gi meh da spoon on deh table.*"

Glass bottle garn' in mey foot—A common occurrence and expression in the earlier part of last century (not a common occurrence now). There are at least two explanations for why this expression is no longer common. 1) The number of existing paved, concrete, or asphalt surfaces now, versus then 2) Today most children wear shoes or sneakers when they play outside. Many in my generation of the 50's and 60's did not.

Go arn/goin' arn—To act, to behave. "*Ah doan ask 'im notin' 'cause sometimes he duz go arn so funny.*" // "*Ah doan like how dem chiren duz go arn wid dey parents dem atarl.*" "*Deh boy was in deh supermarket goin' arn bad, trowin' heself on deh groun' an' ting.*"

Go if yoh goin'—Make up your mind and leave if that is your intention. "*Stap wasin' time an' go if yoh goin'.*"

Go si'down ('tain/'ain bes' he/she go si' down?) —This expression has a whole range of possibilities. Someone reading or hearing this expression out of context may not be aware that it goes far beyond the literal. Several possible implications are that the person is incapable, or in some ways a person may seem inappropriate for a given task. Consider the following: Speaker I: "*Dat man plannin' toh return toh play baseball.*" Speaker II: "*Ain/Tain bes' he go si' down? He ole self. He carn play ah ting.*"

Go so come—Don't waste time. Go and come right back. "*Ah you go so come soon, we geh tings toh do.*"

Go toh deh well an' draw wata' toh bade—This is an ideal example of how times have changed. This notion would have no relevance to most people younger than sixty years old, even though they may have been born or raised in the Virgin Islands.

Go up in deh heart (reference to a coconut tree)—Going as high as one can go in a coconut tree. The boys from Pearson Gardens who had much access to the trees used this term regularly. Not too many people climb coconut trees these days; hence this expression is virtually lost.

Goat mout'—Used in reference to someone who may have seemed to predict something correctly, or may have only coincidentally mentioned something that later did take place. Some people just seem to be always right with their predictions. Even though to a newcomer this might seem to connote something negative about the individual, in reality it is primarily complimentary. *"Ms Lindie ha' done say it gon happen. She geh ah goat mout, yoh hea'?"* Still prevalent today.

Goby—(see also "**cope/copey**"). This refers to a person's head. We still hear in our islands the expression, *"He geh hit in 'e goby (in his head)."* Unlike the expression "clean cope," the phrase "clean goby" is not an expression heard in our Creole.

God ah mercy (*See also* **Lawd ah mercy**)—An exclamation that expresses disappointed, frustration, anger, or surprise. It is a symbolic appeal to "the God of mercy" to intervine.

God bless 'im (ha) in he (ha) grave—An expression often heard after a reference was made to someone who died. *"I tink dat house use toh be Mr. Ceto own, God bless 'im in he grave."* It is roughly equivalent to the American expression: *"May he (she) rest in peace."*

God spare life—A frequently uttered interjection, sometimes preceded by "*if*." This is roughly equivalent to "God's willing." *"Call meh tomorrow, God spare life."* (or "*if God spare life,*" generally not used with the possessive, "*my life*").

Goin' dance—Going to a venue to dance; it was quite a popular activity in the 50's and 60's, and hence a popular expression. With the virtual disappearance of these places where this function took place, the natural extinction of the expression has occurred. Whereas residents will still say, *"We going' party tonight,"* it is no longer common to hear *"We goin' dance tonight."*

Goin' in—Often used when someone is announcing that he or she is going to go to bed: *"Boy, I sleepy. I goin' in now."*

Goin' sleep—To go to bed. *"Ah goin' sleep now cause Ah gatoh wok tomarro'."*

Goin' toh come back—Indicates that the person will be returning in a short while. *"Ah gon tark to yoh soon. Ah jus' goin toh come back."*

Gon—Going to, will. An extremely popular verb in Virgin Islands Creole: *"We gon do it now."* It is one of those creolized words, with its own life, and creates unique structures: *"Ah gon go now."* To the newcomer or the individual trying to unravel our Creole, it is important to highlight that even though one can say, *"He gon do it,"* it is not allowed to say *"He gon movies."* This is a good example of how "logical patterns" may not work when we try to interpolate from one language to another.

Gon be me an' he—This expression is used to indicate the intent of someone to confront another. An interesting feature of this saying is that it does not have to be in reference to a serious issue; it could simply be in jest. Consider the following examples: *"Ah see mey frien' yesterday, an he play like he didn' see me, e'gon be me an' he."* Here it is expected there will be friendly interchange. In contrast: *"David thief mey mango dem, when Ah see him i'gon be me an' he."*

Gon check yoh—An informal way of ending a conversation. *"Ok, man, Ah gon check yoh lata."*

Gon dead bad—This is an expression that speaks negatively about the way an individual is living. In many cases the speaker is referring or alluding to something bad that the person has done. A prime example is mistreatment of a parent. *"Deh way he treat he mudda he <u>gon dead bad</u>."* No one ever knows for certain what "bad" means in the various contexts. However, maybe the idea is that the person might suffer irreparable harm, or might die alone. The emphasis is not on the manner of death, but more on the certainty that it will not be pleasant because of the mistreatment of others, through selfishness, greed, or malice.

Gon meet it—This is still a popular, and very powerful Virgin Islands expression that is stated in a prophetic manner, but the inference is always negative. *"He gon meet it fo' deh way he treat he mudda'."* No one ever wants to hear this, especially if coming from the mouth of a parent. The idea is that the individual will be punished in some way for his or her past transgressions. This may not happen immediately, but whenever it does, the reason will be clear to the predictor.

Gon see—A very popular expression used as a warning of possible consequences. Language associated both with children and adults. In some ways it is a subtle dare: *"Touch meh marble dem but, an' yoh gon see."*

Gongolo—Millipede. I have never heard anyone use the word *"millipede,"* except for science teachers using it in the classroom. Now that this particular arthropod is rarely seen in our islands, naturally the frequency of the usage has been significantly reduced. It is still the word used however in U.S.V.I. Creole. As children growing up in the Virgin Islands we would encounter them with regularity.

Good—This rather conventional word has some elasticity in our culture. Generally used as an adjective it often functions like an adverb: *"He good stuiepid."* The trick is to place the correct emphasis on the word *"good."* The closest translation of this word in context would be "very." **Ex.** *"She good strong."* The position of the word is key; it must be placed immediately before the adjective.

In addition to all of this, the oxymoronic and paradoxical Virgin Islands expression: *"good bad"* deserves some explanation, since it is so confusing. There are two possible meanings derived from this contradictory formula: 1) The person may be seen as a very *bad* person (as is explained above) where *"good"* suggests *"very."* 2) The person may also be viewed as a very good person, where *"bad"* is the intensifier. Only the individual very familiar with the language will be able to follow such a construction. [See the earlier entry where the usage of the word "**Bad**" is explained (*"Dis mango sweet bad."*)]. The intonation, inflection, and context help to make the interpretation crystal clear.

Good fo' heself—Selfish. This is an expression used as tongue in cheek, or at times as a serious indictment of someone. *"Doan waste time wid he. He jus' good fo heself."* There is an indication of self-centeredness. The criticism may be that the person in question does not seem to want to associate too much with others. Or the commentary may be an inference with respect to that individual's arrogance.

Good fo' notin'—Generally speaking, this refers to a bad person; a selfish, insensitive individual. *"He is ah good fo' notin. He doan treat he chiren dem good atarl."* Among the most negative characterizations in our Creole this ranks in the top echelon. It suggests a lack of faith and confidence in someone. No one wants to be described in this way. At times the expression is preceded with the words, *"ah ole"*: *"He is ah ole* *good fo' notin."* At the same time, however, recognizing the frequent ironic feature in Virgin Islands Creole, this can also be used in a light-hearted way, actually in an endearing manner. Consider the following: Daphne: *"Wen las' yoh see Elton?* Carmen*: "Ah donno wen las Ah see deh ole good fo' notin.' Ah geh toh call 'im."* It is clear in such cases that Carmen and Elton are friends.

Good fo' yoh ('tis good fo' yoh,' " / 'im/ah/ha etc.)—This is another expression in Virgin Islands Creole that might leave the uninitiated scratching her or his head. How does such an innocent sequence of words result in something so negative? Here the speaker is not complimenting the listener; on the contrary. Consider the following scenario: Mother: *"Nicole, stop jumpin'."* Nicole later falls and cries: *"Mommy Ah fall down."* Mother: *"Tis good fo' -yoh, Ah tell yoh stop jumpin."* Another example: *"Tis good fo' 'im. He too harden'."* (See *"harden"* defined in a later entry.) It is frequently said as an aftermath to someone's disobedience, or simply failing to heed advice. Often the acerbic response, *"Tis good,"* may be sufficient: The speaker's tone and inflection tell the entire story.

Good night—In the Virgin Islands, *"Good night"* is a greeting as well as a farewell. Someone just came to a house at 8:00 pm where there are 3 people and greets the group saying: *"Good night eveybardy."* When it is time for the individual to leave that person will also very likely say: *"Good night eveybardy."*

Good ready—Even though Virgin Islanders use the conjunction, "and" to separate these two words, they are also used without the conjunction, in particular circumstances. Consider the following: **Question: "***When yoh gon cook deh food, man?"* Answer: *"Ah gon do it wen Ah good an' ready."* Contrast this with the following statement: *"He cou' be ignorant wen he good ready."*

Good ting!—Often used at the end of a conversation; one speaker is often acknowledging something said or done by the other. Eddie: *"We gon tark lata', man."* Clark's response: *"Good ting!"*

Good well—Extremely, very very. *"Mr. Manny good well ignorant."*

Good yoh—An interesting expression that often shows approval, or acknowledgement. Phillip: *"Ah gon finish deh ting today."* Arthur: *"Good yoh."* This continues to be used in our language.

Goonk— Swelling in one's head. *"Partna' fall down; now he geh ah* *big goonk.*" Not a term used in the 50's and 60's, but eventually became popular among younger Creole speakers.

Gouch—To scream at someone in a dismissive or castigating manner; used both as a noun and a verb. *"I went toh ask 'im fo' ah fava' an' 'e gimme ah gouch. Me ain' acksin' 'im fo notin' else."* Also, as a verb, *"Meson, she gouch' me up."* This is still a popular expression used to describe a person's negative verbal reaction.

Groun' apple—This was frequently an expression that referred to a "rock stone," frequently a phrase popular among children. *"We tro mo' groun' apple at dem."*

Groun' sweat—Perfuse sweating. *"He was so frigten' he was unda' ah groun' sweat."*

Guirl chile—Often a reference to one's daughter. Used often to emphasize the gender of the child. *"Yoh carn have any an eveybardy come heh, specially wen yoh have yoh guirl chile heh."*

Guirly—A common pet name used in several families to refer to a girl. (See its opposite "**Bayie**"). *"You know ha, man, dey duz call ha Guirly."*

Guirlin' –A word made popular a few decades ago that typically referred to young men seeking dates. It was always expressed in a lighthearted manner and was never directed toward the girl. *"Man, Ah carn see yoh atarl. Ah hea' yoh went guirlin'."* Interestingly enough, there is no such expression as "*boyin*," most probably due to societal taboos in a patriarchal system. This was generally language used among teenagers and not associated with the utterance of adults.

Ha—Interesting auxiliary verb used for both the English words "have" and "had."

"Man, Ah ha' done leave wen yoh geh heh." // *"Ah tell 'im Ah ha' eat it once."* (See the discussion on the formation of present and pluperfect.)

Ha—Very often used as a personal object pronoun for "her." *"Sen' ha' deh money."* Also used as one of the possessive adjectives: *"Dat's ha business!"*

Had ah conduct—To behave badly. Like other expressions in this collection, some of these words may seem like typical and generic English words. However, the important thing once again is the context. The following phrase is considered non-grammatical in English, but very popular in our Creole: *"She had a conduct. She was acting so rude."* In Virgin Islands Creole: *"Boy, she had ah conduct. She was ackin' so rude."*

Hail up—Used for direct or indirect salutations. For example, some younger residents may use it to directly greet someone. Frank sees Wayne and in greeting him simply says *"Hail up."* It is also common to hear: *"Hail up yoh parents fo' meh."*

Hair like okum—This expression was used to refer to a perceived toughness of a person's hair, especially if another person had the task of combing it. Of course the reference is to "oakum."

"Man, yoh hair tough like okum. How Ah gon comb it?" As is the case with many Creole words, the stress is on the last syllable, <*kum*>, a major departure in stress from the English word.

Hair tun back—An expression used to refer to the *reversal* of hair to the natural texture. *"Elaine hair look so different now. Ah tink it jus' tun back."*

Half-crazy—A kind of euphemism for unpredictable or inexplicable behavior. *"Da man half-crazy, yoh see 'im de."*

Half-Dead—Lacking energy, somewhat boring and disengaged. This can function both as an adjective and adverb. *"Look he half-dead self, no."* *"Sometimes she duz ack so half-dead, like she ain eat."*

Halfa—Exclusively the language of children. Several decades ago this was a tacit agreement among childhood friends. When one heard the word "halfa," that person was expected to share whatever she/he had, including if the person was eating.

Hall—Referred to what would be called today the "living room" of a house. *"Pu' it in deh hall."* Sometimes, though rarely, this word is still used, obviously by older Virgin Islands very familiar with it. In earlier years, people's "*halls*," were place of great importance. Sometimes chairs were covered with plastic and of course, under some circumstances it was forbidden to sit on them!! Occasionally, one can still hear: *"out in deh hall."* In my family this expression seemed to have lasted for many years, clearly because of our matriarch who used it throughout her 98 years of life.

Han'—A folksy unit of measurement, to indicate "a few," "a small amount." Often used in the absence of a scale. *"Miss, How much mango yoh wan'?* Response: *"Jus' gi'me ah han,' please."*

Han/hanin –To be unfaithful. *"Ah hea' he duz han' he guirlfrien'."*

"Yes somebardy say how he duz be hanin' ha arl deh time."

Han' in deh fire—I can or maybe can't vouch for anyone 100%. In fact, I WILL NOT vouch for anyone. *"Ah ain puttin' mey han' in deh fire fo' nobardy."*

Hans it—To try out something. *"Lemme hans yoh new bike, no."* Very likely this comes from "hands." This was popular with young children anxious to use their friends' toys for the first time. When it came to such new toys, as can be imagined children were very protective and not too anxious to let others "*hans it.*" Adults also at times used the expression, but it has generally faded. It is also used as a noun, *"Man gimme ah lil' hans on yoh bike, no. Ah gon bring it back right away."*

Hard back—Refer to someone who is tough, but it is often used sarcastically. *"Ah hea' yoh geh ah new guirlfrien.' Man, yoh is ah hardback."*

Harden' —Stubborn, does not listen, hard-headed. *"He too harden, meson. Ah stop givin' 'im advice."* Often though, this is heard after the fact. Example: Someone is relating something negative that happened: *"Man, Ah miss' deh bus dis marnin' again."*

Reaction: *"Yoh too harden. Ah tired tellin' yoh toh geh up early."*

Harl (Haul)—Used in an assertive way. In context, it means "to come", but always in a commanding way; this represents a DEMAND, not a REQUEST. *"Tell 'im Ah say harl heself heh right now."*

Harl (Haul) in deh do'—Close the door. *"Ah you haul in deh do' so da dem guana doan come in deh house."*

Harl (Haul) up—To pull up, adjust. *"Boy, haul up you pants. Dey hangin' on yoh."* Also used to negatively describe how someone looks: *"He look so haul up in da clothes."*

Harols—Someone is experiencing withdrawals symptoms from alcoholic consumption, clearly from "*the harrows.*" *"He geh deh harols."*

Hattin up people house— Refers to someone who cannot stay out of other people's houses. Culturally, Virgin Islands families still continue to be close knit neighbors, but "*ovastayin' yoh welcome*" is naturally frowned upon in our islands: *"Yoh neva' home. Yoh always hattin' up somebardy house."*

Have ah Min'—Having the will to do something, a desire, or determination, to utilize one's talent or abilities. *"Jackie cou' do good, bu' she geh toh have ah min."*

Have (had) someone goin' an' comin'—To harass someone, or have the advantage over someone, as for example in an argument: *"Deh candidate was very smart; ha opponent cou' not match ha. Boy, she had 'im goin' an' comin' in deh debate."*

Hawk up—Spit of mucous, vomit. *"Partna' look like sometin' wrang wid 'im. He out de hawkin' up."*

He/She 'ain arl heh—A person may have a mental illness. Or it could refer to someone who is comical and the expression is used in an endearing manner. *"He always tarkin' stupieness; he ain arl heh atarl"* (meaning he is humorous). Very often the tone is sympathetic: *"Yoh have toh forgive 'im 'cause he 'ain arl heh. Ah doan know wa happen toh 'im."*

He 'ain in notin'—He is not impressive. He is unappealing in some form. This is primarily a dismissive attitude. *"Donald tink he know eveyting bu' he 'ain in notin."*

He (she, you) <u>duz</u> look!—Not an expression that you want to be directed towards you. In every case it indicates an undeniable disapproval of the person's appearance: *"But look he, no, he duz look!"* The speaker can be referring to the person's physical traits, or the reference can be to the way that the individual is dressed. In any case, the comment is never ever favorable. Very often, though, it is a very harmless expression: *"Boy, you duz look; yoh betta' change dem clothes. Dey too big."* Not as popular an expression as it once was.

He (she) duz wok' obeah—Clearly, the main duty of "deh obeah man or woman." This is a phrase that is so endemic in our cultural fabric that it is important to include it here. It is understood by all sectors of our community, even though people may disassociate themselves from the practitioner of the occult.

He/she garn ajay—A person is doing strange things. *"Ah doan understan' he behavior atarl. Look like 'e garn ajay."* The person is exhibiting behavior that is not considered acceptable or "normal."

He garn deh rum shap— This was not necessarily a reference to a liquor store, but a place that sold alcoholic drinks. Islanders of the 40's, 50's, and even part of the 60's use the word "shap" to refer to places where people went to buy items. The "rum shap" had its own peculiar character and attraction!

He maybe geh ah jumbie on he/she—A commentary on a person's inexplicable behavior. These are expressions that are now only probably exchanged among close friends, since there is a fear of cultural reprimand. The fact is there are still many people who adhere to this belief; there is just a great reluctance to divulge how they feel. *"How come he ackin' so dese days, he maybe geh ah jumbie on he."* A lost expression.

He maybe went' Manda school—Often a negative comment about someone who said something that in the listener's opinion was wrong, or somehow did not seem very sensible. The metonym *"Manda School"* was used in a pejorative sense, and in all probability without justification. Even though many made fun of that school with its limitations, the owner of the school in St. Thomas provided invaluable service to our earlier generations of Thomians in her quest to educate the masses. Interestingly enough, the term still resonates today even though the referent (the school) itself has disappeared. But once again, older islander occasionally may utter the expression in jest in conversation with a friend. The school had its positive impact on scores of children.

He went Macorís toh wok' (ex. To cut cane)—A metonym for Dominican Republic used in the early part of the 20th cent, used with a lesser degree later. Today, no one ever says this, except of course, if he or she is going specifically to San Pedro, or San Francisco de Macorís.

Hea' me no (or "hea' me")—A popular self-imposed interruption used when the speaker, mis speaks, and wishes to correct herself/himself. Example: *"Ah' pu' deh ting' on deh table,...hea' me no, Ah mean on deh chair'."* Often the interjection occurs before the word or phrase is complete. *"Ah giv'im five.., hea' me, no, "ah mean ten dollars"* preceded by the sound made by the *"suckin' of deh teet'."* (see **"Ah lie"**). Also used without *"no"*: *"Dey live Grove Place, hea' me, dey live La Valle."*

Heen—This is a popular contraction used to connote *"he+ain,"* meaning "he is not." For example, Lelia asks her cousin, Deo, *"Warren home?"* To which Deo responds: *"No, heen home now. Pass back lata."* The same meaning can be rendered using "ain," cited earlier in the entries. See also **"Sheen"** later in these entries.

Heen self— "Even." *"Heen self live heh."*

Hees—This is a word used only in one situation as part of the possessive (see the section on possessives). The speaker might say: *"Tis hees own."* Generally used in combination with the word "own."

Hef—Lift with the purpose of testing something to see if it is heavy. *"Lemme hef dis ting befo' Ah lif it up. It look heavy."*

Heh deh odda' day—A very interesting expression for more than one reason. In the first place, the idea of "the other day" seems rather routine, with a very vague reference to the past, secondly when this vagueness is combined with the adverb "heh,(*here*)" in general the construction refers to a recent event. *"Ah see 'im heh deh odda day in town."*

"Ah carn believe he so sick, man jus' heh de odda day he was in mey house."

Hers own/his own, yours own etc. —A special construction of the possessive in our Creole, emphatic possessive. Of course, people also say regularly: *"It is his or it is hers."* It is important to note, however, that our local construction is vibrantly alive. *"Dis heh is mine own; it 'tain yours own."* Also heard is the word *"mines."* *"Dis heh is mines own. An' nobardy betta' doan touch it."*

Hidin' from meh—This phrase is often used when one person is indicating the inability to make contact with another. It is similar to an earlier expression in the entries (*"carn see yoh atarl"*). Jimmy has been trying to reach his friend Tara for some time. Finally he sees her and laments: *"Meson, look like yoh hidin' from meh."* As in the case with the other expression (*"carn see yoh atarl"*), there is generally a light-hearted tone to the expression.

High Day—Generally thought of as that point of the day after 12:00 noon. The popular expression, *"Wa you doin' in bed high day?"* was indicative of the fact that Virgin Islanders were early risers. They frowned upon healthy people who chose to stay in bed, rather than be up working—cleaning etc.

High Perspiration—Used to indicate offensive odor. *"Juniah, yoh perspiration kina high. Go bade."*

High School—This always referred to the Charlotte Amalie High School in St. Thomas. This had nothing to do with the relative importance of other schools. This was actually the first secondary school built on St. Thomas, hence people only referred to it as "high school." Interestingly enough, it is still a rather common expression, even though other secondary schools have since been built. *"Dey live close toh High School."*

Hit me, but—Very unique expression with the conjunction at the end, it is presented as a challenge; it is almost the equivalence of "I dare you to hit me." (Variations: "***Do it, but***"; "**Touch it, but.**"). An expression more associated with children, even though adults are not totally averse to using it. "*If yoh tink yoh bad, hit me but.*" At one point these were considered fighting words.

Hol' fas' toh—To grab. The idea here is that this was done with force. Often, it suggests a level of aggression, at times justified, for example in the following statement: "*Boy, he wuz bein' rude an' he mudda hol' fas' toh 'im, an' give him some licks.*" In addition, it also means holding on to something: "*Yoh betta hol' fas' toh deh railin' so yoh doan fall.*"

Hole in yoh bum—This was an expression used to refer to a boy who had on trousers that were torn in the back. Very popular was the expression: "*A hole in yoh bum is coco plum.*"

Hookin' cars—It would be totally anachronistic to have this "activity," given the high number of vehicles in the U.S. during this century. But with the scarcity of vehicles in the 1950's young children, mainly boys, would run and grab moving cars or trucks to get a "ride." It was a dangerous act done because of the innocence and sense of invulnerability of young individuals. "*We gon' hook some cars lata'.*"

Hat/ hat up—In U.S.V.I. Creole this word is used as a verb, substituting in a unique way for "to heat, to warm up." "*Hat deh pot fo' meh. Ah gon fry dese plantains.*" "*Ah you hat up deh food. People hungry.*"

Hat—Mad, angry. "*Ah so hat wid Sindy, Ah doan wan' toh see ha'.*"

Hat, Hat, Hat like fiah—An expression used to indicate that the location of something is not too far, used to suggest to someone that that person's guess is not too far off. Calvin is looking for a watch that his brother hid. Clavin starts searching, and approaches close to a box where the watch is hidden. His bother tells him: "*Yoh hat, hat, hat like fiah.*"

Housin'—Recently while speaking of the talented Rock City Boys one of my great-nieces remarked: "*Deh Rock City Boys from Housin'.*" Thinking that she had simply made a mistake, I responded: "*Actually, no, dey from Harris Court.*" Her response: "*But Uncle, dat **is** Housin'.*" We spend the next hour arguing about the word. For my generation, *housin'* was (and still is!) Paul M. Pearson Gardens. Even today those of us from the 1960's still self-identity as "*Housin' man, or woman.*" Because Pearson Gardens was the first development of its kind on St. Thomas, people simply referred to it as "*Housin'* an abbreviated expression locally understood, very much like *"High School,"* listed before. The Oswald Harris Court, built a few years later, was generally called *"New Housin'."* I suppose that my niece's interpretation and her uncle's will just have to coexist until a new social context once again imposes itself on language.

How come—Meaning, the reason; why *"Dat's how come Ah didn' go wid dem."*

How yoh comin'?—A very traditional, informal greeting, generally, (not exclusively) used in second person communication. Consider the following, casual encounter of Myron and James:

Myron: *"How yoh comin', man, 'tis larng time Ah ain see yoh."* James: *"Ah good, meson. Jus' wokin'."* As an interesting sideline to this, my mother once asked one of our in-laws visiting from the United States, *"How yoh comin'?"* To which he responded innocently: *"I came by plane."* Culture, tradition, and language collided to create a state of confusion (and humor) for our valued relative.

How yoh do?—This is a greeting, similar in spirit to the one above. The individual is being asked about his state of being. Speaker A: *"How yoh do, partna?"* Speaker B's response: *"Ah good, man, how you?"* The question *"How you?"* itself is a creolized expression.

How yoh mean!—There is no *doubt*, of course. Question: *"Yoh goin' wid us?"* Ans. *"How yoh mean man, Ah don' ready."* One of the Virgin Islands rich expressions. To the uninitiated this may seem to be a question that the speaker uses to seek more information; this however, is not only not the case, but quite the opposite since the speaker is affirming his or her intention to do something. Pauline: *"You would live in such ah big house?"* Marie: *"How you mean!"* Marie's answer is unequivocal, and it does not connote anything other than "absolutely."

Humbug ('in)/humbug up—Used as a verb in Virgin Islands Creole to express disgust, annoyance. *"Ah doan like people humbug ('in) me up."* Also used as an adjective with "up." (See the entry "up" later in the section.). *"Meson, I leavin' he alone; he too humbug-up fo' me."*

Hurry hurry—To rush. *"Take yoh time. Yoh too hurry hurry."* This expression is generally used with "so" or "too." Always suggests something negative. *"Eveytime yoh do tings so hurry hurry, dey aways duz tun' out bad."*

Hush (up) yoh mout'—A command to not speak. *"Boy, hush (up) yoh mout,' people tarkin'."*

I self—Even though there is a separate section on the word "**self**", the structure of this phrase is so rare that it deserves its own space. The expression means "I don't even." "*I self ain have de ting.*" Knowing when to use it is tricky, unless you are intimately familiar with the parlance.

If !?–This special exclamation has a unique application in Virgin Islands Creole. The following situation illustrates how this functions in a simple exchange between two individuals. Randy: "*Brenda, yoh feel hot today?*" Brenda: *If*!? Brenda's response is a confirmation. There is no need to say anything else. It is tantamount to saying, "*of course!*"

If he (she) foh yoh, he(she) foh yoh—You will receive unequivocal support from this individual, as long as the person likes you. The expression highlights the personality of an individual who many might consider reserved, or very particular. When that individual believes in another person he or she will unequivocally defend that other person. The categorization is of someone who tends to be rather selective with respect to friendship and comradery. "*He maybe geh he ways, but if he foh yoh, he fo yoh.*"

If yoh tink yoh bad (also **If yoh bad**)—An expression that puts out a challenge. This was often language used among children, although not exclusively. "*Do it if yoh tink yoh bad, an' you gon see.*" A child my say to another: "*Touch meh if yoh bad.*"

'Im—Him. "*Tell 'im toh call meh.*" Or, "*Ah gon call 'im wen Ah don.*" Can never be pronounced in this manner if it is not part of the structure of the sentence. (Refer to the section on the pronunciation of the "**H**" in Virgin Islands Creole.)

In ah way like dis—A unique local expression that signals a consequence of something, or simply an expectation that the speaker predicts. "*Helen, yoh wokin' so slow. In a way like dis, yoh gon neva' don.*"

In deh foat (fort)—This was an expression that survived long after **Fort Christian** in St. Thomas ceased being a jail. It referred to the incarceration of someone. Many older citizens occasionally still use the expression. But undoubtedly, it is virtually unknown among the younger generation of islanders, and certainly unknown to recent immigrants to the St. Thomas. At one point this expression was so ingrained that some people would say: "*Ah hea' he geh in trouble in deh states, an' he in deh foat up de.*" This monumental structure holds secrets of our past.

In deh place—An expression that roughly can mean "here," literally, "in this place." "*Man, ah you stap makin' noise in deh place.*"

In deh street / out in deh street—A popular expression that initially referenced sites in the town areas of the islands. "*Ah goin' in deh street lata'. Ah gatoh buy someting.*"

"*Yoh doan stay home? Yoh aways in deh street.*" It is an expression emanating from a time when the range of shopping areas was limited. For example, people went on "Main Street" or "*toh deh markit*" to buy items. In spite of much expansion, the term still survives, but in a much more generic sense.

In facs—A once popular expression meaning, "in point of fact." This was an expression that was heard with regularity last century. It is not heard which much frequency these days. "*Cedro still in Sin John. In facs, Ah jus' see 'im.*"

In ha;' ('im; we; meh)—A truly unusual prepositional phrase used in U.S.V.I. Creole, with no equivalence in English. It is an emphatic expression "*Da team tro' some licks in we, meson.*"

"*He mudda tro some blows in 'im fo' misbehavin'.*" While watching boxing, for example, it is customary to hear excited viewers around you saying, "*in 'im*" as they follow the blow by blow account.

In mey (ha;'he; yoh) bed—Contrast this with American English, particularly with the construction in American speech: "I am going to bed." Local Creole expression: "*Ah goin' in mey bed.*" // "*She don in she bed.*" "*Yoh goin' in yoh bed already?*" vs "Are you going to bed already?" in the "standard" vernacular.

In mey (he, ha etc.) name—The individual uses this expression to underscore the fact (or perception) that something is lacking. The reference is generally, although not always about money. For example, "*I ain geh ah (one) cent in mey name.*" Note the difference to the American expression that uses the preposition "*to*", versus "*in*" in Virgin Islands Creole.

Inside?—This single word is used when trying to determine if someone is at home, always as an interrogative. "*Inside?*" In essence, "*Is anyone* at *home?*" What is particularly significant about this is the tacit agreement between the parties involved. The person or persons who may be in the house upon hearing this shouted out, will have no doubt that the speaker is inquiring whether or not there are occupants in the house.

Is—This linking verb is often used as a contraction, in place of "*it's*." Note the following 3 examples: "*Is good fo' yoh*." "*Is good dat dey comin' now*." "*Is he dat do it yes*."

It (e') cou' eat—*The* speaker uses this phrase to indicate that something does not taste particularly good; however, it might, for example satisfy one's hunger. Brenda: "*How deh food?*" Shirlene responds: "*It (e') cou' eat I hungry*."

It get/ E geh—This is an expression that is totally disconnected from American speech. In addition, this expression has its variation, "*e' geh*." It is an expletive (Not a swear word!), a grammatical formula: "*There is*." "*There are*." For example, "*It get (e' geh) ah latta' people heh*."

It (eh) have—(there is or there are)—(see the entry, "**get**" explained earlier). "*It (eh) have ah latta people de*."

Jesum Bread—An expression used to avoid the blasphemous enunciation of *Jesus Christ* uttered "in vain"; the moral imperative is not to disobey the Third Commandment of the Bible. It can also stand by itself: "**Jesum!**" The Virgin Islands is a very strongly religious community and islanders are generally conscious of not disobeying the unwritten rule "do not blaspheme!" The implicit Biblical references are Exodus 20:7, Deuteronomy 5:11. "*Jesum bread, man. Ah you stap deh noise*."

Jak—A word often used as an interjection. It is normally at the beginning or end of an expression. Example, "*He funny, Jak*." "*Jak, he duz ack crazy*."

Jesum Bree—A variation of the previous entry. "*Jesum bree, e' so hot*."

Jokey- This refers to something or someone that is funny, but can also be used to suggest the incapability of a person. "*Dat man so jokey; he duz aways make me laugh*." "*He ideas so jokey, Ah even ain studyin' im*."

Jumbie beads— Often used to make necklaces. The beads come from a tree. The expression is still occasionally heard but not with the same frequency as the 50's or 60's.

Jus' be—The expression is the rough equivalence to the adverb "simply" or "only." "*We duz jus' be heh tarkin*." "*She duz jus' be in deh house arl deh time*."

Jus' he/she—That is exactly who it is. Juan: "*Darn deh boy who wuz heh las' night?*" Her friend responds: "*Jus' he*," or "*Tis jus' he!*" or "*Jus' he self*."

Jus' heh—In this statement the person is implying that nothing exciting, different is happening. This is a common phrase heard on St. Thomas. Things are normal; the person is ok. Orlando: *"How yoh doin', man?"* Edwin: *"Man, Ah jus' heh."* (*"Ah jus' de heh."*) Sometimes, *"Ah jus' de' ya,"* heard in St. Croix.

Kasha (or Casha*)—Children may know it or heard of it, but hardly see it, or FEEL it these days in a fairly industrialized Virgin Islands. Walking through Virgin Islands thicket ("bush") you were bound to make contact with this annoying, prickly, and painful "thorn." For Virgin Islanders the word "thorn" never came in to play. The word Kasha captured the essence of annoyance and discomfort. *"Some Kasha hol' arn toh meh yestaday in deh bush."*

Keep ah bir'day/keep up ah birday—To celebrate a birthday. *"We gon keep up he bir'day nex' week."*

Kenip—Popular fruit, green on the outside, pink in the inside, also genip. Among the favorite of Virgin Islands fruits.

Kerchif—Handkerchief. *"He sweatin' bad. He need ah kerchief."*

Kerosene lamp—Popular words for an essential device used in the first half of the last century. For a younger generation, these words should be cherished as they try to imagine rows of wooden houses with flickering, intermittent light illuminating an immense darkness. *"Tun arn deh kerosene lamp, lemme see wa Ah eatin'."*

Ketch an' keep—Local thorns. *"Wen dem ketch an' keep hol arn toh meh Ah bawl out."* Clearly people are not walking through the Virgin Islands "bushes" in the same frequency as decades ago, and are thus spared this uncomfortable experience.

Ketch myself/heself/sheself—To recuperate physically, financially, emotionally. *"Ah so tired Ah need ah minute toh ketch myself."* *"Ah ain wokin' now, bu' gon buy ah ca' as soon as Ah ketch meyself."*

Kiakin' kiakin'—*"Dey jus' Kiakin' kiakin',"* talking a lot, onomatopoeic expression.

Kina how—An expression used to indicate incompleteness, imperfection, or dissatisfaction. Karen: *"Wayne, yoh fix deh ting?"* Wayne: *"Ah do it kina how."*

Randy: *"Yoh understan' deh lesson."* Dora: *'Kina how."*

Knack-down—In the Virgin Islands if you hear someone says *"Yestaday he geh knack down,"* there is no need to guess what is meant, so ingrained is that expression. This expression is somewhat similar to "run down" given in a later entry. The assumption is always that the person was hit by a vehicle. It is unlikely that the listener would think in terms of boxing or some other event or activity. In our language this has a very unique ring. In the United States the statement, *"Yesterday he got knock down,"* would not resonate at all. It would be a meaningless statement without a context to substantiate it.

Koka deh Bear wid deh halfa ear an' he brudda—Perennial St. Thomas Carnival entries in the 50's and 60's; now part of Virgin Islands folklore What little child did not want to see Koka deh Bear? Along with Shorty deh Zulu this was for many of us a highlight of the Carnival.

Kuno muno- Foolish person. It is an expression that has not disappeared from our language, but is heard much less than it was decades ago. There is the sense, however, that even many of the younger generation are still familiar with the term. *"Doan study he man, he ain notin bu' ah kuno muno."*

Ladda 'e (ha) behin' (ladda 'im (ha) wid blows)—A reference to corporal punishment. *"Wen he geh home Ah gon ladda 'e behin' fo' ackin' so rude."*

Larg giarlin—Very skinny person and tall. *"Yoh know 'im. He was a larng giarlin boy from deh Bayside."*

Largnside—Next to. *"Come heh largnside (ah) meh."*

Larmie (Larm)—As alluded to earlier, we live in a Virgin Islands community that is generally religiously conscious. Like with *"Jesum Bread"* this expression tries to steer away from what could be conceived as a Biblical violation. The word is a substitute for *"Lord,"* used to avoid blasphemy. *"Oh larmie, Ah forget deh ting."*

Larng lip—A contemptuous expression used to criticize the physical attributes of an individual. Especially heard during verbal sparring matches. Another one of those Creole expressions in which two or more words function as if they were one adjective: *"Look 'im no, he larng lip self."* (See also **Poung' ah lip**).

Larng out yoh tongue—To stick out one's tongue as a sign of disapproval, or disrespect. *"Look 'im, no, he so rude, largin' out he tongue at people."*

Larng time—An expression used to emphasize that something (a task for example) was done expeditiously. Dora: *"Yoh do yoh homewok? // Ans: "Larng time, mammy."*

Another example: *"I don eat larng time."*

Las' lick—Children's play, sometimes when a child was leaving another. Also can be interpreted as *"until we see each other again."* The children would try to see who could hit each other last. As can be imagined this could last a while!

Las' up—To defeat someone in a race by a comfortable margin. But this does not capture the tone of confidence and braggadocio: *"Meson, yoh carn beat Carmen in ah race. Da guirl gon las' you up 'cause yoh too slow."* Fortunately, a Creole expression that is still very much in use: *"Yoh gon race me? Boy yoh maybe wan' toh geh las' up?"*

Latta in ha face—*"Yoh know ha, man. She geh Latta in ha face."* A temporary skin ailment that was believed to be related to the heat. Many children got it at some point; others were seen with it on their faces regularly. The expression barely survives because the condition is no longer common.

Lawd-ah-mercy—"Lord, (of) mercy," or "Lord have mercy." Expressions frustration, anger, disappointment. The way that this is stated is certainly a creolized expression. *"Lawd ah mercy, man; ah you stap deh noise in mey head."* It is a symbolic appeal to "the God of mercy" to intervine.

Laydin down— Lying down. Carol: *"Wa yoh doin', Marvin?* Marvin responds: *"Ah jus' heh laydin' down 'cause Ah tired."*

Leave—This word is included here because in Virgin Islands Creole it is used in place of "let." Allow. *"Leave 'im eat it if he hungry."* Also *"Leave ha go wid us."*

Leave meh ('im etc.) stay—Leave me alone. Do not bother me/him. *"Boy, leave meh stay. Ah geh wok toh do."* This Creole expression have several applications. For example, *"Leave 'im stay, he too rude."* In this case, the speaker has decided not to be bothered with the other person. *"Leave 'im stay, meson; he gon fin' out fo' heself."* Also, *"Leave ha stay de wid ha nonsense."*

Also, this means to allow the person to remain where he or she is. *"Leave it stay de 'til lata."*

Leh me ("leeme")—Interesting entry because the word can mean both "leave me" or "let me," depending on the context. *"Leh meh alone, man, Ah busy."* Here this word is used to mean *"leave."* However, by contrast *"leh me (leeme) do it"* means *"Allow me to do it."*

Less man—Negative expression often used by boys speaking of sports, often of rival players. *"He carn play ah lick, he is ah less man."* This was a designation that was truly dismissive of an individual. If you were classified as such, it also meant that no one would choose you to play on his side, for example in a basketball game. Some people used the phrase outside of the context of sports, in obvious denigration of someone.

Liard—Word for "liar." *"Ah even Doan wan' toh talk toh 'im cause he is such ah Liard."*

Lick—Used to indicate quantity when preceded by "ah." *"Ah lick,"* therefore, would mean "any," "no," or "none." For example, after tasting a particular meal, someone might remark: *"Man, tis ting ain get ah lick ah salt."* In other words, the food does not have enough (or any) salt; it is bland. Other examples; *"Da boy ain get ah lick sense."* This particular sentence could be interpreted in a light-hearted manner. It could well be a reference to a humorous individual.

Other example of how the expression is used: Joe: *"Check toh see if it geh wata in deh cistern."* Lelia: *"Meson, tain (ain) geh ah lick in it."* Also someone might say, *"I ain' care ah lick."*

Lick down—This expression can be used with respect to an assault: *"Doan tell 'im notin' meson befo' he lick yoh down."* In addition, it can be used in reference to an accident: *"Ah ca' lick 'im down yestaday."*

Lick in—Collide. *"She wuz drivin' crazy dat's why she lick in deh wall."*

Lick up—Collide, essentially the same as the previous entry. *"She wuz drivin' crazy dat's why she lick up toh deh wall."*

Licks—Spank/hit. *"He gon geh ah latah licks fo' 'e bad behavior."* In addition to referring to disciplining someone, it is also used when speaking of aggressive behavior, for example a fight. *"Boy, she give 'im some good licks yestaday. Come bet he ain gon trouble she again.'*

Ligh' bill—In the United States Virgin Islands this refers to any bill that is generated from kilowatts hours. Therefore, even if there is no light being used, the term *"ligh' bill"* is the preferred terminology. *"Ah you turn arf da' rajo man. Mey ligh' bill too high."*

Like—Apart from its general meaning, often this word is understood in USVI Creole to mean "love." "*Da guirl like yoh bad, yoh know.*" (meaning, *She is in love*).

Like ah lot—With this expression the force of the meaning is in the vagueness of the phrase. One can fill in the blanks; for example "*He like ah lat a foolishness, stuppidness*" etc.

Like nonsense (**like stuiepiness**)—A light-hearted commentary about someone's attitude that suggests a sense of humor: "*Calvin was heh las' night makin' jokes. Boy, he like ah lot ah nonsense.*"

Like notin'—This is an expression with all kinds of variations and inferences. Interestingly enough, it can be used in an affirmative way. Consider the following unique Virgin Islands constructions: "*Dis mango sweet like notin'.*" Or "*Dis ting hot like notin'.*" In the first case, the mango is *very* sweet. The second case, the item is *very* hot. The inference is that there is "*nothing else like this.*" The construction may also be used in other ways. "*He stuiepid like notin'.*" These expressions defy facile rules and regulations; however, the speaker of Creole knows exactly when to use them. Anyone not part of the community of language would be very confused with this expression ("**like notin**") that at first glance seems to make no sense. But it is truly an emphatic expression and quite a popular one for that matter.

Like peas—Indicates a large amount or quantity of something. "*Man, Ah tell yoh, e' ha' people de like peas.*" Clearly not as popular as decades ago.

Like rain—Indicates a large amount or quantity of something. "*It had people like rain.*" Definitely not as popular as years ago.

Lil—Often directly precedes a noun for emphasis when a person describes an action that will be taken or was taken: "***Befo' ah go sleep ah like to drink mey lil' bush tea.***" Sometimes it is accompanied with the adjective "nice." For example, "***Befo' ah go sleep ah like to drink mey nice lil' bush tea.***" There is no appreciable change in meaning.

Lil' small (variation, "**lil' smalie**"/ **small lil'**)—One of the numerous redundancies in our language: "*He live in a lil' small house.*" Also once popular was the phrase "**lil' smalie**," for example: "*Dey live in dis lil' smalie house.*" Such an expression is not as frequent as 30 or 40 years ago, but is still heard. "*Yoh know ha, man, she is a lil' smalie guirl.*"

Limin'—Idling, relaxing, out enjoying oneself. "*Las' night we went limin'.*" "*Man, we jus heh limin'.*" "*Las' night we wuz unda ah piece ah lime.*" Not generally known in the U.S.V.I. before the 1970's.

Lindy—A special, frozen beverage, heard primarily in St. Croix, the equivalence of "special," heard primarily in St. Thomas and St. John.

Lock arf—Turn off. *"Lock arf deh wata."* The expression, *"Lock arf deh rajo"* has fallen into disuse these days.

Locus'—A powdery fruit that is seen and eaten less and less. It is noted mainly for its powdery texture and the awful smell it leaves in one's mouth. It was common to hear: *"Locus' duz stink up yoh mout'."* Such a rare fruit now, its entry is essential here. In Jamaica, they are right to refer to it as "stinking toe."

Look (See) deh devil fo' meh *(variations: "Bu' look...meh"; "Ah you look....meh")*—An expression of surprise or disapproval often in reference to something not expected. *"Bu' ah you, look deh devil fo meh, wa' yoh doin wid da knife?"* In a religious community such as ours the inference is that the act is so egregious that the devil had to have had some hand in it! This situation is unacceptable. Still a popular expression. A similar expression is *"Hea' deh devil fo me."* (variation: *"Wa'deh devil fo' meh."*). In the Creole of the U.S. Virgin Islands, the preface, *"Bu' ah you (yoh)"* is a common introduction to the phrase.

Look (lookin') hard—A very disparaging expression used to describe the features of a person, most specifically to the face. Most times it is an indication that the individual has undergone some kind of change, caused, for example, by lack of sleep, stress, excessive drinking, drugs or any number of reasons that the speaker my imagine: *"Meson, Patrick drinkin' too much, now he face lookin' so hard."*

Look 'im/he /ha'/ no—There is something about the individual that is not particularly appealing. In general, it is presented as a criticism. The sense of the expression is captured in such statements as the following: *"Bu' look she, no, who she tink she is?"* // *"Look 'im no, wid 'e marga self."* *"Look 'im, no. He tink he bad"* (or *"tink he so hansome"* etc.). There is, however, an alternate meaning because this expression is also used in a friendly manner, *"Look she (he), fo' me, no."* As in the previous entry, and in fact in a manner typical in U.S.V.I Creole, the word *"Bu"* often introduces the statement: *"Bu look he, no."*

Look it (dem etc)—Used in combination when drawing a person's attention to something, meaning "Here or there it is." Consider the following: Bernard asks Akeem: *"Wey deh book?"* Akeem responds: *"Look* *it right heh.*" The response translates to "Here it is." In another sense, it can also mean "there he (she, it etc.) is." "*Look 'im de sittin' down.*" Also used: "*Watch 'im de sittin' down*" and "*See 'im de sittin' down.*" Common words, creolized usages.

Look out deh way—A command that is telling the person to "get out of the way." See also "**Watch out deh way**" in a later entry. "*Ah you look out deh way, people passin'.*"

Lookin fo' rain—Rain is imminent. This is another one of those statements that defies logic. Someone trying to decipher its meaning through analysis of the structure of the sentence would come up empty. Clarice: "*Let's go inside 'cause it lookin' fo' rain.*" (In other words: "It looks like it is going to rain."). The use of the preposition, "for' " performs an unusual function in this structure.

Lookin' fo' weadah—Bad weather is coming. "*Ah you betta close dem window 'cause it lookin' fo' weadah.*" If the previous entry seems illogical, then this one may seem even more so. The idea that there will be **bad** weather is not in any way implicit in the expression; yet, in the Virgin Islands the idea of imminent bad weather is indisputable. The person who utters the statement is affirming that fact.

Lookin' toh—Trying to; seems like. This requires some explanation. The phrase is a kind of pseudo prediction; it expresses what someone might do, with or without thought of intentionality. For example, "*Wa' yoh doin', man? Yoh lookin toh break deh ting?*" In other words, what the person is doing may cause the item to break, though it may not be the individual's intention to do so. Consider the situation where Jerry and Clara have been waiting for their friend, Louis for 2 hours. Jerry might say to Clara: "*Man, he ain lookin' toh come atarl.*" In other words, it does not seem that Louis is going to appear. At this point his intention is not known. Other notable examples of the expression: 1) "*Thomas ain lookin toh do notin fo' he'self.*" 2) "*Careful, da' ting lookin' toh break.*"

Loose—To release; a common word but the Creole expression is unique. For example, someone is holding something and is told: "*Loose it.*" In order words "let it go." "*Meson, loose mey han';Ah have toh go.*" It is very common to see two children struggling over some item, for example a toy and one might say: "*Meson, loose deh ting; tis mine own.*" For those unfamiliar with the language, in this context this does not mean "untie."

Love City—A reference to St. John

Mahogany bird—A euphemism for the cockroach. An obvious sarcastic play, giving importance to an annoying pest—the roach.

Mainlan'—Refers to the contiguous United States, in addition to Washington, D.C. *"She movin'; she gon live in/on deh mainlan'."*

Makin' ah scene—A once popular expression that refers to making jokes at another person's expense. *"He was makin' arl kina ah scene on meh. Everybardy was laughin'. I had feel so bad."*

Makase—Hurry, literally "make haste." The pronunciation of this English expression makes our Creole expression a totally new word. Children growing up did not generally associate the Creole expression with two separate words. Hence, *"makase"* became and is still its own independent word. *"Ah yoh makase; we geh toh go now."*

Make it do (Make do)—This suggests that a particular thing, matter, or situation will have to suffice; whatever that thing is, it will have to fulfill the purpose. Consider the following: *"Ah only have a lil' piece ah bread toh eat. But Ah gatoh make it do."* *"Dis gon **make do**."* See also "**Dis (Dat) gon do**" and "**cou' do**."

Make it hunt—An expression used to refer to a person's desire to avail himself or herself of something. The phrase was often used to indicate the intent of the individual to take control. In speaking of food, for example, it was not uncommon to hear: *"Da' fish look good; Ah gon make it hunt tonight."* This means that the person will devour the food; will really enjoy it.

Makin' Birday—To celebrate another year. *"Charles makin' birday tomorrow. He makin' five."* *"Wen yoh makin' birday?"* *"Wen you duz make birday?"*

Makin' chile—A reference to pregnancy.

Makin' up yoh face—Facial expression that shows objection to an act, statement, attitude etc. Very often associated with children. Parent to child: *"Yoh betta' stop makin' up yoh face like yoh mad."* The typical child knew that such a gesture was culturally prohibited and that there could be consequences for violating that code. My sense is that children are still aware of this!

Man—Like the word "meson" this word is popularly used in Virgin Islands Creole. It does not matter the gender of the person speaking or listening. Conversation between Doris and Rita: Doris says: *"Man, call meh* *lata,' no."* It is safe to assume that the frequency of use of this word has not changed much over the years. The many ways in which this word can be used as an interjection are impossible to enumerate. Suffice it to say, it is one of the staples of Virgin Islands Creole: *"Man, he is sometin' else." "Go do deh ting now, man." "Man, da wuz good!" "Stap it no man!"*

Mangy darg –This expression generally referred to stray mutts, always part of Virgin Islands folklore. I choose this expression because in the 50's and 60's this simple, wayward mutt was such a staple of our community. This dog, present everywhere, is as legendary as the Green Face Man. *"Me 'ain fraid ah no mangy darg."*

Manisible—A unique Creole word; respectful, polite, exuding good behavior or manners. *"She is such ah manisible young lady."*

Marble terms**—Marble playing was popular pastime for children. The terminology surrounding the game was itself unique. It represented a different type of language known and shared by the participants. It was a game of prearranged stipulations and general cooperation, but often fiercely competitive, often with onlookers who were "rootin'" for one player or another. Below is a list of some expressions associated with the game:

****ah side yoh buttin' full**—Another player's marble will occupy the space of the original "setter."

****Barly**—A metallic piece used to substitute for a real marble, a ball bearing. Often players objected to its usage in a game because it was capable of shattering the "legitimate" marbles. It was perceived to give the user an unfair advantage.

****Big Bum**—A big marble, several times the size of the regular marble.

****Budget** –A collection of marbles.

****Linguis'**—The line in marble to initiate the game. Each player tried to toss the marble as close to the line as possible. Whoever came closest to the line without going over, played first.

****Mama say fall in scratch**—A signal by a losing player or onlooker who wished to end the game or to walk away with marbles not belonging to him or her. At the sound of such an utterance, players rushed to the ring to retrieve marbles. Never considered good gamesmanship.

****Number + "up"**—The designation that indicated the amount of wager. For example, 5-up, each player must put 5 marbles in the ring.

****Ova'**—An opponent's marble has gone over the line (*linguis'*) in the initial toss. The unfortunate player whose marble went over the line plays last. *"Yoh garn ova."*

Picha—The principal marble used by a player.

Pokin'—A player forcibly ejecting the marble from between his/her fingers, using his/her arm and body to increase the velocity of the projectile, one of the clearest violations of the rules. This illegal act was a big reason for censorship by other players who very quickly recognized this major infraction. The individual played again, returned marbles, or lost his turn.

Quaksa- The very best marble player, the Michael Jordan of marble players. This individual was able to hit your marble, even if you *"set behin' ah rock."* This was the person whom you hated to see in the game, unless of course that individual was an ally—for example not going after your marble. Even though marble was an "individual sport," there was quite a bit of "team play." The Quaksa was the most envied of players.

Ring—A circle inscribed in the dirt by one of the players. The marbles were enclosed within this prescribed space. It was located at a particular distance, from linguis' agreed upon by the players,

Set—The player designated a spot for his or her marble. *"I set heh."*

T(h)ree hole—*An alternative to the typical marble game.* It was truly remarkable how there was an inherent "honor system." When one player stipulates what his/her remaining moves were in order to win, there was not much argument. A popular expression that spoke to the process of the game was: *"Ah have toh' go up toh come down toh go come down toh win."* Very popular game that attested to the creativity of Virgin Islands children. This is a game that young Virgin Islanders would love today if it were revived. I have absolutely no doubt about this.

Yoh fat—The player tried to knock the marbles out of the ring, but instead his/hers became trapped. He has to leave the game.

==

Marga self— (really from the word "meager")—*"He marga self,"* a very thin person. This always has a negative connotation.

Mash an' go—An expression used to refer to cars with automatic transmissions. Not too many people were familiar with cars in the 50's and 60's, and this was a convenient expression that simply connoted in the most basic manner the operational capability of the vehicle. A term that is now loss to technology and modernization.

Mash off—To leave quickly. *"Wen he fin' out wa wuz happenin', mey boy mash off."* Heard with less frequency these days.

Mash up—To destroy, used as a verb. *"Doan' mash up yoh toy."* But it may also be used as an adjective: *"Deh ting don' mash up."* The expression can be used to allude to injuries or even violence. *"He geh mash up in ah ca' accident."* Unfortunately, too often it is used as a threat.

An aggressive individual might say, *"Keep troublin' meh, Ah gon mash yoh up."* In lighter moments, younger people use it to express enjoyment: *"Dey gon mash up deh party."* The popular expression *"Watta mash up!"* is often a response to news that a person may have just received, or someone may use it as she/he describes a particular situation: *"Lemme tell yoh; when she hea' 'bout dis, dat gon be ah mash-up."*

Maubi—A popular local drink that has various ingredients, among them maubi bark, ginger, anise, and orange peel. This is a staple of Virgin Islands culinary culture.

Maybe ain' geh—Speaks to the lack of something, but in a somewhat ironic or even sarcastic manner: *"He maybe ain' geh no frien'; he aways de by heself."* *"Dey jus' sittin' 'roun tarkin' stuiepiness arl day; dey maybe ain geh notin' toh do."*

Me' 'ain in da' wid yoh (dem, he, she)—I reject what you are doing; I am not even paying much attention to your rhetoric, or your situation.

Meen (+self)—A contraction for *Me+ain*, meaning *"I am not."* See discussion under the section on subjects and objective pronouns. *"Meen goin' no way today."* *"Meen self studyin' he."* This means, *"I am not even…"*

Meen (I doan) give yoh wrang—This means that I understand what you are saying. Your action is right, from my perspective: Debbie: *"Johnny, I gon stap tarkin' toh Richard."* Johnny: <u>*"Meen (I doan) give yoh wrang. He doan ack right atarl."*</u>

Meh—Pronounced like <M-a-y>. Me. *"Tell meh deh trut."*

Melee—In Virgin Islands Creole this is often used to refer to gossip. Also it is heard in situations when there is a disturbance of some sort. 1) *"Da man like too much melee. Doan let 'im in yoh house."* 2) *"Las' night it had mo' melee 'roun heh. Two people wuz cussin.'"*

Melee in deh air—There is a whole lot of gossip.

'**Memba**—To remember, to recall. "*Yoh 'memba wen we use' toh play in dat yard in Grove Place?*"

Meson—The quintessential U.S. Virgin Islands expression. Various usages of one of the Virgin Islands most uttered, unique, and cherished words; it is the utterance that brands and identifies you as a Virgin Islander:

Meson, how yoh doin' (greeting)?

*Wa' wrang wid yoh, meson? (*I object to your attitude and/or behavior*)*

Meson, I take off....—used as a marker in storytelling

Da ting' bother me, meson—an end marker, in storytelling

Meson, guirl (boy)—an expression of surprise, astonishment, or an introduction to a question or reprimand. *Ex. "Meson guirl, wa YOU doin' wid da ting in yoh hair?*

"*Hey meson, also heard as "ey meson"* —as interjection, initiation of a discussion- "*Ey meson, dat food wuz good!*" I cannot imagine that this expression is used anywhere else in the West Indies outside of the United States and British Virgin Islands.

If you are any place in this world and you hear someone saying "*meson,*" you can be sure that that person has lived in our islands. If we lose this one, we lose our linguistic heart and soul.

Metee—An adjective; overly inquisitive, used in a negative fashion. "*Yoh too metee acksin' arl kin' ah questions. Betta' min 'yoh own business.*"

Mey—Possessive, my. "*Yes, dat's mey sista.*' " (more on this in the section on the **Possessive**).

Mey dear chile—An expression of endearment used in a variety of ways, especially when relaying information, as part of the story telling formula. "*Mey dear chile, ah coun' believe wa Ah was seein'.*" It is also used as an expression of confirmation, acknowledgement: Consider the following. Patsy tells her friend: "*Dey aways causin' trouble in deh place.*" To which her friend responds: "*Mey dear chile,*" supporting Patsy's assertion. A sociological footnote is that the expression is more frequently uttered by women and girls. The explanation for this social reality is far beyond the scope of this study.

Mey (He etc.) eyeball—An expression that suggests an exceedingly close familial connection, friendship, or other relationships between individuals. "*Da lil' gran'daughta ah mine is mey eyeball.*"

Milk tea—Milk with hot water and sugar; not really "tea." See "tea" later in this listing of words and phrases. In the 1950's and 60's this was a staple for many families: *"Befo Ah go sleep, Ah like toh drink mey lil milk tea."*

Min' (Minin') chiren—to take care of. Jack: *"Way Laverne duz wok?"* Clarence: *"She duz min' chiren."* Clarence is referring to Laverne's job; maybe she has a small day care.

"Ah carn stay heh wid ah you 'cause Ah geh toh go home toh min mey chiren dem."

Min' he/she (doan min')—Interesting expression with much variation that deserves some discussion. What seems to be an affirmative, is actually a negative. Joan to Kelvin: *"Ah jus' buy ah big house."* Allen responding to this, tells Kelvin: *"Min' she wid she stuiepiness"* or *"Doan min' she. She aways talkin' stuiepiness."* Tony to Pauline: *"Ah geh ah thousan' dollars."* Tony: *"Min' me, Ah jus' jokin'."* The negative sends the same message: *"Doan min' me."* The individual may also respond: *"You minin' she/he?"* (meaning *"If you are paying attention to her or him, don't!"*)

Min' eh—Advice, warning. *"Min' eh, Ah puttin' dis ting in yoh han' doan drap it."*

"Min' eh, yoh betta' do wa Ah tell yoh." *"Min' eh, doan' say Ah didn' tell yoh."* *"Min', eh, make sho yoh call befo' yoh come."*

Mincin'—Very similar to the "standard" English word, however, in the Virgin Islands context the usage is quite different. It is generally reserved for eating. Example: *"Boy, eat yoh food, stap mincin'; yoh have toh go toh school."* The idea is "stop eating so slowly," or as people often say, *"stap playin' wid deh food."*

Mo'—In Virgin Islands Creole this <u>is not</u> the comparative, "more." The meaning is closer to *"a whole lot."* This can only be understood in context. *"Boy, e' geh mo' food on deh table."* This does not mean "there is more food on the table than elsewhere," but rather that "there is an abundance."

Mo' dan—Used in the non-conventional sense this construction highlights a situation already alluded to. Always used with an adjective. Consider the following: Carolyn: *"Da man ignorant, yoh hea'."* Charlene, in support of the statement responds: *"Mo' dan ignorant!"* This response is at once vague and rather specific, at least in the mind of the responder. Charlene confirms the man's "ignorance," but wants it be known that Carolyn's description of the person is really a conservative and benign one!

Mocko—Not smart: *"Yoh is ah mocko"* (West Africa). *"Man, stop ackin' like ah mocko an' do deh ting."*

'Mong—The word used instead of the English preposition "among." This word cannot be used indiscriminately. Only members of the community of Virgin Islands Creole speakers would know exactly how to use it: *"Look boy, go play 'mong yoh friens' dem."* See the section on APOCOPATED PREPOSITIONS.

'Mongst yoh sex— *"Boy, 'mongst yoh sex,"* meaning, stop trying to get into the affairs of adults. Definitely something said by grownups, and not considered appropriate for children to say. No longer a popular expression.

Monkey know wa' tree toh climb—The person knows what he can get away with.

Moo moo—Someone who is not too smart; silly person. *"Stop it, yoh ackin' like ah real moo moo."* *"Yoh de cryin' like ah moo moo arl deh time."*

Mopin'—-Gazing, day dreaming. *"Yoh de mopin'. Go do yoh homewok."*

Mount—Amount. *"No 'mount ah money gon save yoh."* Again only the speaker of the language will be able to tell when this word is allowed. For example, it would not be correct to ask, *"What 'mount yoh wan'?"* to mean *"What amount do you want?"* See the section on APOCOPATED PREPOSITIONS.

Much—In United States Virgin Islands Creole this word often replaces *"many."* As in numerous Creole constructions, knowing exactly when this is applicable is a great challenge for the new speaker of Virgin Islands Creole. *"How <u>much</u> people goin wid us?"* // *"We see so <u>much</u> animals in deh zoo."* *"How <u>much</u> mango yoh say yoh wan'?"* *"How <u>much</u> ah you e 'tis?"*

Much it ––Can't tolerate something; don't care for a particular food, for example. This was a real popular Virgin Islands expression. People used it to express their disapproval: *"Ah doan much it atarl, it tase bad."* Can only be used in the negative. In other words, no one would say: *"Ah much it."* Not as popular in contemporary Virgin Islands society.

Muck-up—Mix things together, always used negatively. A parent to a child: *"Boy, stap muckin'-up in deh food an' eat it."*

Mus/ mus'n—In the sense of "should," "should not," "don't." *"Ah you chiren mus' behave ah yohself."* A child speaking to a parent: *"Mommy, we mus' go now?"* *"Daddy, we mus' eat now?"* The questions are not whether or not they are obligated to go, or to eat, but whether or not they "should," if the parent would like them to go or to eat at this point. **Mus'n** implies both "should not" and "do not." Parent to a child: *"Ah yoh mus'n make noise in deh house." "Ah yoh mus'n stay out toh late tonight."*

Mus'be / Mu'be—An interesting expression. The idea is "has to," "maybe, "probably." But its usage in Virgin Islands Creole at times has a kind of ironic tone to it. *"He mus'be tink I (Ah) stuiepid. Bu' he wrang."* This is also rendered as *"He mu'be tink I (ah) stuiepid. But he wrang."* In this case the "s" is not heard in the utterance. In this context the expression is tricky and really has no direct equivalence in English. Here it is used in place of "probably."

Nable—A reference to a person's belly botton. In the Virgin Islands it would be unusual to hear the word "navel." Generally, the stress is on the last syllable: *"Deh baby barn wid ah big naBLE."*

Nack arf somebardy—To terminate a romantic relationship. *"I don nack he arf ah larng time. Ah couldn' stan' 'im no mo'."*

Nackin' about ('bout)—This suggests carefree action; idle; irresponsible. *"He de nackin' about, not doin' anyting."* Also used to indicate an unkempt place. *"Look at dis room; everyting jus nack about."*

Nackin' darg—Another expression that speaks to the creativity of Virgin Islanders. It is a typical Virgin Islands hyperbole. It is still a popular expression that refers to abundance: *"Man, las' night dey had people toh da party nackin' darg."* Simply put, a lot of people attended the event.

Nana—This referred to the woman that took care of children. Not used these days. Actually a word prevalent in Ghana (from where many Virgin Islanders can trace their ancestry.) that saw the woman as royalty. *"Miss Melba was mey Nana."* Who is more important than the individual that cares for a child?

Nat—Naturally a word connoting something negative; it is the way that it is used that makes it so distinct. *"Nat ah man call me dis marnin.'"* Such a statement could be ambiguous in the Virgin Islands. In one sense it could mean: *1) "No one called me this morning"* or 2) A warning, *"Don't anyone call me this morning."* In addition to this, there are expressions such as *"Nat ah ting in deh house toh eat."* (Meaning: "There is nothing at all in the house to eat."). In the following conversation the phrase is quite emphatic: Lorna: *"Yoh have ah dollar?"* Marilyn responds: *"Nat ah cent."*

Nat dat! / Nat da de! —-The general sense is that the speaker does not expect a particular thing to happen. The speaker might be one of the reasons that this will be the case. Example: Randy shoots a basketball and shouts confidently to his friend, Roy, "*2 points.*" Roy, while trying to block the shot, shouts: "*Nat dat!*" or "*Nat da de!*" Meaning, that is not going to happen, and in this case, I am ensuring that it does not.

Nat he/she/you!—This is in a very different context from the next expression on the list. It is an emphatic rejection of a comment about someone. The scenario: "*Man, Ah hea' Eric cou run" 5 miles in 30 minutes.*" Responder: "*Nat he!*" Sometimes the reaction is given in regular cadence, but often the speaker stresses the first word: "NAT he (she etc.)." "*Dey say bu' how Karol rude toh her mudda'.*" Responder: "*Nat she! Dat guirl too nice.*" Notice that the tendency is to use the subject pronoun (he, she), except with the first person singular, where "*me*" tends to be more natural and prevalent than "*I.*" "*Nat me.*"

Nat it—A game. "*Let's play 'nat it. You is it.*" Once a popular game that children played. Americans use the word "tag." In the 1950's and 60's Virgin Islands children were not as familiar with the word "tag' as they may be in 2017. The game is certainly not as popular; the expression has all but disappeared.

Nat you—Abrupt expression used to inform someone that the speaker is not addressing him/her. Some Americans consider this a rude response; however, the tone of the voice and the context would determine the nature of the response. Consider the following:

Speaker #1: "*Dougie, Dougie…*" Speaker #2 whose name is not DOUGIE responds: "*Yes, yoh call' me?*" Speaker #1: "*Nat you, man, Ah was callin' Dougie.*"

Neighbors—Referring to a section of hair in the back or side of the head that often seems resistant to a comb: "*Her neighbors so ba(r)d, dey hard toh comb.*"

Nenny—Godmother. (also "Nen"). "*Miss Ana is mey Nenny. She stan' fo meh in deh Anglican chuch.*" In the Virgin Islands this was among the most serious relationships. A person's "Nenny" was an extended family member in whom one could confide, and one who was always available for support. It was truly a unique and valued relationship. As children we were often required to go to our "Nenny" to see what chores she wanted us to do.

Nex'—At first glance this may seem like a typical word, from "next."

In Virgin Islands Creole, however, its usage can be radically different to that in English. It can mean "<u>in addition to</u>": "*Ah don sen' yoh one aready, so Ah ciarn sen' yoh ah nex' one.*" Or "<u>different</u>": "*Miss, dis ting ciarn fit, yoh cou' gimme ah nex' one please?* Or "<u>another</u>"—"*Tain have ah nex' person heh who cou' do dat.*"

Niapa—"A little bit," "*Jus' ah niapa.*" Often the word is preceded by the adverb "lil," making the expression redundant, emphatic. (A similar grammatical arrangement is seen with the word "*Tunchie,*" discussed later.)

Nigga' man sardine—A reference to a type of food for people with *little* means. During the lean days of the 50's and earlier people with little means cooked this dish with "fungi", or rice, or simply ate it with bread. There was no brand called *Nigga' Man Sardine,* but again this is indicative of the people's imagination and creativity. Rarely uttered today.

Night dew—The words themselves are common words, however, the usage is special: "*I doan keep night dew.*" The idea is that I am not the type of person that stays out late.

Nite Soil Man—That committed employee, whose responsibility it was to transfer wastes from the outside latrines to a waiting trucks. (See the following entry.)

Nite Soil Truck—As mentioned in the Introduction this refers to the vehicle that transported human waste. This very important activity was always done in the early hours of the morning, maybe in part to protect the identity of the workers. These faithful employees were undervalued and unappreciated in spite of the valuable service that they provided. This is clearly an expression that is unfamiliar to the majority of people. Only those who have lived in the islands during the particular historical period (50's and before/and very early part of the 60's) would have a clue as to what the speaker is referring.

No—Special use, not used as negative: "*Do it no, man*"; "*Come no, man*"; "*Help me no, man*"; "*Call meh lata' no, man*"— Unique expressions that build on a negative word "no." The "*no*" does not suggest a lack of desire, but precisely the opposite. In our language the "*no*" in this paradoxical construction is used for emphasis. The negative is deceptive, (other examples, "*call meh, no man*"; "*help meh, no—yoh jus' de watchin*'"). In this verbal arrangement one is being asked in an emphatic way to do something, a type of exhortation. It could very well be a softened request, even though it can be used in a more insistent manner. Still extremely popular in Virgin Islands vernacular.

No place—Meaning "anywhere." Another expression which at first glance may appear to be a common English phrase. While it is a phrase used in English, never in the same context as in U.S. Virgin Islands Creole: *"We ain' goin' no place today."* Also, *"We ain goin' 'ah place' "* as reference earlier under "**ain**."

No way—Anywhere. Similar to the previous entry ("**No place.**"). *"He ain' garn no way dis marnin."*

No way—This entry is a different connotation to the manner in which the phrase is used above, and not at all like the **American** expression, "No way am I going to do that." In U.S. Virgin Islands Creole, "**No way**" means *"anyhow."* For example: Carma to Joe: *"Dis pen ain wokin."* Joe: *"Dat's ok; meen need it no way."*

'Noint wid oil—Anoint with oil, for example if someone has a pain. *"Ah geh toh 'noint mey head wid oil. Ah geh ah headache."*

Noise in mey head—This expression has a character all its own. The idea of course is that the person is being disturbed. But it is the way how the sentence can be phrased that gives it a special character—for example: *"Ah you stap deh noise in mey head."* Similarly to *"Stap makin' noise in people head."* All colorful Creole expressions.

Notice—There is a special use of this word, for example, in reference to child support: *"Da man doan notice he chiren dem atarl."* In this case, the person does not support his children financially. But the word also is used in a general sense—for example, to pay attention to someone: *"One ting wid she, she duz notice ha' mudda."* This means that she calls or visits her mother regularly, is concerned with her welfare.

Notin' bu mo' craziness (Notin' bu' mo' stuieppidness*)*—The situation is so utterly ridiculous that it defies explanation. *"Las' night Ah went to deh ting, notin' bu mo' craziness. I coun' stay de meson."* *"Listen toh dem two deh tarkin, notin bu' mo' stuiepiness."*

Notin' go so—I am not going to accept that. It did not happen that way. Also, I am not going to allow that. A variation is *"Tain notin' go so."* Speaker #I: *"I gon sen' yoh deh ting dem in two weeks."* Speaker # II: *"Notin' go so; Ah need dem tings today."*

Notin toh me—Not related. This is an expression that at times causes a problem because the uninitiated interprets it incorrectly. I recall that some years ago a Virgin Islander living in Rhode Island said about an individual: *"She ain notin toh me."* Another person listening to this interpreted the statement as, *"She means nothing to me,"* and felt offended. The Virgin Islander was actually saying: *"She is not related to me."* The difference is significant.

Nuff ah dat—No more of that.

Nyam — To eat, an onomatopoetic sound. In Spanish *"Ñam Ñam."* A once popular expression: *"Ah goin' toh nyam."*

O—The conjunction *"or."*

Oh Fathers—An allusion to God for help in a difficult situation. *"Oh, fathers! Ah you hea' deh news?"*

Okro—Okra, used primarily with fungi.

"Ole" + an adjective plus the emphatic **"self"**—A construction that is used frequently to criticize, *"He ole maga' self,"* but it is also often used in jest, *"Dat's mey frien', he ole crazy self."* It is important to note that the person may well be young, so that the expression is not necessarily in reference to the person's age.

Ole Years—December *31st*. In general, Virgin Islanders do not use the expression: "New Year's Eve." *"For Ole Years mey mudda' gon cook some callalou. Yoh carn have ole years widout dat dish." "We goin' chuch Ole Years night." "Wa ah you doin' fo' Ole Years?"*

Once ah man, twice ah chile—The idea that if one lives long enough he/she will at some point become dependent in very much the same way as in infancy.

One—This is an entry that might raise eyebrows, but it deserves some explanation. It is used for emphasis. *"He was ackin' rude. Boy, Ah give 'im one look, an' he stap.'"*

// *"Ah yoh betta' stop makin' noise befo' Ah give ah yoh one lick."* It is important to note that "one" may not necessarily mean *"only one."* The word could also be used in the following way: *"He come in heh wid he craziness. Ah tell yoh, he had one conduct."* In this example it is used for emphasis; also heard, *"He had ah conduct."* (See also earlier entry **Had ah conduct**). In both of these sentences, the person was behaving unruly.

One time/one time an' don—Here the idea is to take advantage of the time you have to accomplish an additional task. *"Ah ain have ah* *appointment today, but Ah don heh, so Ah might as well see deh doctor one time an' don."*

One ting Ah know I (me)—This often used phrase is so characteristic of our speech and reflective of the tendency towards emphasis. This is used as a kind of self-affirmation, or reaffirmation. The speaker is stressing in no uncertain terms that he or she will or will not do something/ or did or did not do something. The following examples illustrate this special usage:

Ricardo says: *"Dey say dey goin' party. One ting Ah know meen goin'."*

In another situation Priscilla asserts: *"He ain do he taxes. One ting Ah know I don do mine own."* Typical English words, distinct usage.

One ting wid she/he/dem etc.—This is a phrase used to highlight a particular situation, for example a person's position: *"One ting wid she, she doan like rude chiren."*

One way—An expression used to convey a friendly kind of teasing. *"I was tellin' her arl kin' ah tings, teasin' ha'. Boy, Ah had she one way."*

Oney—Used in place of the English word, "only." *"Laverne was deh oney one who help meh clean up deh place."*

Onlis'—Used like "oney" (see above). These days this expression is not at all as prevalent as "oney" which fortunately is used with regularity by the young and the old. *"Dell is deh onlis one dat went wid me."*

Out—In Virgin Islands Creole this popular preposition can be used as verbal command: *"Ah you out deh stove. Deh food don cook."* The expression was made popular during the days of the small one or two burner kerosene stoves. And that was preceded by the coal pot with its flames—*"out the flames."*

Out deh light—An expression that very likely came from a command connected to candle light, or kerosene lamps. Often one would "blow out the flames." The expression carried over to some electric gadgets during the period of modernization. *"Man, ah yoh out deh light. Ah yoh wasin' current."*

Out he/she head—Could refer to someone with mental issues, or someone who is not acting right. *"She just' start screamin' like she out ha head."*

Outside chile—In the Virgin Islands this refers to a child born from an extramarital affair.

Outta—This creolized word results from the combination of the prepositions "out" and "of." *"Meson, Ah geh toh geh outta heh now. Ah late fo' wok."*

Outta orda—-The person is not acting right, has a bad attitude etc. Sometimes it is associated with such vices as rudeness, disrespect, and forwardness. "*He come pushin' out he mout';he outta orda.*" In other words, how dare he act to me in the way that he did!

Outta place—Forward; fresh. "*Dat young' chile come callin' meh by mey fus' name. She ain geh no manners. She so outta place.*" Also this is used to refer to a person's action that someone might consider uncouth. "*Man, Ah tell yoh he too outta place. He aways cussin' an' carryin' arn.*" "*Dat's wa' she tell yoh? She too rude an' outta place.*"

Own—Possessive; "*Dat's mines own.*" "*Dat's his own.*" (Belongs to me; belongs to him."). No question, an emphatic, or stressed possessive. This item certainly does not belong to anyone but to the particular individual cited. (See Section under **Possessive**).

Pai'as— For those who always thought that this was a "cuss word," relax. Actually it is an apocopation of the Spanish word "*payaso*"= clown. Again this is a clear "hand me down" from Puerto Rico. When someone is referred to as "ah pai'as" it is a shortened version of the Spanish. In essence, the person plays around a lot, is not a serious person. At times the criticism could be in jest, for example speaking about a friend. It can, however, be a derisive comment that suggests the incapability of someone.

Pail— Bigger container used to transfer waste from the *po'* (later in the entry) to the outhouse.

Pam pam—This was a reference to someone, usually a child, being punished corporally. "*Yoh gon' geh pam pam if yoh doan behave.*"

Pants foot—Creole expression for the leg of one's pants. Example: "*Roll up yoh pants foot.*"

Papa God gon punish yoh—"Papa God" is an expression that was used frequently for "God," but is now disappearing. Very often parents would say, pray so Papa God cou' help you. In Spanish, <*Papá Dios.*>

Papai—Papaya. Very much like "**tarmon**," "**ponguana**," and numerous Creole words, this word stands as a separate word from "papaya," even though my sense is that its usage is slowly slipping away.

Pappy—This was once a word used frequently with "no" or "yea/yes." Still heard among older Virgin Islanders. It is used as a type of emphatic confirmation, or negation. For example, in the following situation Lorne says to her friend, Petula: "*It hat outside, yoh hea'?*" Petula: "*Yea, pappy. Ah* *know I stayin' inside."* Or with negation. *"Yoh ain goin' wid we?"* Response: *"No, pappy. Me ain goin' ah way."* (Similar, to **"Buddy"** addressed earlier.)

Pappysho'—A clown. *"Boy, Danny is ah real pappysho.' He aways foolin' aroun.' "* This could be used to refer to a person being humorous in a given moment. It could also suggest a person's general personality. However, it can be used symbolically to suggest a person's incompetence, or unreliability. *"Doan listen toh 'e, man, he jus' ah pappysho. He' ain know ah ting wa 'e tarkin' 'bout."*

Para—Acting out of the ordinary; the person is believed to have a problem. The prefix comes from the paranormal. *"I duz stay away from he. He too para."*

Pass back—A Creole expression that is frequently used. Again, here is one of those phrases that appear to be quite regular, using 2 common words. However, this is a very localized express which means "to return." *"Man, wen yoh gon pass back toh see meh?"* Another example, *"Heen home, pass back lata wen he don wok."*

Pass by—An interesting expression that at first might appear to mean only "pass in the vicinity of a place." In Virgin Islands Creole, however, this can be the equivalent to visiting.

"Last night Ah pass by dey house an spen' some time wid dem."

Patience— This word is used to indicate an understanding of a situation. Consider the following circumstance: Mr. Lendell is seen begging for money to which his friend, Mr. Ford, objects because he knows that his friend is wealthy. *"If he ain ha no money, Ah woud ah say 'patience.' "* In other words, Mr. Ford would have understood Mr. Lindell's panhandling, if his financial situation were truly dire.

Pear— Many people still used this word in place of *avocado*. It may be more popular with the older population but still somewhat known among the younger generation of residents. Clearly heard with less frequency these days. *"Ah love toh eat bread wid pear."*

Peas an' rice—Really refers to rice and beans. It would be rare, however, to hear someone call this dish "rice and beans" or worse, "Beans an' rice," or 'Rice an' peas." Not only the words but the order, is important. In other words, in general no one says, "rice an' peas an' chicken." Such phrases would be a total departure from the particular local culinary dish—which, in the biggest note of ironies is in fact, Beans and rice. *"Ah like me peas an' rice."*

People—This is probably a surprise for many to see this word on the list, but this word has its usage for Virgin Islanders beyond the general one. Here is the situation: A child is hitting another child, and the victim screams: *"Stop hittin' people, no."* Another example: **Caller**: *"Cheryl, Cheryl."* **Response**: *"Stop, callin' people arl deh time, no man."* The person complaining places himself/herself in a generic category. Yet another use of the word is the following: *"Robby was sick yestaday, now he look like people again."* Simply put, Robby is doing fine now. In expressions such as *"Go cook no ma; people so hungry"* and *"Stop deh noise, people wan' toh sleep,"* the speaker could actually be referring to herself/himself, but uses the generic as part of a popular Virgin Islands phrase.

People dem—An expression that is used to refer to relatives, or good friends. *"Dat's he people dem."* (Cousins etc.); "comado," "compado" etc. (See entries explaining these last two terms). *"Liz garn toh she people dem."* (Her friends)

People (dem) wok—An expression used at times to refer to a job. "People" is employed here generically. It could be a reference to "the boss," or the owner of a business, etc. In a broad sense it means "*my job.*" *"Look heh, no, Ah carn tark no mo' Ah gatoh do deh people (dem) wok."*

People (out) in deh street—An expression used to indicate that people are out doing chores etc. It is never a reference to any particular segment of the islands. *"Man, e' geh ah lot ah people out in deh street today."* In other words, "they are out and about."

Pepe—Godfather. This was quite a serious responsibility. Many children lived with their "nenny" and "pepe" even when their parents were alive. Like the "Nenny," this individual played a crucial role in family affairs.

Pickin' wilks—Searching for whelks, a frequent activity. Those who went looking for whelks would roll up the leg of their pants to prevent them from getting wet from the water rushing against the rocks. From this social-economic reality if a person's pants are too short someone might say: *"Look he pants,' no; he pickin' wilks."*

Picky hair/head—Short hair, generally said in a negative manner, never as a compliment. *"Geh from here, yoh picky head self."* (Also, *"picky hair self"*)

Piece- This word can be used in an expression to emphasize the intensity, size, or amount of something. Consider the following examples: *"Wat ah piece ah rain!"*(a lot); *"Wat ah piece ah house!"* (Huge, or also could refer to the quality)! But also, *"Arn geh ah piece ah money."* In this case only the negative can function. That is, one **cannot** say: *"Ah geh ah piece ah money."* The expression, *"Dats ah piece ah lie"* is used to point out the hyperbolic (exaggerated) nature of something said—it is a very big lie.

Piece—There is a different usage to the previous one in that the speaker is referring to something appealing, very often food. *"I cou' eat ah piece ah fish."* This does not mean "a part" of a fish, but rather that the person has a desire for fish. *"Da man de like ah piece ah rum."* Very much a Virgin Islands expression. *"You like ah piece ah nonsense, yoh hea'."*

There is no question that ours is a culture of magical realism in the sense that our "realism" has always been infused with the "unusual" and the inexplicable, given our traumatic history this should not be at all such a surprise. I speak of the same kind of magical realism often used to reference Latin American in its literature.

Piece—Also used to connote the bad quality of something. For example, *"I geh ah piece ah phone dat duz neva' wok."* Also, *"She geh ah piece ah foot de dat always causin' problems."*

Piss an ah rock an' smell it—This was a reference used to condemn the attitude of a child who was being rude, or was exhibiting behavior that suggests that he/she was trying to act older that he/she really was. This person is trying to act like a "man" or "woman." *"Yoh' ackin' so forward'. Yoh mus' ah piss an ah rock an' smell it."* Language exclusively of adults.

Plat her hair in Guinea—Style from Guinea, West Africa. *"Tell ah toh plat yoh hair in t(h)ree— an' tell ah toh plat yoh sista own in guinea."* Many girls in the 50's and 60's were experts at "plattin." Sometimes girls were sent to these "experts" to have their hair done.

Play—In this context it does not refer to engaging in an activity for fun. The main sense in Virgin Islands Creole is to act, to pretend, to fake. In some usage, it could mean "believe" or "think." *"Ah see ha in town yestaday, but she play like she (dain) ain see meh."*(She pretended). But also very popular is: *"He playin' bad"* or *"He playin he bad." "Playing bad man."*

In these cases the person is acting as if he is tough, or the person, based on his/her action believes he or she is tough. *"You playin' woman, no."* Some very popular expression with this word are *"playin' crazy," "playin' stuiepid."* All suggest a level of pretense.

Play ketcha—Actually this comes from "to catch." It was once a popular children's game similar to the American game, "tag." *"Who wan' toh play Ketcha?"* The word "tag' in this context was virtually unused in this context in the 1950's or 1960's in the U.S.V.I. (See also "**Nat It.**")

Playin' + ADJECTIVE+NEG (Tain, Ain')—Used to express an affirmative in an emphatic manner. Example: *"Tain playin' hot outside."* This means that it very hot!

Please God—If it be God's will. In a society characterized by its religiosity, this is an important and cherished interjection. *"Ah gon call yoh tomorrow please God."* // *"Ole Years please God Ah gon cook mey callalou."* In all likelihood this is generated from the idea *"if it pleases God to let me live this long."*

Plug out—Unplug something. But also at times it is used to mean "turn off" a device. Consider the two examples: *"Plug out deh machine."* *"Plug out da TV right now"* could very well be a command to turn it off—actually using a button or switch!

Po'(poochy)—-Kept in the house, often under the bed, used in the 60's and earlier as a kind of miniature portable toilet. Many of us who were children of the 1950's did not see an indoor toilet for roughly the first 10 years of our lives. The use of the *"po"* was the convenient and conventional mode of operation.

Poke 'im/ha etc.—To hit intentionally and deliberately with force suggested. *"She poke me some licks."* *"Ah was de standin' an' he poke meh one fist."* See this word also under the heading *"Marble Terms."*

Poke it in yoh mout'—Stuff your mouth with a lot of food at one time. It is a contrast to eating slowly. *"Look, doan poke deh ting in yoh mout; take yoh time an' eat it."*

Polybuck—Used often in place of the official name, Polyberg, a staple residential area in St. Thomas.

Ponguana—A translation of our Creole word is pomegranate. *"I love dem ponguana. Dem ting sweet, yoh hea'."* There are certain Creole words that might have resulted from "mis pronunciation, or misunderstanding" that persisted for generations. Eventually the creolization became the "standard." Ponguana (like **tarmon**") is a good example of that phenomenon.

Poochy-A variation of the "Po."

Porah—Rushing. *"Take yoh time. Yoh too porah."*

'Pose—Suppose. One of several apocopated words. *"He' pose toh come heh next week."* // *"I was pose toh go toh chuch, but Ah ain went."*

Posin arf—Idle, milling around, acting rather stylish, standing. Ofen this word in English refers to a position that a person assumes, for example to pose for a picture. In U.S.V.I. Creole, the suggestion is that the individual was just standing, as if positioning for a photo shot.

"Las night ah see yoh by deh carna' jus' posin' arf, yoh ain geh notin toh do?"

Poung –To hit; to knock. *"Ah de minin' mey business, deh boy poung meh one lick." "Look, stop it befo' ah poung yoh ah fis'." "Who out de poungin' on deh do?"*

Poung' ah lip—Said often to refer to the perceived thickness of a person's lips, often said in a derisive manner: *"He poung ah lip self."* For those very unfamiliar with pronunciation in our islands, the idea is that the lip "weighs" a pound! (See **Larng lip**).

Poung' melee—Gossiping: *"out de poungin' melee." "She/He duz poun' too much melee fo' me"*—the person gossips too much. This is a perennially popular Virgin Islands expression, of course sometimes said in jest, but frequently suggesting a serious situation because of the possible discord that can come from idle gossip. *"I ain' gon say too much toh dem 'cause dey like toh poung too much melee."*

'Preciate—To appreciate. In Virgin Islands Creole there are numerous words that are shortened. Even though there is a discussion in this book focusing on prepositions that follow this tendency, there are also some verbs. *"Ah really 'preciate wa yoh doin' fo me."*

Press—Not interested in something or someone/ don't like it very much. Judy: *"Yoh like mango?"* Sandy answers. *"I ain' so 'press wid it."* Chances are this comes from the word "impress," but whatever the origin of the word, it does have a unique ring. *"Yoh wan' toh go sho' lata?* **Ans**: *"Man, Ah ain' 'press toh go atarl."*

Pries' Yard—Term used in the 1950's when speaking of the yard at

St. Thomas' Catholic School. Now only heard among a few older citizens. *"E' geh ah bunch ah chiren ova de playin' in deh Pries' Yard."*

Pu'arn yoh school clothes—Don't ever mistake this with *"chuch' clothes."* During the middle of the last century children would often have clothes for school, and one set for church. *"Chuch clothes"* and *"School clothes"* were very popular expressions.

Pu' arn ah yoh sleepin' ting—Whatever you slept in was called "**sleepin' ting**"—in the early years of the 1950's (and certainly earlier) and 60's. Whatever you could find that was convertible enough was good enough. Sometimes one would hear *"Pu arn yoh night gown."* Needless to say there was no "gown" involved in this.

Pu'arn yoh 6 o'clock beeny—Very common for children of the 40 and 50's to do this—to put on a felt "tam" to ward off "deh dew."

Pu' deh lock on deh do'—This expression would not have much relevance today. Those of us (most) who lived in wooden houses in 40's, 50's etc. recall these locks, even though it is true that very often doors were left unlocked, even when the entire family was out.

Pu'in fo' (**Putin' fo'**)—Tricky construction and usage. The first thing is to observe the various ways of expressing the sense of this phrase, which could be "to defend," "to protect," "to intervene," "to side with." The following examples demonstrate how this saying works. Jimmy: *"Tori, wen me an' yoh cousin' Ladell geh ah fight, you aways pu'in fo' he."* This means that Tori sides with Ladell; he intervenes in order to protect and defend his cousin. The phrase is also used in reference to purely verbal confrontations. James: *"Me an' she wuz arguing an' you come pu'in fo' she wi'out knowin' wa happenin."* In other words, you sided with her, also arguing against me.

Pu' it in deh sho' case—During the first decades of the 20th century almost every house had a particular piece of furniture made of mahogany and glass case that we called the *"sho' case."* The show case is where items, such as dishes were displayed. People who sometimes would want to be "proper" in their speech would say *"Put it in the SURE case,"* an expression that totally betrays the original. Clearly "sho" comes from "show," exhibit.

Pu' lil macuricome on it—Really the American word is **mecuricome.** This was a cure-all medicine, and was as legendary as the "mangy darg," *"Deh Green Face Man"* and *"Deh Cow Foot Woman."* Any kind of cuts or scratches was treated with *"macuricome."* Unquestionably, this word deserves in special place in the annals of Virgin Islands vocabulary because of the versatility of this antiseptic iodine.

Pu' mo' loggin' an deh bed—A very important, but, not surprisingly, lost expression. For me, this is a sentimental entry that deserves recognition. Because most people did not have mattresses, they would put old clothing on their beds that served as mattresses. This consisted of any fabric that would help to create a comfortable sleeping space. Naturally with modernization and the creation of high quality mattresses the term "loggin" has become lost.

Pu' up deh food—This expression is used to refer to the act of storing food in the refrigerator, generally (but of course, not always) overnight. *"Ah yoh pu' up deh food fo' tomorrow."*

Pull in deh do'—Close the door. An expression frequently heard in yards with their big doors. In Grove Place, St. Croix, my aunts and grandmother used that expression, along with one mentioned earlier (*Haul in*).

Pull up yoh pantaloon—Pants, British, Spanish (*pantalones*). Virtually no one uses this expression, but many years earlier it was heard with regularity. I would venture to guess that today teenagers have never heard it, even though if they did in context, the meaning would be clear.

Pushin' out yoh mout—You are being rude; I can see from the way you are positioning your mouth. A child exhibiting such a behavior to an adult, especially to a parent, is inviting serious reprisals. *"Yoh betta stap pusin' out yoh mout an' do wa Ah tell yoh toh do."*

Quadrille—United States Virgin Islands square dance with French and African influences.

Quail up— Wrinkled. Virgin Islanders creative way of describing people has no limits. This is an expression that speaks specifically to wrinkles, however, it suggests a general negative description of someone's face or other parts of the body. *"He is ah young man, bu' he face don' quail up." "Yoh eva look at ha han' dem? Dey arl quail up."*

Quelbe—Virgin Islands original music.

Raben—Ravenous. The person simply eats a lot, maybe too much. *"He duz eat eveting. Da ting raben, yoh hea'."* {See "**ting**" in later entry}

Rah rah—A person who talks a lot *"He duz talk too much. He is notin but ah rah rah."*

Rain wata—This redundant express is generally used to refer to water in people's cistern and often used to distinguish from portable water or water from a well: *"Ah want some tea; make it wid rain wata, not well wata."*

Rajo—Radio. *"Turn on deh rajo toh hea' deh news."* No question this is still heard with relative frequency these day.

Raslin—The Creolized word for "wrestling." *"Dain fightin'; dey jus' raslin.'"* This was an important pastime for young boys in the 50's and 60's. It was done with such regularity that one could consider it a kind of "unofficial sport." There was no organized wrestling as such in the Virgin Islands, but boys spent a lot of time *"rootin' in deh grass."*

Ratta- A temporary swelling cause by a strike to the arm. *"Yoh hit mey arm so hard yoh gi' meh ah ratta."*

Reach back—*To return.* This is another example in which the words themselves are commonly used in English; however the expression is uniquely ours. Of course someone can "reach back" and retrieve something. In the case of U.S. Virgin Islands Creole, however, the usage is in reference to travel, moving from one venue to another. *"Wa time yoh reach back las' night?"* *"Wait fo' me, Ah ain reachin' back so late tonight."* Some Virgin Islanders informed me that they had assumed that this was a prevalent expression in American English, and were most surprised to discover that its prevalence is really local. The statement in Virgin Islands Creole, *"She reach aready"* would be virtually unintelligible to the person not familiar with our language. To the local resident it would be a clearly articulated pronouncement.

Red peas soup—Some who are not familiar with this dish might well ask, "Why this entry?" My response is, there cannot be a discussion of Virgin Islands language without referencing this dish. Apart from the fact that it is part of the Virgin Islands rich culinary tradition the word "peas" is a misnomer, since in fact the dish main ingredients are in fact **"red beans."** People unfamiliar with the Virgin Islands are always surprised when they hear the word "peas," while looking for *"Beans."*

Red skin—Still used often to describe the hue of one's skin. This is in contrast to a person with darker complexion. *"Yoh know 'ha, man, she is ah shorty red skin lady."*

Red Wall—(St. Thomas) refers to Fort Christian. For most of last century the expression, *"He in deh Red Wall"* meant that the person was a prisoner at Fort Christian (1671) in St. Thomas. These days one can go years without hearing this expression as a synonym for Fort Christian. It is losing its relevancy, even though the referent (the fort) is still a major St. Thomas landmark. This structure embodies the United States Virgin Islands glorious and inglorious past.

Res—Rest, to place. But also to relax, such as in the following: Child: *"Ah feel sleepy."* Mother: *"Jus' res' yoh eyes."* It is interesting that this is also used for objects, as if the object themselves could "rest." The sense is to "leave," or to "put" something in a particular spot, usually the indication is that it will be temporary. *"Man, jus' res' yoh ting dem in deh carna' 'til yoh geh back."*

Ritarearin—Acting wild; uncivil; noisy, not well behaved, loud, unacceptable conduct. *"He really surprise' me deh way he wus ritarearin right in front deh chuch. It wuz shameful."*

Roas' ah time—An expression general associated with carnival in years past; it is occasionally still heard when speaking about enjoying oneself during carnival. *"Evey carnival he duz roas' ah time. He duz really enjoy heself."* No longer a popular concept.

Rock City—A term of endearment used by many Virgin Islands to refer to St. Thomas; see also **"Deh Rock."**

Rock-stone—The unique combination "rock-stone" is typical of our speech that is often hyperbolic and paradoxical. *"Ah wuz walkin' tru deh alley an' somebardy hit meh wid ah big rock-stone."*

Roosh it up—In cooking, to mix things together, to sauté. *"Afta' yoh put deh fish in de pan, jus' roosh it up."*

Root-up— To unravel, to undo. *"Ah jus' make up deh bed; ah yoh doan root it up."*

Rootin'—Playing. *"Come inside deh house now. Ah you out de rootin' in deh dut."*

Rough dry—Refers to a person who looks unkempt, especially if it is clear that the person's clothes was not ironed, or not ironed correctly. Metaphorically it can also refer to a general sloppy look. *"Ah hope you ain goin' no place wid dem rough dry clothes."* *"Secko, how come you look so man, Ah mean so rough dry."* Similar to "wash-out," discussed later, but with a major exception: This expression refers primarily to how a person is dressed, and not the physical aspects of the individual. See **Wash out** in later entry.

'Roun. –Generally speaking, it signifies the preposition "around." However, this Creole word functions differently to the English preposition. Its *usage* highlights the unique nature of the structure of our language: "**Way she is?**" Ans. "**She 'roun deh house.**" The response refers more to the location of the individual, rather than movement. Also see earlier grammatical section on APOCOPATED PREPOSITIONS. In St. Thomas, the expression, *"She live roun' deh fiel'* is still in vogue."

Roun' deh coas'—A reference to the area north of the old Knud Hansen Hospital in St. Thomas.

Roun' deh fiel— A reference to the area where the Lionel Roberts Stadium is located in St. Thomas.

Rubbers—-Word used for sneakers in early to mid-20th century. *"I buy' mey rubbers dem from Bata."*

Rude song—A song considered to have perverse lyrics. *"Ah you stop listenin' toh dem rude songs dey playin' on deh rajo."*

Rugadoo—Confusion, trouble, situation. This is a word that often speaks to a situation of conflict and disorder: *"Ah stayin' away from dem people because dey duz cause arl kina ah rugadoo." "Wa' kin-a rugadoo goin' arn here, man?" "Wa rugadoo dis is, man?"*

Rum bubbla'—A person who drinks too much. As far as anyone knows, it may just be the consumption of beer. But if the person seems to consume alcoholic in excess, the word "rum" is often used to describe the person or the situation—no matter the beverage.

Rummy—A term reserved for those who drink too much alcohol: *"He is ah real rummy."* As noted in the previous entry, even though there may not even be any proof that the person consumes "rum," the characterization is sufficient to describe someone who seems regularly inebriated—even if the inebriation is a result of excessive wine or beer.

Run behin' deh smoke (flit) truck—A dangerous act that children mistakenly thought was fun during the 50's. Anything could be converted into play during that era, and this is a prime example of a play that could have worked to our detriment. No one knows what long term effects resulted from this practice. Hopefully, none.

Run down—In general, this means to get hit by a car. *"She was walkin' in deh street wen she geh run down."* Like the expression "knack down," this needs no qualification. It is immediately known in the community of speakers of the language that the reference is to someone being hit by a vehicle.

Sacabo—Finished. Barely heard, sometimes among older residents. Clearly a loan from Spanish- "*Se acabó*" which indicates that something is finished. "*Mey rice sacabo, Ah have toh buy some mo' lata.*"

Safe—A place where people kept food and other items, a kind of make shift cabinet. "*Put deh food in deh safe 'til lata.*" With the construction of modernized kitchens and sophisticated cabinets this is an expression that is totally extinct. The "safe" was in essence a place for "safe keeping."

Salt—Having no luck. "*You keep losin man; you salt, yoh hea'.*"

Sal'ting—Refers to meat, generally when speaking of a meal to distinguish this from the meatless portion. For example: "*Man, you servin' me arl kina rice, but wey deh sal'ting?*"

Santapee—Translation *of the word from our Creole language is the word centipede*

Santo—A term often used to refer to a person from the Dominican Republic. Two interesting points: 1) In Spanish nouns ending in "**o**" are generally masculine, and those ending in "**a**" are feminine. In this case, the term refers to both male and female. 2) Ironically, the Spanish term for Saint Thomas is *Santo* Tomás."

Savesoul—A term reserved for a person who became a "born again Christian." Here it is written as one word because it was always elaborated in that manner, and never "saved soul." It was generally a reference to a person who was a Pentecostal. It is an expression that at times could have a negative connotation from the perspective of the speaker. It was a type of intentional verbal affront: "*Man, she doan go ah place. She is ah savesoul.*"

Say one, say two—An expression that gives two sides of an argument. "*Say one, say two, dat man duz do some good tings.*"

Scal'—To burn with excessively hot liquid. "*Dat crazy man try to scal' meh, jus' because Ah tell him he wrang.*" "*Wa wrang wid dat woman skin?*" Ans. "*She geh scal-up yestaday.*"

Sciam—As a noun, this means it is "a scam." As a verb, to get away from here. "*Boy, you betta sciam.*" "*We gon sciam outta here.*" A term that is heard less today.

Sciamp—Rascal. "*Da man is a real sciamp. Ah ain trus 'e atarl.*"

Sciatta deh jumbie—According to legend, "*If yoh tun' yoh back on* *deh jumbie, yoh gon sciatta' deh jumbie"* (You would get rid of it). This is a segment of our culture from which many people try to disassociate themselves. The combination of shame and the notion of "jumbie" and "obeah" as satanic in some people's minds, have kept such expressions lying dormant. Present day Virgin Islanders are not very familiar with this myth. No matter how it is viewed, however, this is an integral part of Virgin Islands lore and belief system.

Sciatta yoh self—Get out of here. A disrespectful, emphatic command. *"Look meson, yoh betta' sciatta yoh self from heh', yoh hea'."*

Scoot out ah here—To leave. This is definitely an expression that is no longer popular. It was used often when indicating departure. However, it was never universally used, but seemed more common among young boys. "I *gon scoot out ah heh now; Ah geh toh go."*

Scrub yoh mout' (Teet')—Brush your teeth. *"Make sho yoh scrub yoh mout' (teet') befo' yoh go toh school dis marnin'."*

Scrumble—*Crumbs.* One of many words that took on a life of its own. Like "**tarmon,**" it has its own character, with no regard to the referent. *"Look, no, Ah hope ah yoh pick up arl deh scrumble from deh flo'."* Not heard frequently.

Sea cat—As a boy this was commonly used for octopus.

Sea moon—Jelly fish. *"Dey say dat dem sea moon duz sting bad. I 'fraid ah dem."*

Secko—Hardly heard these days; the word was used like, "pal." It was only used when speaking directly to the person. *"Wa happenin', Secko?"*

Self—In some cases it means "even;" a "utility" suffix that emphasizes a particular situation. It is often used to describe someone in a negative way. *"He 'ain self know wa' he doin'"* (the person does not understand for one reason or the other); variation, *"He 'ain know wa' he doin' self,"* this could also be an allusion to or a suggestion of a person's mental illness: *"Po ting; heen self know wey he is."* The person is so sick that he or she is not aware of what is happening.

Self—The choice to separate this from the previous entry is because the difference is so radical. There is really no way to adequately translate a phrase such *as "He no-teet self"*— said even if the person was missing only <u>one</u> tooth, as long as it was from the front. Another example, *"She picky hair self."* Of course, the creativity of the language permits our own inventive expressions: *"she big-foot self"; "he big belly-self." "Yoh marga' self;" "Yoh raben self."* The suffix basically serves as an intensifier highlighting the adjective.

Self—"Precisely," "exactly," "just." This suffix is used in yet another context very different to the descriptions above. It must be made clear, however, that the inference is <u>not</u> that the words listed ("precisely," "exactly," "just") are interchangeable with "self," but they represent approximate interpretations in a particular context. Consider the following: Ellie asks Hubert: *"Wen yoh gon do deh ting, man?"* Hubert responds: *"Ah gon do it today self."* (This is precisely the day that he will perform the task.)

"It was yestaday self dat we wuz talkin' bout 'im." (Just yesterday)

"Yes, tis he self Ah wan' toh talk toh." ("He is exactly the person that I...")

It is important to note here that the expression *"he self"* is different to *"heself"* (See section on **Reflexive**), both in meaning and pronunciation. As indicated above, in the sentence *"Tis he self Ah wan toh talk toh,"* the idea is that "he" is *precisely* the person. On the other hand, *"He gon do it heself"* means that he will do it alone. With respect to pronunciation, in the expression *"he self"* the stress is on "he" (HE self) whereas in "heself" (heSELF) the emphasis is on "self."

Setty fowl—Here is an expression that has its roots in the patriarchy and the notion of masculinity. It was clearly a negative gender reference. Fortunately, it is not heard with the same frequency as decades ago. It generally was the portrayal of someone as "restless" and "edgy" like a fowl laying eggs. It is an expression that is by its nature sexist.

Shak shak— Musical instrument created from the flamboyant tree, a staple of the Virgin Islands fauna. Localized "maracas." These days the expression is not heard with the same frequency. Since it was mainly used by children and the present generation of children does not have frequent contact with the tree, it is natural that the term would be employed less today. Also, as explained in the preface, it is the word that launched this book project!

Shaks (Oh Shaks)—An exclamation used with regularity in our islands under a variety of situations. For example, someone might say: "Oh *Shaks, Ah foget mey phone."* Or, *"Shaks, dat ting bun mey han'."*

She duz wok' out—Not a reference to exercise, but that she has a job outside of the home; an expression barely uttered these days. In a historical context, opportunities for women were limited, the expression speaks to the fact that the woman was working in the public or private sphere. Of course, she also assumed the awesome responsibility of running the home. *"Gloria doan be home ah lot 'cause she duz wok out."*

She geh he bassidy (He geh ha bassidy*)—A reference to someone's erratic behavior caused by the fact that he/she is madly in love. *"John walkin' 'roun town` like he ain know way he goin. He guirlfrien' geh he bassidy."*

She/He Name— Certainly one of the Virgin Islands staple phrase because of how it functions with respect to expressing one's identity. *"Wa' she name?"* (What is her name?) Response: *"She name Luz."* In Virgin Islands Creole at times the personal pronouns are used in place of the possessive (This is discussed in more details under the section on **The Possessive**). But this is not simply a case of the possessive, it is more about a construction that is creolized. The statement *"Ah name Joan"* turns the English sentence, "My name is Joan," on its head. In the first place, in the Creole version there is the subject pronoun (Ah), instead of the actual possessive "my." But also there is no verb. A warning to the person unfamiliar with this structure: The sentence, *"He name Juan"* would not work if an actual possessive was substituted. In other words, "His name Juan" would not be an admissible Creole sentence.

Sheen (also used with "self")—This contraction is used for *she+ ain*. *"She home?"* Ans: *"No, sheen heh."* See also **"ain"** and **"Heen"** in earlier entries. Also meaning "even self." *"Sheen self know mey name."*

Sho'—Movies. Back in the 50's hardly anyone said *"We goin' toh deh movies."* Instead the expression was: *"We goin' sho."* This is a lost expression.

Shorty deh Zulu — Perennial carnival entry in the 50's and 60's; now part of Virgin Islands folklore, along with *"Koka deh Bear wid deh halfa ear."* A legendary folk hero well-beloved by Virgin Islanders in the 50's and 60's. Shorty brought so much joy to our community with his yearly commitment to carnival and his typical Zulu dancers and sounds.

Shub—This is yet another example of a word that has its own life. "To shove" in English is "to "push," but "to shove" does not capture the essence of the word; it does not resonate in Virgin Islands Creole. The word *"shub"* is creolized and universally expressed and understood in the U.S. Virgin Islands. *"He was lookin' fight an' so he shub me fus."*

Shut up—Closed. "*Deh shap shut up.*" The store is closed.

Sick foot—An expression that covers a wide variety of ailments, including but not limited to injuries and diseases. "*She carn walk good 'cause she geh ah sick foot. She fall down yestaday.*"

Side—Adjacent; next to. From beside. "*Si' down side meh.*"

Simpavivy—Virgin Islands word for aloe. This is a type of plant that has been a cure all for islanders for centuries. Its potency is still very much recognized and appreciated.

Sin John, Sin Croix, Sin Thomas—Even though the word Saint when used by itself would never be pronounced "Sin", that is the local pronunciation when referring to our islands. In other words, no one would say "*He is ah sin*" to mean "*He is a saint.*"; however: "*Eddie from <u>Sin</u> John, bu' he granmudda from <u>Sin</u> Croix. He geh cousin in <u>Sin</u> Thomas.*"

Sixteen-Seventy-One—This is placed here only because numbers are not alphabetized, the actual numeral is more compelling—**1671**. One of three designations for Fort Christian in St. Thomas, also called "**Deh Foat**" and "**Deh Red Wall.**" This imposing building sends profound messages of the history of the U.S. Virgin Islands.

Skinnin' up yoh face—A facial gesture that suggests the disapproval of something. But like some of the other gestures referenced before, children can be accused of being rude and disrespectful if they direct such a gesture toward an adult.

Skounch ova—Move over some more; I need some room here. "*Skounch ova ah lil' bit so evebardy cou fit.*"

Skounch up—For example, clothes that fit too tightly. "*It feel all skounch-up on me.*" "*It look so skounch-up an yoh, man.*" Other: "*Stap skounchin' up yoh face like dat.*"

Skrounch up—Similar to the previous expression; just another variation

Skylarkin'—Fooling around; clowning around. There are several usages of this expression. For example: "*He/she like to skylark too much, dat's why he ain' doin' good in school.*" (There could be serious consequences to this type of behavior.). Sometimes the word suggests physical contact: "*Yoh keep skylarkin' arl deh time, yoh make meh break deh glass.*"

"*Quit skylarkin', no*" (More of a playful reaction). But as shown in the first example it could be symbolic of a person's lack of seriousness.

Slingerin'—Staying away from home and going different places without permission. Often places where you do not belong. A translation of our word is the English "lingering." Mother to child: "*Yoh betta' stap slingerin' an' come straight home wen school done.*"

Slow up—Reduce speed, sometimes used instead of "slowin' down." But one has to be careful because these are not always necessarily interchangeable expressions. Note the following examples: "*Deh car in front keep slowin' up.*" This is the same as: "*Deh car in front keep slowin' down.*" However, the statement," *Mr. Ruben is gettin' ole, he really slowin' down*" <u>cannot</u> be rendered as: "*Mr. Ruben… he really slowin' up.*" Such an expression in Virgin Islands Creole would not be recognizable. This shows once again how usage depends on the context, and not just on the words themselves.

Smell ah—A reference to a smell that is pervasive, strong. "*Man dis place smell ah fish.*"

Smell dis—Often a child challenging another by telling him to "smell" (notice) his/her fists. "*Smell dis, smell dese.*" It was one of the first steps in the initiation of a fist fight. From the perspective of the 21st century, this may seem rather benign. Often the speaker had "*ah lot ah chat.*"

Smoke truck—Vehicle used in the 1950's and 60's to spray chemicals in order to reduce the infestation of mosquitos in the United States Virgin Islands. See earlier entry **Run behin' deh smoke (flit) truck.**

Snat—This refers to nasal mucous. "*Yoh geh snat in yoh nose. Wipe it.*"

So—Uniquely used to mean "like that," "like this," "in this manner." This can be rendered in many different ways. "*Stop ackin' so, man.*" "*Do it so.*" "*Do it like so.*"

The expression "**He duz go arn so,**" represents yet another usage of this word, in which the sentence suggests negative behavior. No need to add another word at the end; the sentence is self-sufficient. For example, Evelyn tells her friend, David: "*Ask yoh neighbor toh give us some mango, no.*" David's response: "*Not meh, meson, 'cause sometimes he duz go arn so.*"

So' foot—An expression that was used to refer to an injured or diseased foot or limb. "*Mr. Mikey geh ah so' foot. He need toh go doctor.*" As discussed earlier (Section on Grammar), this particular expression defies any logic because "foot" may in fact be referring to the person's leg. Notice here that the words "toh deh" before "doctor" is not necessary. (See Section on Prepositions.)

So help MEY (Gard/God)—At first glance one might assume this to be a "standard" English expression, but it is not. This saying has nuances in pronunciation that truly makes it special. The capitalization of MEY indicates that the stress is on that possessive. Following are some prime examples of how this popular expression is used, and has been used for many years:

"So help MEY Gard wen Ah see him, Ah gon pu' *'im in he place."*

"Ah don wid he, so help MEY Gard"

For many Virgin Islanders the expression is blasphemous. Some simply refer to it as "swearing," and hence children are culturally forbidden from using such an utterance,

Soak ah—Indicates something done with some degree of intensity. *"Deh darg soak' ah bite in meh."*

Soak deh cloth in bay rum an' tie up yoh head—A typical remedy to stop headaches, treat fever etc., the same magic as the macuricome. Said with less frequency now.

Sofy—Referring to the texture of something; but metaphorically, it means easy to control; kind to a fault; based on the English word "soft" but clearly a word that has taken on a life of its own. *"Dis pillow feel so sofy, Ah carn sleep."* But also, *"Yoh cou' do wa' yoh wan' wid he 'cause he so sofy."*

Somebardy do sometin' toh he/she—A reference to the occult, to obeah. One of those once popular sayings that people say less frequently these days because no one wants to admit that he/she adheres to such beliefs. *"She ackin so strange; somebardy mus' Ah do sometin toh she."*

Sometimish—Moody, somewhat unpredictable. *"Pedro duz tark to yoh wen he wan'; he too sometimish."*

Sometin' in deh mata' beside deh pestle—Something else is happening that we are not addressing.

Sometin' toh—A relative. *"He is sometin' toh we."* For example, the person may be a cousin.

Soon ripe soon rotten, soon forgotten—An expression used to suggest dire consequences when someone tries to act beyond his or her age. (See **"force ripe"** earlier in the listing)

Soon tell—To be aware of something, and to emphatically state this: *"Ah cou' soon tell dat she wasn' feelin' good."*

Sorey—A reference to a sore or sores on one's body, often used in a kind of derisive manner. **"*He geh arl kin ah ting on he skin, he so sorey.*"**

Souce—Pork fairly spicey and often cooked and served with potato salad.

Soul—This word was once used frequently in two different contexts, one of which has been virtually in disuse: 1) *"Man, dat's mey soul."* The speaker has an intimate connection with or affection for the individual. 2) Not ah soul— This second expression is translated as "no one or nobody." It is used for emphasis and always in the negative. *"Not ah soul wake me up wen Ah go in mey bed."* // *"I ain talk toh ah soul arl day today. Ah ben heh by meyself."* Interestingly enough, it is generally not used affirmatively in this context. For example, we do not say: *"Yestaday, ah speak toh ah soul."* Also the expression *"in her/he/yoh soul"*—Example: *"He geh one lick in he soul."*

Sou'sap—A creolization of the fruit soursap. Without doubt one of the favorite fruits of the Virgin Islands.

Spall de pot (cup)/ spal up—An expression used for example if the enamel was damaged; *"Doan drop da pot 'cause yoh gon spall it up."* // *"Man, Ah doan wan' toh drink out dis cup, it arl spall up."* This is an expression that is no longer heard frequently.

Spanish—*Ah Spanish*, (with emphasis on the last syllable) was a type of kite, constructed out of paper. Those who were the best at constructing this type of kite had a good grasp of aerodynamics, even if they did not know that they did.

Spanish Town—*[Virgin Gorda]* *"Dey from Spanish Town."* Today almost everyone refers to our sister island as Virgin Gorda. There was a time in the last century when many people used the expression, "Spanish Town." My mother, who grew up on Virgin Gorda, once told me: *"Ah 'memba wen eveybardy use toh say 'Spanish Town.'"*

Speakin' calypso—An imposed designation that was used to characterize the manner in which Virgin Islanders speak. There was always something about this characterization that made me uneasy. These days the expression is not heard as much. The designation of our speech as "Virgin Islands Creole" is not only more palatable, but more accurate, even though still rejected by some.

Special—Fortunately virtually everyone in the Virgin Islands is familiar with this word; in this case used only as a noun. Residents loved (and still love) this frozen delicacy. The bold underline indicates that the stress of the word is generally on the last syllable. In St. Croix, **Lindy**

SPECIAL SOUNDS**: These are not really words but sounds made in our islands to express series of impressions, reaction etc.

****Ah ha**— The stress is what really counts here. The stress sometimes is on the first word, other times on the second. This expression is used to express various modes of thought. For example, a person may say it to express surprise after receiving some news. *"She jus' lose her house."* Reaction: *"Ah ha! I didn' know dat."* The speaker is expressing surprise. Also, *"Ah ha, Ah forget toh bring deh money." "Ah ha, look wa Ah do, no. Ah put on deh wrang shoes."*

****Ay ya yay!**—Oral expression in response to pain (also used in Spanish); or a sigh. Sometimes one would hear something like *"Ay ya yay, man, yoh mashin' on mey toe;"* or even the sounds repeated up to five times: *"Ay ya yai ay yay."* It does not work if it is uttered less than three or more than five times. Again, it is only by language consensus that we would know this.

*****Oh yo' yoy***!—A sigh, often used when somewhere is tired; at times used as an alternate expression of pain in place of *"ay ya yay." "Oh yo' yoy, lemme si' down heh ah wile,* Ah so *tired."* Often heard after a yawn (or sometimes when the individual stretches) followed by such expressions as *"I so sleepy."*

—**The sound that results from "suckin' yoh teet,' an expression that is described later in this entry. Some would find it unbelievable that this is not a natural sound, but a learned one. In Virgin Islands culture it is taken for granted that everyone can produce the sound, but I have learned over the years that many outside of the African or West Indian cultures have a difficult time imitating this sound. The sound suggests disapproval, disgust, anger, disappointment etc. See explanation in entry under *"Suckin' (up) yoh teet."* Often times this gesture is considered rude and disrespectful. Yet, at other times it is an interjection that suggests something humorous. For example, when the sound precedes an expression such as *"he so funny."*

Cha-cha-cha—This does not refer to the famous dance that originated in Cuba. This is a sound of disgust upon seeing or smelling something repulsive: *"Cha-cha-cha, wa' smell so bad, man?"* [A variant of **chi-chi-cha**, later entry]. Not an expression with which many younger residents would be familiar.

Chi chi cha—A sound made as a reaction to something that is nasty or repulsive. *"Chi-chi-cha, look ah dat dead rat."* Interestingly, as popular as this impression once was, it was primarily the language of children. [A variant **of cha-cha-cha**]. Probably now mainly familiar in circle of older island residents.

Eh eh—A popular interjection of all our Virgin Islands, even though in St. Croix the emphasis is slightly different, with a sharper inflection at the end. Expresses surprise, *"Eh eh, Ah ain know he garn states."* At times the expression is said by itself as a response. Speaker 1: *"Ah hea' Marlene jus' geh married."* Speaker II: *"Eh eh!"* Depending on the inflection and the tone of voice of Speaker II, the listener would be able to determine disapproval, surprise, sarcasm.

Hay—This is the expression that is often used when giving something to someone, meaning "take." It is ALWAYS said with the gesture of the hand. Pauline to her child: *"Hay, put dis on deh table."* Even though it may sound logical, one cannot say *"Hay dis"* to mean *"Take this."* *"Ok, hay, go wid it, bu' doan foget toh bring it back nex' week."* This is one of those words that stands by itself. *"Hay"* is understand to mean, *"Take this."*

==

Specially—Popular shortened form used for "especially."

Squeeze he gundy—How to stop a crab from biting you, supposedly a sign of one's cultural IQ.

Squeeze up—An expression used to refer to one's physical stature, or limited space. *"He so tin; he look so squeeze up."* *"Dis room so small and squeeze-up."* In addition, we see it used with respect to one's clothes: *"He look so squeeze up in dem clothes."* The outfit does not fit the individual well.

Stale drunk—Still displaying the effects of being drunk; still not sober. *"Look 'im, no; he still ain walkin' straight. He mus' be stale drunk."*

Stan'—To desire something. *"I cou' stan' ah good piece ah fry fish now."*

Stan' fo'—A once popular expression which carried very serious implications because someone agrees to be the godparent of a newborn. *"She is mey godmudda'. She stan' fo' meh wen Ah geh crisen."*

State—A bad condition. *"Dis house in ah state."* The house is particularly dirty/messy. Probably comes from "a state of confusion."

States—This is a very popular expression used to refer to the United States mainland. At one point it *almost always* meant "New York city." These days the statement, "<u>Ah goin' States nex' week</u>" would evoke the question, "**Wich one yoh goin' to?**" In order words, because now people travel to just about every state, more clarity is needed. These days the word could be referring to any of the contiguous state. Included in the idea of "states" is Washington D.C.; excluded are Hawaii and Alaska.

Stew' tarmon—A Virgin Islands delicacy among a long list of other cherished creations: among them Stew' mango and Stew' cherry. A syrup resulting principally from the fruit "tarmon," combining water and sugar. The stew converts a "bitter-sweet fruit" into a mouth-watering culinary treasure.

Stick ah fiah—Quickly, very fast. *"He come, an' leave like ah stick ah fiah."*

Stick up—In one place, most notably in a house, and not coming out frequently enough in the judgment of others: *"Darwin, come out an' play, no, yoh always stick-up in deh house."*

Sting'ah nettle bite meh—It would be very rare for islanders to feel the sting of that plant these days. No doubt, though, everyone is familiar with this thorn than can cause irritation, discomfort, and actual pain. *"Ah sting'ah nettle grab arn toh meh. Ah still in pain."*

Stink ah—Smells like. *"He stink ah rum."* In the Virgin Islands this means one can smell the rum coming from his pores.

Stoppage ah wata—Once a reference to a condition, a likely reference to the prostate; for example a blockage.

Strenk—Strength. This is another case of a word that even if we concede that it results from the mispronunciation of the English word is nonetheless and independent Creole word. *"Mabel geh some strenk. She lif up dat heavy rock-stone."*

Strumoo—Trouble, confusion, popular expression: *"Watah strumoo!"*

Study yoh head—Literally pay attention to what your mind is telling you. In other words, think. *"Look, befo' yoh make dat decision, yoh betta' study yoh head."*

Stuiepid bush—Symbolic; *"You maybe eat stuiepid bush"*—you are talking nonsense.

Stuiepid idiot—A very common, often heard phrase. This hyperbolic combination of negativity speaks for itself.

Stuiepidy—Used to describe a person or persons negatively or even in a lighthearted manner among friends. It can be an adverb or adjective: *"He duz act so stuiepidy." "He such a stuiepidy man." "Move from meh, yoh stieupidy self."* When used with the word "feel," the meaning changes and the sense of the word changes to mean "strange" or "weird." *"Man, ah eat so much Ah feel stuiepidy."* It is a vague usage that suggests a general malaise.

Stuiepiness/stuiepidness—In the Virgin Islands this word is stated with impunity. It is one of the very popular Virgin Islands words that in all probability will never disappear. Used in infinite contexts in the U.S.V.I. A word with its own life!

Very common are: *"Bunch ah stuiepiness," "Stop tarkin' stuiepiness," "Ah neva' hea' mo' stuiepiness." "Aways doin' stuiepiness." "Full ah stuiepiness." "He cou' tark some stuiepiness."* It is used in so many contexts that it would be impossible to capture all of them here, but it is important to note that the mood of the utterance may vary drastically according to voice inflection and intonation. In each of the examples cited here the situation may well be referring to something very light hearted, or its opposite. In other words, the statement, *"Boy he cou' tark some stuiepiness"* is not necessarily negative. It may very well be complimentary of the individual's comedic skills.

Such ah look—To look at firmly and scornfully or with some sense of disgust, or to give a subtle warning. *"Deh chile was ackin' up. Boy I give she such ah luck. She behave right away."*

Such ah one—This means "such as." It expresses real particularity about person. *"I neva' meet such ah one like he yet."*

Suck finga' La La—Refers to someone who sucks his or her finger, teasing gesture, the language of children. *"She is ah suck finga' La La."*

Suckin' (up) yoh teet—This is a sound that is difficult to make by those who are outside of the linguistic community. Very often considered one of the most disrespectful gestures; an especially socio-cultural code violation if done by a child in front of an adult; a close equivalent to cursing. But its usage is much more extensive, impossible to be all captured here. However, a person might do this, in a more lighthearted manner, as an introductory to something that she or he is going to say. Often it is a response of sheer defiance that stands by itself. *"He say he gon hit yoh."* **Response**: the sound of *"suckin' yoh teet,"* followed by: *"Yoh tink I fraid ah he?"* Often when the sound is more prolonged, that is an indication of more disapproval.

Suga'- In context, this refers to diabetes. *"He ain doin so good. Ah tink he geh suga'."*

Suppose toh be some kin ah family—The person is in fact my family!

Swatsy—A pejorative word use to describe someone who is considered to be "overweight." The description of an individual using this adjective can never be deemed to be complimentary under any circumstances.

Sweep deh yard—The circular or rectangular yard with its signature well was kept clean by residents who swept them regularly with a special "yard broom." The surface was often dirt. It is still possible to see this, but the changed architectural contours of the islands have made this a less common sight.

Sweet bread—Both the name and the product are unique. Certainly this is not a bread in the traditional sense of the word. This Virgin Islands delicacy looks more like pastry, with its nuts and fruits. Mention Christmas in the Virgin Islands and this culinary specialty will be at the top of the list.

Sweet eye—An expression that suggested a kind of intimate suggestion. Once popular this is likely more confined to older residents who would understand its contextual usage. *"Doan come givin' meh sweet eye. Ah still doan like yoh."*

Tain—Means it is not. Example: *"Tain' da, man."* "It is not that." *"Ah don tell yoh, 'tain he."*

Tain from larng (From larng)—A long time ago. *"From larng ah tell 'im toh fix da ting an he still ain do it."* Also the expression suggests that the individual was being advised or told about something consistently over a period of time. In other words, *"I have been telling him/her over a protracted time period."*

Tain' now ah…—Popular introductory. *"Tain' now Ah tell 'im clean deh place. Ah 'ain know wen he gon do it?"* (See also **"Tis now?"** later in this section). The general meaning is that this is not the first time that the person was informed, advised, or warned.

Take in—To become ill. The expression is generally used in unexpected situations. *"Ah wus tarkin' toh her den wen look she jus' take in so."*

Take yoh toh Michael—In St. Thomas this was a very popular saying often uttered if a person was threatening to bring charges against another. Cyril Michael (1898-1978) was a folksy, well-respected St. Thomas judge whose name was synonymous with St. Thomas courts in the 50's. Every one living in St. Thomas and St. John knew exactly how to translate the threat.

Tambran—Popularly used in St. Croix for "Tamarind," "tarmon" in St.Thomas and St. John.

Tantie—Often used in place of the word aunt, but also used in reference to a neighbor or family friend whom children must address with respect. In many ways it can be considered a term of endearment.

Tarmon—*Tamarind* is the English word. Our word is clearly a distinct and equally valuable denomination of a very important fruit still popular in all of the islands. The notion of *tamarind stew* seems rather unhinged from Virgin Islands culture; "tarmon stew" is the appropriate local phrase.

Tart—Creole word used for the variety of local "torts." Among the variety of delicacies: pineapple, guava, guavaberry, coconut. *"Ah love mey guava tart."*

Tase' yoh (he / ha') han'—The expression alludes to a person culinary skills. It is a phrase that tends to be lighthearted. *"Man Ah hea' yoh is ah good cook, but I neva' tase' yoh han' atarl."*

Tatalo // Totola—-The U.S. Virgin Islands Creolized pronunciation of our neighboring island, Tortola with whom we share an unbreakable bond—we are really one people!

Tea—This is not a drink defined in the limited way as it is in the United States. It is always confusing to a visitor when someone speaks of *"cocoa tea,"* or *"milk tea,"* both of which are referenced in this list of entries.

Tee tee—Creole word for breast.

Teifin'—Used as verb or gerund/ participle; stealing. *"Yoh geh toh be careful 'cause he aways teifin people ting."*

Tell arf—To let someone know in no uncertain terms what you feel. *"Boy, she was mad wid me, she had me well tell arf."*

Tell cow howdy—Used for excessive talking. *"Yoh duz talk so much, yoh cou' tell cow howdy."*

Tell 'im (ha'/yoh) 'bout heself—An expression which, as in typical Creole form, can be present, future or past. It is a response to someone, "to put that person in his/her place" for having said or done something objectionable. *"He come tell meh forwardness. Well, ah had toh tell 'im 'bout heself."*

Tesik—Reference to a general respiratory condition that is highlighted by a pronounced coughing spell. *"Wa wrang wid da one de, he coughin' so; he mus' be geh deh tesik."*

Tie' tongue —A reference to a speech impediment; this is often uttered in a negative way. *"Ha tongue tie self."*

Tie up mey mout—give your mouth a tart taste. *"Ah carn eat dat cashew, it dus tie up mey mout."*

Tightin' yoh (meh) up—An old expression meaning a person is going to give money to another person; at times it referred to money owed, a repayment of a loan. Example: Leroy sees Conroy and asks. *"How 'bout deh ting, man."* Conroy: *"Ah gehin' pay Friday, an' Ah gon tightin yoh up."* Definitely an expression that is virtually lost, except to an older generation of Virgin Islanders.

Tin nin—A noun, the English translation is "galvanize." *"Deh man dem pu' tin-nin on deh roof toh stop deh wata from comin in deh house."* This material was also used extensively for baking bread on a coal pot. Bread done with this accessory could not taste better! Bread baked in the oven these days can never recapture the special taste of that done with the aid of the "tin nin."

Ting —A versatile expression; varied utility of the word "ting" in the language. *"He so ting up."* In this case it may be a reference to a person who does not have a good attitude. The listener of this expression as part of the consensus community of the language somehow understands what the speaker is intuiting. *"Ah gon try ah lil' ting"*—a useful expression meaning that the person will do something; there is really no lack of confidence here, in spite of the word "try." I am fascinated by the flexibility of this word usage. Consider the hypothetical conversation: *"Wa' yoh doin' meson?* // Ans: *"Man, Ah heh tryin' toh ting dis ting."* No amount of English mastery would enable a listener outside this community of language to follow such a conversation. Who outside would understand: *"We jus' heh tingin' "?* Consider the following conversation between a parent and child: *"Mommy, deh aspirin yoh gimme 'ain helpin' meh."* **Response**: *"Doan' worry chile, it gon ting' soon."* The members of the community of language know exactly how to interpret the parent's response without asking: *"wa' yoh mean?"*

There are many other expressions that include this elastic word: such as "*Wattah ting!*" This is an exclamation that can be used to express grief or happiness: "*Wattah ting! Ah feel sorry fo' deh family.*" "*Watta ting! Tina win so much money.*" And the popular, "*He/She like toh be in ting*" in reference to someone who likes to be involved, even when the person is not welcomed. Finally, in this non-exhaustive list, "*Da ting crazy, yoh hea.*'"—a reference to person, often said in a light-hearted manner.

Ting in yoh eye—Usually a reference to mucous, "yampy" (see this entry later).

Ting toh eat—Food. "*Ah lookin' ting toh eat. Ah so hungry.*"

Ting wid you/yoh—This expression deserves its own category. It is used when there is an indication that something unusual is happening to the person; in general, it deserves praise. Seen as a kind of deviation from the norm, but generally positive. "*Ah hea' how yoh wokin' Government House now. Man, tis ting wid you. Keep it up.*" At times there is a kind of satirical utterance, especially if the individual in question is showing some kind of exaggeration. "*Yoh dress toh kill. Tis ting wid you.*"

Tink it (so) hard—Is not inclined to do something. "*I tink it hard toh go out tonight.*" It expresses a reluctance to engage in some activity for whatever reason. "*It look like yoh tink it (so) hard toh call meh.*"

Tis+ an adjective repeated for extra effect—Always in the form of a question: "*Tis lazy he lazy so?*" "*Tis stuiepid yoh stupid so?*" In fact, the speaker is not really asking a question, but is affirming his or her position. The question is rhetorical.

Tis now?—In the form of a question. "*Tis now Ah tell 'im toh clean deh place?*" The expression is similar to one given earlier: "*Tain now Ah tell 'im toh clean...*" One major difference is that one is a question. Also consider the follow: Speaker I: "*You fix deh ting?*"

Speaker II: "*Tain now!*" or "*Tis now?*" Translation: "*I have done it a long time ago.*"

Tis woman (man) yoh tink yoh is?—Generally speaking, a rebuke of a child, or adolescent by a parent, or another adult. It is a reminder to the child that he or she is NOT an adult. "*Yoh carn be comin' home wen yoh feel like. Tis woman (man) yoh tink yoh is?*"

Tis...yoh say, yoh know- -*In the first place "tis" is used in place of the English* contraction, "It's." The expression itself is quite special as exemplified by the following example: Ruben to a friend: *"You have ah $100 yoh cou' give me*h?" Friend: *"Tis ah 100 yoh say, yoh know."* The implication is that the friend does not have that amount of money to give to Ruben. Clearly, a playful, satirical response.

Tol' mundo—From the Spanish *"todo el mundo"*; everyone. This expression originating from Spanish fuses several words together. Example of its usage: *"Out out, tol' mundo."* This was once a frequent expression. Even though it has not disappeared, it is more likely heard only among older citizens of our community. *"Wen dey see deh Green Face Man walkin' toward dem tol' mundo take arf."*

Tomian—Someone from Saint Thomas, an expression that never sat quite well with most residents who prefer the term St. Thomian. *"She ain no Crucian; she is ah Tomian."*

Touchin up (see feelin' up)—Unwarranted touch or excessive or exaggerated touching. *"Stop touchin' meh up." "Stap touchin' up deh ting people gatoh eat."*

Toul mon'— From the French meaning "tout le monde." *"Ah yoh geh outta heh right now, toul mon."* A variation of the entry above, **Tol' mundo**. Virtually lost expression.

Two ba'wod unda'—To curse someone in an emphatic manner. *"She was so mad. She put two ba'wod unda' im."*

Tra la la—Confusion. *"Yoh jus' tarkin' ah bunch ah tra la la."*

Tramp—Dancing in the streets, especially during carnival or festivals on any of our three islands. The word can be used in multiple forms: Noun *"Deh tramp comin' up de road."* Participle: *"Deh wuz trampin' las' night."* Active verb: *"Yoh gon tramp lata'?"*

Trash (out) deh nut—Open the coconut. As children picking coconut we did not travel with machetes. We relied on our ability to *"trash (out) deh nut,"* in order to open it. For example, hit it against the ground, or *"ah big rock-stone."*

Trow down—To take in excess, used specifically for eating and drinking. *"Da man de cou' trow' down some food, meson."*

Trow someting on yoh boy (guirl) de, no—It is important to note the fact that "the boy" or "guirl" is very likely an adult speaking. The speaker is telling someone, with whom he or she is most likely familiar (but not necessarily) to spare some change, give some money: "*Deano, Ah know yoh geh pay today. Trow someting on yoh boy de, no.*"

Trowin words—Cussin,' carryin' on, talking through inferences. "*She outside trowin' words. Ah donno wa' she tarkin' 'bout.*"

Trus'—A type of folksy system of commercial credit: "*Ask Mr. Denton if he cou' trus meh ah poung ah lard.*" Very often these store owners, Denton, Davis etc. did not write anything down; I have seen this custom continued at a few select small "community" stores. With the dwindling of these small venues, the concept has also faded.

Tudoo—A happening function, often used with adjectives, like big. "*Man ah hea' how yoh had a big tudoo las' night. Yoh even ain invite meh.*"

Tump—Fist. "*Ah gon bus 'im ah tump.*"

Tun' foot—This could refer to a sprain or a permanent injury or natural condition. "*He geh ah tun foot.*" "*Ah wuz walkin', step on ah rock an' tun mey foot.*"

Tun 'im loose—To get rid of someone, as in a personal or work relationship. "*Man da good fo' notin' woan look wok. Ah had toh tun 'im loose.*" Or, "*She keep comin' late toh wok, Ah had toh tun she loose.*"

Tun loose—To release, but also used in a figurative sense, as to suggest an exaggerated action. "*Wen he tun loose nobardy cou' stop 'im.*"

Tun meh ('im/ ha/ dem) crazy—An expression which is roughly equivalent to the English notion of "driving someone crazy." "*Man, ah yoh stap de noise, ah yoh tunnin' meh crazy.*"

Tun 'roun (so/too) slow—The person moves slowly. "*Hurry up, man, yoh duz 'tun 'roun too slow.*"

Tun' up—Over turn, turn over as in an accident, to flip over, to spill. "*Ah wata truck tun' up goin' from Cruz be toh Coral Bay. Arl deh wata run out.*"

Tun' up deh stove—This is asking someone to making the flames higher. "*Tun up deh stove; deh meat cookin' so slow.*"

Tun' up yoh face—Contort the face generally in an expression of dissatisfaction. "*Look no, stop tunnin' up yoh face like dat. Yoh gon do wa Ah tell yoh toh do.*"

Tunchie—A measurement used in a general sense. "*Not much, jus' ah lil tunchie.*" Interesting how the word itself suggests a small amount, but is still often accompanied with "*lil.*" In this sense it is similar to "niapa" also often preceded by "lil." They are both redundant expressions, part of the vibrancy of the language. Not heard so much these days.

Twin City—A reference to St. Croix, particular allusion to Frederiksted in the West and Christiansted in the East.

Two-cent—Often used to represent an unspecified amount of money. Interestingly, the stress is frequently on the first word. *"Ah geh mey TWO-cent in deh bank toh bury meh."*

Two two's—Quickly. *"Look, wait fo' meh, man, Ah gon be ready in two twos."* The speaker is conveying that she/he will be ready right away, that the friend will not have to wait long.

Undah ah root—Generally lighthearted expression; to tease. *"We had he undah ah root, meson."* This means that we were teasing him constantly.

Undah deh Bongolo—This venerable site at Market Square in St. Thomas was not only a lively place of business—fruits, fish, local candies, etc.—but one of the focal points for socialization. The expressions, *"Meet meh undah Bongolo,"* or *"Ah gon wait fo' yoh undah deh Bongolo"* are no longer understood by everyone on St. Thomas. Clearly, the center of commercial activity in St. Thomas has not only shifted, but there are now multiple "markets." This radical transformation has taken with itself the language associated with the Market Square in its heyday.

Undah deh house—Popular expression when wooden houses were very popular in the architectural landscape.

Untrut'—Children were (and still are) discouraged from using the word "lie" which in the opinion of adults was an inappropriate expression for them. The children would be considered rude. Hence such expressions as *"Yoh untrut"* and *"He duz untrut' too much"* not only have survived but remain popular. *"Yoh lie"* or *"Yoh duz lie too much"* are reserved for conversations between adults, or a one-way accusation—a parent to a child.

Up—This is a very elastic adverb that functions as a special suffix to intensify or exaggerate a situation or a description of a person. It is in some ways a very illusive suffix that it would take quite a while to dominate. In Virgin Islands Creole, for example, one can say the following: *"funny-up"* (difficult to please, unpredictable); or *"Man, dis ting arl twis-up."* Some people may very well say: *"Yoh know'im man. He iz ah strong-up man,"* a reference to the physical size of the person. This is not universally said, but is often heard, and universally understood. Imagine the challenge for the uninitiated. *"Dem good fo' notin' kick-up deh man."* Interestingly enough, no one would say *"strange-up,"* *"nice-up,"* nor *"stupid-up."* However, one can hear *"Man, he arl sweet-up,"* a reference to how the person smells, for example if the person has put on cologne or perfume. Given a list, Virgin Islanders would know instinctively whether or not the addition of the prefix "up" would be permitted.

Up an' down deh place—This expression can best be seen as a kind of preface to a description of the behavior of a person. It is truly a very prevalent island expression. In the Virgin Islands its special nature lies in the fact that there is no generation gap with its usage. The expression, *"She up an' down deh place helpin' people"* is not incorrect, however, neither is it as common as the negative. More natural would be *"She up an' down deh place causin' trouble."*

Up deh road (down deh road)—Old expressions once used to indicate that someone was leaving. *"OK, Ah goin' up de road now."*

Us Crime—An expression once used to avoid the blasphemous enunciation of *Jesus Christ* uttered "in vain;" the moral imperative is not to disobey the third Commandment. It is a fading expression probably used only by a few nostalgic individuals!

Valise—Once popularly used in the Virgin Islands for suitcases of all sorts without distinction. It was a direct substitute for the word "suitcase." *"Ah yoh pu' deh ting dem in deh valise. We have toh leave soon."* Not used today.

Vex—Anger, frustration, to be fed up with someone or a situation. *"I so vex wid he, Ah even doan wan' toh see 'im."*

Wa become ah he/ha/yoh?— Rather than emphasizing the verb "become," I have chosen the entire expression for its unique usage. It is used in an unconventional sense, roughly equivalent to "How is"? or "How are?" *"Wa become ah yoh mudda?* Res: *"She good. She jus' retire."* Also, often used when a person has not seen another in a long time. Basically, what has happened to,,,? *"Wa become ah yoh, man, ah carn see yoh atarl.* What has happened to the person? —-with the stress on the infrequency of contact. *"Wa become ah he chiren dem?* Meaning, how are they doing?

Wa' cat duz play wid darg duz wan'—If you don't think that something is important or useful, someone else will avail herself or himself of it.

Wa doan kill duz fatten—Generally speaking, what does not kill or harm you will make you strong. Very often children would say this if they drop a candy, for example, and then decided to eat it. If the candy does not cause any harm, then it should give benefits. At least that is the logic of the statement. Dorothy: *"Carly, doan eat da ting. It full ah dut."* Carly: *"You cou' stay de. Wa doan kill duz fatten."*

Wa he look like?—This is not asking for an answer to what seems a routine question but rhetorically is affirming that someone does not look good. *"Bu' wa he look like atarl wid dat ole hat?"* Often it is a reference to a person's features, but also a reference to how the person is dressed. Often one can hear: *"Ah doan know wa he look like atarl."*

Wa' She (He) Name—Used often even at times if the speaker knows the name of the person. *"Ah tink she is Wa' He Name daughta.... son."* // *"You tink Ah ain see yoh walkin' wid Wa She Name yestaday, no?"*

Wa' tis dis!—This is never ever a question in the language of the Virgin Islands. It is more of an interjection that people use to express surprise, disappointment. The intonation of the voice can radically alter the interpretation of what the speaker is saying: *"Wa' tis dis! Ah carn' believe wa' yoh tellin' meh."* *"Wa' tis dis, man, ah you stap deh noise."* Sometimes it is the only reaction after receiving some kind of news: *"Wa' tis dis!"* Still a popular Virgin Islands expression.

Wa yoh buy yoh duz wear—You brought this problem on yourself. You are responsible for this situation and the consequences. So now don't look for someone else to resolve it. The inference is always that the person failed to heed advice. *"Yoh ain wan' toh listen toh wa Ah tellin yoh, bu' wa yoh buy yoh duz wear."* The warning is clear.

Wa' yoh sayin'?/ Wa' yoh sayin' fo yohself? Sometimes a greeting, but also a reaction to a comment, indicating surprise, or disbelief. For the uninitiated this could be tricky; so if a person addresses you in this manner, you can consider it the same as *"How are you?"* Paco: *"Wa' yoh sayin', man?"* Ruben: *"Man, I awright."*

Wa' yoh sayin!—A secondary usage of this expression is to express surprise or disbelief after hearing a comment. "Carolyn says: *"Meh sista' Daphne jus' buy ah bran' new car."* Myron reacts: *"Wa' yoh sayin!"* In this case it is not a question, but rather an exclamation, of surprise, happiness.

Wack—This old word was often used to refer to the idea of quantity, but in the sense of "a lot of something." A popular statement was: *"Dat's ah wack ah nonsense."*

Wail he tail/ he hide— Corporal punishment. *"He too disgustin'. Ah go wail he tail wen he geh home."*

Walkin' Stick—Once used to refer to a cane. *"He carn see too good; he need ah walkin' stick toh geh aroun."*

Walk on yoh/ on people—An expression often used to express an individual's sense of self-importance; or his or her lack of friendliness or general manners. *"He duz jus' see yoh an' walk on yoh widdout even sayin' hello."* Often this can have consequence, for example, for a politician. *"I will nevar vote fo' he. He duz jus' walk on people widdout sayin' 'marnin.'"*

Wall house—Concrete house; an expression used back when most people mainly saw wooden houses. With the proliferation of concrete buildings the expression is much less frequent, but still used. *"Dey doan' live in a wood house; dey live in a big wall house."*

Wash arf befo' ah yoh go in ah yoh bed—Since at one time there was no running water in many areas, one was often told to wash his/her feet in a basin— *"Wash arf dem dutty foot."*

Wash mey han' from—No one wants to hear a mother say this: *"Ah wash' mey han' from he."* Unquestionably this has Biblical roots; it is to disown a child, for his/her disrespectful behavior toward the parent. It also can refer to other types of relationships. Symbolically, it is a very powerful sign of the ultimate disassociation.

Wash out—An expression that could refer to an individual, or to the clothes that the person is wearing. *"How come she look so wash out? She need toh iron dem clothes."* *"Da man doan take care ah heself atarl. He look so wash out."*

Wash out yoh mout' wid soap—Was literally done often to children who were disrespectful, especially to parents, or for those who would curse. Children who cursed were often told by adults: *"Yoh need toh wash out yoh mout' wid soap;"* in this case more of a symbolic statement to condemn the "forwardness" or "freshness" of the child.

Wash up—In the Virgin Islands this generally means—"to wash dishes" without ever mentioning the word "dishes." *"Who gon wash up?"* Ans: *"Not me, I wash up yestaday. Tis Shirlene turn."*

Watch ah joke—Roughly translated, "see what happens" or, simply "look." But this phrase is really a flexible one used in a variety of contexts.

Example: "*Watch ah joke wen he come; he gon start cryin.*" Another example: "*Watch ah joke, no, look who comin'.*"

Watch it—Get out the way. "*Watch it, Ah wan' toh pass.*"

Watch out—Look out; be careful. "*Watch out fo' de ca' dem.*"

Watch out deh way—A command to move out of the way. "*Ah yoh watch out deh way. Ah wan' toh pass.*" (See the earlier entry: "**Look out deh way.**")

Watch yohself—Be careful/ also move out the way. "*Meson watch yohself befo dis ting hit yoh.*"

Wat's deh que pasa?—What is happening?—once used as a greeting, combining English with the influence from Puerto Rico. In Spanish, "¿Qué pasa?" "¿Qué te (le) pasa?" It would be rare to hear this these days, except among a select group of elderly residents.

Wattah crass fo' me— Also "*Wa crass dis is fo; me?*" The reference is to the religious symbol, "cross," and speaks to a particular burden or challenge that a person has. A variation is "*Wa crass I/ Ah hearin'.*" This is the more intriguing expression since the "cross" metaphor presents a mixed structure. Clearly one cannot "hear" a cross, but as we know no language survives merely on logic, but repetitive usage, unusual or not. Still a very popular expression.

Ween (also with "self")—Contraction of "We+ain". For example: "*Ween goin' wid dem.*" Used as a contraction for "even". "*Ween self know dem.*"

Well—*Very.* "*He well stuiepid.*" This is similar to the earlier entry "good" and grammatically functions in a similar way—"*He good stuiepid.*" They are not totally interchangeable, however. The expression, "*She well happy dis marnin*" does not convey the same meaning as "*She good happy dis marnin.*" The first case expresses a kind of surprise, or sometimes is said in a probing tone; or often in a sarcastic manner, sometimes in a suspicious way. "*He look well tired.*" (I am wondering what he was doing.). As is the case with many of our expressions there are at times contradictory combinations, as in the sentence "*He well sick.*" This is a statement that on its face seems nonsensical, but it expresses the view that the individual *is "very sick."*

Well Mey God—Expresses surprise, shock, disappointment, anger. "*Well mey God, look how da lil' chile almos' geh run down.*" Often seen as a blasphemous expression.

Well Mey Peace—There are two prominent expressions used with the word "peace": "*Well mey peace!*" and "*Well my peace!*" These expressions are used to express surprise, sorrow, or, ironically, joy. After receiving bad news a person may use either of these expressions: "*Well mey peace, deh boy almos' bun up heself.*" But you will also hear the expressions in situations that are not at all dire, or serious: "*Well mey peace; me'ain expect toh see you heh. Watta ah good suprise!*"

Wen fowl geh teet'—Whatever you are hoping for is not going to happen anytime soon. In the Virgin Islands when you are told this, there is not much probability that you will get your wish. Lionel: "*Wen yoh gon len meh yoh bike?*" Caba's response: "*Wen fowl geh teet.*" Still uttered, recognized throughout our three islands.

Wen look— (also **Wen yoh look**) used in narrating. "*I was minin' mey own business, wen look dis ca' almost run meh down.*" But this expression is also used to explain why someone would not do something in particular: "*Ah ain' goin' toh ha' house cause wen look deh people dem start tarkin' 'bout meh.*"

Wen yoh doan see me, expec' meh—I am going to come at some point.

Wen(t) sleep—to fall asleep. "*Wa time yoh wen(t)'sleep las' night?*"

Went toh call (or other verbs)—An utterance used to express the fact that the person made a mistake. Example: "*Sorry, Ah went toh call Luis, not you.*"

Wes'—In St. Thomas this is generally a reference to locations west of the Cyril King airport. In St. Croix, Frederiksted. "*Ah goin Wes now.*"

Wey—Where.

Wey (da) deh one fo' me (yoh)?—An expression often used to asked about someone's friend or companion (See the section on grammar under "Present Tense and Subject and Object Pronouns). Generally, there is a tone of endearment: "*Wey da (da) one fo' you?*" "*Wey da one fo' me? Wey he fo' me?*"

Wey he?—Used when the subject is understood. "*Ah hea' somebardy mention John name. Bu' wey he atarl?*" In other words, what ever became of John? Not necessarily where is he at the moment of the question. Intonation and inflection determine the meaning of this expression and its various nuances.

Wey he (she) de?—This expression means *"Where is he?"* *"Way he de? Ah wan' toh see 'e bad."*

Wey pa'—*"Wey pa 'yoh goin'?"* Translation: *"Where are you going?"*

Wey pa' yoh fin' he/she?—Sometimes in a lighthearted manner a person might use this expression to comment on someone not seen for a while: *"Wey pa' you fin(d) he, meson?* Or often for someone being introduced for the first time as a friend or a partner. For example, someone might whisper, *"Wey she fin' he, meson? He look so wash-out"*—an indication of the negative vibes with respect to the new acquaintance.

Which part—*"Yoh know which part dey live?"* Also, *"Wey pa' he from?"* meaning *"Where is he from?*

Who doan hea' duz feel—When you don't listen to good advice, you suffer the consequences. The clear inference is that the person has been already warned about something. This expression is often a response to a situation, or a comment. Consider the following: Marian: *"Ah don tell da boy come home early, an' he still doan do it."* Carol: *"Well, who doan hea' duz feel."*— I suspect that this is a maxim that is here to stay.

Who sen yoh ('im, her)?—Very often this is a response to something that occurred to someone because of disobedience or presumptuousness. Example: Harry complains to his mother: *"Ah went toh Austin dem house an' dis darg bite meh."* Mother's response: *"Bu', who sen yoh? Ah tell yoh toh do yoh homework."*

With this rhetorical type expression the speaker is basically saying: *"You had no right to go there." "You brought this on yourself." "You deserved it."*

Who tell you?—Similarly to previous expression. The question is roughly, "Who gave you the permission" to do something. Any attempt to change "tell" to "told" would lose the sense of the expression. Child: *"Daddy, Ah fall arf deh bike?* Father: *"Bu, who tell yoh toh ride it?"*

Who yoh fa'?—Who are your parents? "Who do you belong to? *"Lil' boy, who yoh fa?"* In this questioning, there is a great likelihood that the questioner will know the individual's family.

Widout—without

Wi'out—Without. *"Ah ain gon buy dat expensive ting. Ah cou' do wi'out it."*

Wo'—Would. *"We wo' go wid ah you, bu' we busy."*

Wok—The word is so universally used in the United States Virgin

Islands that it must be included, and NOT as a mis pronunciation, but as a Creole expression: *"I goin' wok now."*//

"I dain know yoh wuz wokin' tonight."

Wok up (Wokin' up)—A dance noted for its gyrating moves and carefree style. Naturally it comes from the idea of making the body "work." However, no one would say *"Working' up yoh body"* in much the same way as no one should speak of *"tamarind stew."* Sometimes the use can be negative as in *"He de wokin' up like heen geh no shame."*

Wrart up—To verbally reprimand someone *("Meson, Ah wrart she up")*. This basically means that an individual was told in no uncertain terms how another felt.

"Ah gon wrart 'im up wen Ah see 'im." In essence, verbal wrath was brought on the person.

Wutless—Careless, wanton, carefree but also one who does selfish things. Also, stingy. It does NOT mean that the person has no worth, but that the individual shows a lack of concern. *"Boy, he wutless! He geh money but he'ain wan' toh help nobardy." "Man, she look so wutless, walkin roun' so dutty (dirty)."* Combined with *"good fo' notin'"* you have a powerful, insulting character assassination. *"He is a wutless, good fo' notin."*

Ya—Used as an exclamation to emphasize a thought as in *"He crazy, ya." "Dat music loud, ya."*

This is one of those colorful expressions like "meson" or "man." Popular in St. Croix.

Ya – Prevalent in St. Croix. *"Come ya, now."* As young boys spending our summers in St. Croix my siblings and I tried to adopt many of the unique expressions said by our large Crucian family.

Yabba—To scream at someone disapprovingly. *"I was tryin toh tark toh her, bu' she bus meh such ah yabba. I jus' shut up mey mout'."* When you are given a *"yabba,"* there is no uncertainty about the reprimander's feelings!

Yampy—Refers to "cold" in one's eyes." [At times one can hear, "**Yoh geh ting in yoh eye.**"] *"Boy, go wash yoh face. You eye full ah yampy."* This is a word that is still very much in vogue.

Yankee—This refers to anyone from the United States mainland. There is absolutely no allusion to any specific or particular geographical location in the United States. Also the person's color is irrelevant. A common conversation could be something like the following: *"Way he* *from?*" Response: "*Ah donno, bu' he soun' like ah Yankee.*" There are many offshoots of this, for example, the verb in the infinite: "*Stap tryin' toh yank, no man.*" At times the adjective might be used, obviously in a clearly more sarcastic tone: "*Boy, she so yankify now; Ah carn' even undastan' ha.*" The word "stone" used as an adjective is often added for emphasis. "*Da man is ah stone yankee.*" He is definitely an American!

It is interesting to note the different reactions to such characterizations when the speech being described is that of a local person. Some embrace it as complimentary because consciously, or perhaps subconsciously, they want to distant themselves from the local Creole. Others feel offended and reject the characterization because of their rebellious spirit and the affirmation of Virgin Islands culture.

Year befo'—This is a popular expression (with the stress on the second word, "*befo.*") that refers to two years earlier. In Virgin Islands Creole the tendency is to avoid such cumbersome expressions as "*The year before last year,*" and instead we opt for the more colorful creolized version. "*Year befo' we went on ah trip toh New Yark.*" To be faithful to this particular expression the definite article ("the") is not allowed—"*The year befo'*" is not popular, nor creolized!

Yes—Placed at the final position of a sentences, emphasizing an affirmation. This syntactic arrangement is uniquely local. Mother: "*Tis Edward dat hit yoh?* Ray's Response: "*Tis he, yes,*" rather than, "Yes, tis he."

Yes sa'—Often used in conversation to confirm something than someone has said. Example. "*Yes sa,'dem chiren disgustin.*" Of course, there are numerous variations, for example the interaction of two or more speakers: **Speaker 1**: "*Dem de rude, yoh hea'?*" **Speaker II**: "*Yes sa,'Ah ain able wid dem atarl.*" It is important to note that the use of the word "sa" does not have to be as a response to someone else. A person can simply affirm: "*Dem tools heavy sa.'*" Could this possibly be a carry over the days when subjugated people had to respond with the word "*sir*," when speaking to an overseer? Such a speculation is not at all far-fetched.

Yoan—This is the contraction for "*Yoh+ain*", meaning "you don't." "*Yoh look like yoan geh no money atarl.*"

Yoh—This is a subject pronoun for the second person singular. It is also used as a possessive. (Refer to the sections on **subject pronouns** and **possessives**). There is much discussion on this feature earlier. Examples:

1) "Doreen, wey yoh goin'?" 2) *"Zeke, da guirl is yoh sista?"* In the first case the "yoh" is the subject of the sentence, whereas in #2 it functions as a possessive adjective.

Yoh ain (Yoh'in) geh marnin' (manners) in yoh mout?—You definitely do not want to be told this. The truth is, it is not truly a question; or we can say that it is rhetorical. It is a reprimand: *"Boy, yoh ain (yoan) geh marnin' in yoh mout? Yoh come' heh an' ain say notin' toh nobardy."* If a person fails to acknowledge cultural protocol during these time frames, the reaction most likely would be: *"Yoh ain geh ah bit ah* <u>manners</u> *in yoh mout'."* For those trying to understand Virgin Islands Creole, it is important to note that even though you will hear *"marnin' "* in this expression, *"afternoon," "evening," "night"* are not *frequently* heard.

Yoh cou' pu' yoh pat on deh fiah—You have no doubt that someone will do something or that you will receive something on schedule because the people involved are dependable. *"Wen she say she gon bring yoh money, yoh cou' pu' yoh pat on deh fiah."* In essence, you can begin to cook because you are assured of receiving the money to buy the ingredients for the food. The person's word is golden.

Yoh darg' (don') dead—Meaning, there is nothing else that you can do. Your fate is sealed! *"Too late toh ask ha forgiveness now. Yoh darg don dead."*

Yoh ole darg yoh—an expression often used in jest with various interpretations, for example meaning "you are sly" or maybe "you misled me," or "surprised me." *"Ah see yoh las' night with dat guirl. Yoh ole darg yoh."*

Yoh gon live larng—Your name was just mentioned and coincidentally you suddenly appear. Several similar expressions heard in some countries in Western Africa. *"Boy, we wuz jus' tarkin' 'bout you wen yoh walk in. You gon live larng, meson."*

Yoh gon see—A sort of warning, a pseudo threat, there will be consequences. *"Do it an' yoh gon see."* In other words, "you will see what I will do."

Yoh hea'?/ "Yoh ain' hea'?"—A very popular expression used to end a sentence, giving emphasis to the story. *"Da man lazy, yoh hea'."* The formula does not work if the expression comes at the beginning of the sentence. Sometimes the negative is use to affirm a statement. **Barry**: *"Da boy need some help."* **Ray**: *"Yoh ain' hea'?"* In order words a tacit agreement.

Yoh know—This is an expression often coming at the end of an utterance. The irony in this usage is that it does NOT indicate the possession of knowledge. It is used more as a confirmation of a declaration, similarly to **"you hea' "** appearing in an earlier entry. As in the case of **"yoh hea'"** the expression does not work in the same way if it precedes the declaration.

"Ah wan' toh tark toh yoh, yoh know." The truth is the listener does not necessarily know of my desire to speak to him or her. *"We leavin' now, yoh know."*

Yoh know da kin'ah way—This is an expression used to emphasize what was stated before. *"He was screamin' an' actin wild, yoh know da kin' ah way."*

Yoh know wa Ah mean!—This usage is not to be confused with the English statement: *"You know what I mean?"* In Virgin Islands Creole this is often a response of affirmation to what another person has said. For example: Diann says to James, *"Darwin doan listen. Someting gon happen toh he."* Reaction from James: *"Yoh know wa Ah mean!"* A most unique feature of this exchange is that the person reacting to the statement responds as if he or she had made the comment, with the use of the first person singular.

Yoh (he/she) lie—Used when preceded by the clause, "If yoh/she etc…", and often with verbs such as *tink, believe, expec'* etc. For example, *"He sittin' down de ain doin' notin'. If yoh tink I gon gi' he money, yoh lie."* The speaker is emphatically stating his or her unwillingness to placate the individual in question.

Yoh lyin' meh (Yoh lyin')—This is not accusing the person of not telling the truth. The speaker simply finds the story unbelievable, or very intriguing. *"Yoh lyin' meh. Owen couldn' say such ah ting."* Other example: *"Who yoh say? Charlene? Yoh lyin' meh."*

Yoh see 'im (ha, ah) de—An introduction to a description of a person's behavior or attitude. *"Yoh see im de, he is ah real coward."* *"Yoh see ah de, she wo' do anytin' fo' anybardy."* An equal variation is to have the expression at the end. *"He good lazy, yoh see 'im de."* Often it is pointing out a behavior or attitude of an individual that is not generally known.

Yoh see you?—This is a kind of subtle rubuke, sometime in gest. But the idea is that I know what you are doing. Example: Carl refuses to help his friend with something. The friend responds: *"Yoh see you?* Could mean,

"I am watching you." It is really an incomplete thought even though both speaker and listener understand the gest.

Yoh sleep— An expression that has all but disappeared. It was used to indicate that the person is in trouble and cannot escape it. *"Tain notin yoh cou' do meson, yoh sleep."*

Yoh tellin' I?—Emphatic expression said as reaffirmation. The important feature is the use of the pronoun "**I**" instead of "**me**." Calvin: *"Dat man is trouble."* Carol: *"Yoh tellin' I"?*— in other words, tell me something new. The listener already knows.

"Yohself" used as reaction to previous communication or action—A rather unusual reaction, in which one individual reproaches another. This is so unique it can only be understood by example. Tina and Cleve had an argument. Shortly after Cleve sees Tina and tries to greet her: "Hello, Tina." Tina's reaction: *"Hello yohself!"* In other words, "don't say hello to me"—literally, "say hello to yourself."

You fo' [usually the child's mother's first name]—Popular way of addressing children of people that the speaker knows. Sometimes you were signaled by your mother's name. Example: *"Yoh fo' Maggie, come heh; go toh deh shap an' buy ah poung' ah flour fo' meh."* — Maggie's son/daughter. Conventional wisdom taught us that we could never say "no" when you were so signaled.

Young ting—Actually an allusion to a young individual, used often in a lighthearted way. *"He or she is ah lil' young ting."*

Yout' man—A reference to a young boy. *"How deh yout man doin?"*

Res: *"Good, he just make ah year."* Understood by all, but not uttered by everyone.

THE NEXT STEP:
RECONCEPTUALIZING USVI CREOLE

The Creole spoken in the United States Virgin Islands in many ways has stood the test of time. While it is true that over the past century or more, many words and expressions have become extinct, it is also true that many are still vibrant and are characteristic components of the islands' language and identity. Some have become so ingrained in the speech fabric that they may even have a sense of "eternity" to them. Clearly, there can never be any guarantee of linguistic immortality, not with the unpredictable nature of society and humanity itself. Nonetheless, Virgin Islands Creole has survived the socio-cultural swings, shifts, and major economic and ideological transformations. For example, as I reflect on the U.S. Virgin Islands accent, inflection, and intonation my own sense is that they have remained remarkably consistent throughout the past 5 or 6 decades. U.S. Virgin Islands speech continues to be identifiable, not only for its words, expressions and syntax, but also because of the idiosyncratic cadence of the language.

There is no doubt that there is much work to be done with regard to the preservation of United States Virgin Islands Creole. This is especially true with respect to our written language. As mentioned earlier, one of the salient features of our linguistic predecessor, Virgin Islands Dutch Creole, is its immortalization in text. It is my hope that contemporary Virgin Islands Creole will eventually move in that direction. To be sure, now there is a sizeable amount of material written - - poetry, drama, and short stories— using United States Virgin Islands Creole as the medium of communication. In fact, journals such as the **Caribbean Writer**,

Yellow Cedars Blooming, **Islands Jewels** and others have helped to facilitate the process of the legitimation of our speech by publishing works of authors employing Virgin Islands Creole as the primary means of articulation. Such publications can be instrumental in bringing a certain level of respectability and authenticity to our language. We need to go well beyond this, however, working toward a linguistic consensus of our *written* Creole. Such a project would entail, as a possibility, the establishment of an academy of Virgin Islands Creole in which linguists, ethnologists, etymologists, and other scholars would work with the general populace to collectively develop strategies that would help us to transcribe our language from oral elaboration to the written word.

The arrival at such a level of transcription must be preceded, however, by a relentless mission of changing the image of our Creole because besides being recognizable our language must be embraceable. At some point we must confront our uneasiness and sense of discomfort with respect to U.S.V.I. Creole, and as we do this we perform the most important and necessary task—that of unmasking ourselves. Consider the fact that speakers of the English language are not ever engaged in perennial debates about the legitimacy of the English language. Certainly there are discussions with respect to grammatical structures, syntax, and morphology, but there is no sustained discussion revolving around the authenticity or legitimation of English as a mode of communication; this is perceived to be a given fact. The same can be said of Spanish, German, French, and other languages. Virgin Islands Creole deserves to be in the same category with respect to its own authenticity and legitimacy.

The United States Virgin Islands are rightfully proud of so many treasures that identify the territory, including beautiful, unmatched landscape, enviable beaches, ideal weather, (Hugo, Marilyn, Irma, and María notwithstanding), and above all its warm friendly people. In much the same way that we rightfully acknowledge and embrace these characteristic features, so too must we herald our speech as part of a wider overarching socio-linguistic reality. Included in our self-adulation must be our mode of articulation, our Virgin Islands Creole—which brands us as Virgin Islanders, and as part of a shared linguistic community. The customs and traditions of our people are not encased and preserved in the rays of the sun, nor in the soothing trade wind breeze, nor in the rolling hills and crystal clear waters, but rather in the rich multifaceted nature of our language—United States Virgin Islands Creole, with its peculiarities and idiosyncrasies. When we embrace it undeniably and unabashedly as ours, we acknowledge its indispensable link to us and ultimately affirm our Virgin Islandness.

The great 19th century poet-philosopher José Martí, postulating the importance of embracing the local (Latin American) culture, posits that *"our Greece is preferable to that Greece that is not ours"* (Martí 223) [my translation].[38] Placing this affirmation within the context of the United States Virgin Islands, it is true that our Creole has not had the recognition, status, or prestige[39] as other languages globally, but it is in fact our mode of speech, and that is the central point; for we must strive for the type of the pride and sense of identity that the Cuban writer advocates in his essay *"Our America"* (*"Nuestra América"*). In his typical symbolic language, Martí accentuates that spirit of creolization, the appropriation and propagation for that which emanates from the core of the local customs: *"The wine made from plantain, even if it turns out sour, is still our wine"* (Martí 224)[my translation].[40] In contrast to some other writers in Latin America (for example, Domingo Faustino Sarmiento[41]), Martí recognizes, acknowledges, and privileges the local traditions, language being one of the important components.

We can certainly take a page from Martí, that guardian of Latin American culture, as we push ourselves to freely engage with our language, to argue for its value and its viability. Significantly, Martí does not employ such comparatives or superlatives as "better," "superior," or "best," but rather, simply affirms his stance, opting for the adjective "preferable" (Spanish— *"preferible"*) to underscore the importance of cultural embracement. We can also learn valuable lessons from the Dominican essayist, Pedro Henríquez Ureña whose essay, *"Six Essays in Search of Our Expression"* [my translation][42], argues enthusiastically for the authenticity of the local (Latin American) expression. Although in his work Henríquez Ureña emphasizes the need to establish a regional (Latin American) literary tradition, underpinning this is the exhortation for general cultural embracement. It is a critical posture, not only promoted by Martí and Henríquez Ureña, but by other 19th century writers such as Andrés Bello who maintains that there must be a general consciousness with respect to originality and the claiming of the collective identity. Bello in very poignant language warns that if we were to avoid our cultural responsibilities then *"the [critics] will say that [Latin] America still has not shaken off its chains..."* (Bello 108).[43] Defending Virgin Islands Creole affirms its independence as a language, and its national (territorial) significance.

There has always been resistance to creolization, resulting from a confused ideology set in place by false claims that Americanization—being American—should be the major factor in determining the dominant language. Over the years, because of the colonial arrangement between the United States and the United States Virgin Islands, attempts to appropriate the lingo of the mainland sometimes seem more persistent and pervasive. A prevailing myth is that the English as spoken in the United States would represent the "best" speech model for Virgin Islanders to follow; that is, the authenticity resides in the linguistic norms of the U.S. Undoubtedly this is an inverted way of thinking, for in point of fact the authenticity of the citizenry is connected to their naturalness of speech, to their linguistic normalcy gleaned from their interaction and engagement in the local domain.

For a long time now the idea of a Virgin Islands language has been considered repulsive by many. The too frequent criticism of articulators of Virgin Islands Creole speaks volume as to how we ourselves view our cultural legacy. In this vein, Speakers of Virgin Islands Creole might not always be taken seriously when they express a particular point of view because to some, their local utterance signals a lack of understanding or an inherent incompetence. Changing this attitude in favor of an enthusiastic embracement of United States Virgin Islands Creole can never be attained through simple means, certainly not through some process of natural linguistic osmosis. This would be akin to someone waiting for his or her fate in life to change without becoming a protagonist in the transformative process, depending on some arbitrary timetable. The likelihood that future generations would automatically swing the pendulum in the other direction, and re-gravitate toward the Virgin Islands Creole as the default language, is decreasing with time. Waiting for this to happen would be an investment in fool's gold.

The fact is, any change that we can engender must begin with a conscious effort to transform minds, an effort that can only emanate from recognition and admission. Herein lies the most complicated aspect of our linguistic challenge because it would require that we admit that we engage in the process of distancing. What is even more difficult would be an admission of why we do this. But, if we reject the importance of promoting the way we speak or worse, deny the existence of a problem, then we will go in the direction of linguistic extinction. The promotion of Virgin Islands Creole as more than a mere comic relief or "substandard" means of communication can only yield fruits when there is a concerted effort springing forth from various entities—the government, the private sector, our schools and universities, and individual citizens who value language, customs, traditions—- culture.

Some laugh at the thought of using Virgin Islands Creole as a medium for official business. Their argument, however, supports what I have been contending here, that we are too often guilty of approaching the way we speak from an angle of inefficiency. If we were to accept the false premise of an inevitable deficiency in our language, then naturally the idea of using Virgin Islands Creole for official communication would logically seem ludicrous. But what if the exchange between government and other agencies proceeded without obstacles using Virgin Islands Creole as the language of choice? What if the medium of communication was so clear that private businesses or public enterprises operated as usual without interruption or disruption? If Virgin Islands Creole functioned on the same level of efficiency as "Standard English," then what would be the argument against its utilization in similar or equal spheres? The stark reality is, however, that this cannot happen if we do not consciously create the space for a new *modus operandi*, an opportunity for such a possibility.

Is it possible to influence our community to a point where language itself can be securely viewed as valuable? The optimistic answer is "yes." How long it will take to resend subliminal messages of countless years of negativity would depend on many factors, among them, an honest assessment of our language situation, community mobilization, and the consistent inclusion of younger citizens in our ongoing debates concerning our Creole. But of course, no meaningful change will occur without waging a campaign to convince those in authority of the importance of revamping our linguistic image. It may well be true that well-intentioned citizens could be stymied by the lack of capital needed to launch major projects related to the promotion of the language. Yet, no one is suggesting that serious work should not begin without legislature funding or governmental commitment. In fact, it should be the citizens unencumbered and undaunted by financial stagnation who must spearhead the important mission. Following their lead, governmental and private entities could serve as major pivotal forces in a catalytic shift in the way in which we view our Creole.

In the newly envisioned scenario, the government would encourage the use of the language without apology. The role and responsibility of this institution would be to foster the learning and the constant usage of Virgin Islands Creole, and to propagandize its importance as an inherent component of who we are culturally and socio-linguistically. In addition, it would eventually (we would hope) offer financial backing that would speak to its commitment for change. Schools, then, would be encouraged to incorporate the language as a regular part of the curriculum. It is the first step toward re-education, the antidote of years of miss-education that famed educator and historian Carter G. Woodson criticizes in his seminal and classical work. Woodson laments the system, (a "vicious circle (sic)," asserts his editor) "that results from mis-educated individuals, then proceeding to teach and mis-educate" (Woodson vii). In this context, to avert the "mis-education," the schools themselves must undertake the responsibility of emphasizing the importance of language acquisition. But this would be done within a framework that highlights the general principle that in contemporary society the learning of second and third languages is not only important, but essential. The schools' position would be a clear departure from the historically traditionalist approach to the promotion of a monolingual community—English as the centerpiece and the simultaneous suppression of another, United States Virgin Islands Creole.

The promotion and propagandization of Virgin Islands Creole in the Virgin Islands schools would not compromise the viability of other languages, whether it be Spanish, French, Haitian Creole, the Creole of St. Lucia, or that of Dominica, or any other area. In essence, the schools will not be in the business of discouraging the learning of any language, but must stress the importance and indispensable value of Virgin Islands Creole. The school system itself would become a conduit for the local vernacular. This would not represent a contradictory position by any means. In other words, the fact that the school system makes a case for

Virgin Islands Creole should not in any way minimize the relevance of other languages. In much the same way, advocating for French studies in the Virgin Islands school system should not in any way impinge on the legitimacy or importance of teaching or learning Spanish.

There is much irony in the fact that in some cases our Creole is already used even in the most hallowed of places. I think, for example of the courts where countless witnesses or accused regularly express themselves in United States Virgin Islands Creole, and others in various other Creole languages. The court does not (or at least *should not*) insist that the person speak in "proper English," in much the same way that the court would not insist that a speaker of Spanish, speak English, if the individual happens to be more adept and comfortable with Spanish. The court's action would be to request an interpreter in order to ensure the proper, just, and fair procedures and proceedings of its agenda. If witnesses and accused are allowed to speak in "their language," then perhaps the time will come when judges and lawyers also would conduct the proceedings in Virgin Islands Creole, consistent with the fact that this is the language spoken by the majority of our residents. This may be in the very distant future, but it must begin with the idea that this possibility does exist.

The appreciation and respect of our language would reflect a simultaneous respect of traditions and customs— in essence of our culture and ultimately of ourselves. Let us think of the implication of this: our islands will be standing at a different threshold, a point at which we will have reassessed the state of our language. In order for this to happen, though, there must be the cooperation of several entities. The academic institutions cannot be left with the awesome responsibility without support of government officials and representatives from the private sectors of our community. The religious sector will have to view this as a project worthy of its time, and beneficial for the uplifting of our citizenry, Virgin Islanders.

Our present University and any other future institutions of higher learning would also play an important role as a proponent of the language. These institutions may have as one of their core courses the learning of Virgin Islands Creole. Such a course will not necessarily have to be a requirement, but certainly students at the institutions should be encouraged to take at least one such course during their four year tenure. And scholars would be encouraged and funded to study the rudiments of the language and perhaps move ever so closer to the establishment of a consensus of ground rules for representing the language in writing. It is my belief that several goals can be achieved simultaneously: 1) the elevation of the status of our language 2) the emphasizing of the importance of acquiring other languages in general and 3) the insistence that our children learn English well, as they master Virgin Islands Creole without feeling a sense of contradiction, guilt, belittlement, conflict, or disparagement.

In line with this new approach, if the legislature, for example, would commit to conducting some sessions in Virgin Islands Creole, then one of the important branches of government would be in essence endorsing the legitimacy of the language. In this scenario there would be constant campaigns designed to help people to understand that there should be no shame in being who we are. Residents who understand and speak Virgin Islands Creole must resist succumbing to the stereotyping of speakers of the language. More importantly, they must reject the ideology of those who try to convince them of their "improper" way of speaking. In essence, we would be offering resistance to the politics of fear. In the new alliance, the private and religious sectors can join forces in the promotion of our Creole language. The churches for example, can commit themselves to conducting some services in Virgin Islands Creole. Imagine such a scenario that no doubt would elevate the stature of the language. As indicated earlier, during the colonial period the missionaries translated the Bible in Dutch Creole, a singular act that acknowledged the viability of this language in the Danish West Indies. We also know that in centuries past sermons were given in that language.

There is an audacious attitude inherently tied to those who foster linguistic superiority and inferiority. The notion that one speaking "Standard English" would somehow be "superior" to another speaking Virgin Islands Creole is a mythology directly linked to linguistic elitism. The argument against Virgin Islands Creole is replete with faulty premises that render the conclusions invalid, yet accepted as true by those who embrace the ideology of "linguistic superiority." The faulty premises are recognized by many of us, but we nonetheless, do not reject them. I can still hear the sounds of antagonists *"suckin' deh teet"* at the thought of any discussion surrounding legitimating our way of speech. In a sense, I can understand the discomfort because they have been victimized by an ideology that pushed them to reject what is truly theirs. Unquestionably, underlining the failure to resist the linguistic patrol is the chief immobilizer—fear—the most deadly of which is the fear of ourselves, but I do recognize that this is a fear that is profound, tracing back to many decades of mischaracterization.

We need not look too far than to recall that historically governors of our islands were "appointed to serve," often with no clue of who we were as a people. If we closed our eyes to the "reason" (i.e. ideology) behind this process that did not change until 1970, we would be pretending that those "chosen" were more worthy and, certainly more exceedingly qualified to govern our Virgin Islands than those who would have been elected to represent the people, were not for the imposed disenfranchisement. Equally revealing is the lack of confidence that Washington demonstrated in the electorate whose will for self-determination was suffocated by the appointment process. A close look may very well allow us to see that there was always a sense that out islands did not "measure up" to the "American standard." The implications of this position are vast including the false categorization of our islands and its people. Naturally a major part of this mis representation centers on the question of the English language, and our supposed inability to "speak it properly."

This imposed linguistic analysis of our islands unfortunately took root and sprang other branches of the same ideology promoted, not only by Washington but locally as well. Consequently, those who spoke Virgin Islands Creole were denigrated and disparaged and convinced that only the uninformed would "choose" to speak that "gutter language," a term regularly heard. Even though he was directing his attention to Blacks in the United States Wilson gives us pause to think about the rejection of our own Creole: "In the study of language in school pupils were made to scoff at the Negro dialect as some peculiar possession of the Negro which they should despise rather than directed to study the background of this language as a broken-down African tongue" (Woodson 19).

Even more challenging is the fight against our own self-deprecating tendencies. Indeed, this is the biggest challenge of all mainly because it calls for a new way of thinking, a new way of seeing and defining ourselves. One approach that has never been seriously considered is the establishment of a serious dialogue that allows a space for opposing views on our Creole. The idea would be to create a real medium for exchange of ideas that would help us to unravel our language situation at the core. It would also be an opportunity for those who are opposed to the notion of a Virgin Islands Creole to articulate their position.

In the long run, a healthy dialogue would not in any way be detrimental; on the contrary, over a period of time such intellectual exchanges would help us to better understand the nature of our mode of speech. And differences of opinion notwithstanding, a vibrant conversation on this topic by its very nature can only serve to promote our language, if nothing else as worthy of serious inquiry and investigation. Alienating ourselves from a significant component (our language) of ourselves is culturally self-punitive, a kind of socio-linguistic self-flagellation. On one hand we boast of our customs, traditions and culture; yet, on the other, our sense of linguistic shame strikes at the very core of our language integrity. The new counter ideological consciousness would reaffirm the existence of a U.S. Virgin Islands Creole and help to ensure its authenticity and legitimacy. But this cannot be mere lip service. This must be a process that far exceeds the political and the academic, which also means it cannot stop on the level of theory.

We must swing the doors wide open, to expand the periphery as the critic Jacques Derrida[44] would say. Entering into the threshold of the door would be United States Virgin Islands Creole, no longer masquerading and disguised as "sing-song dialect" and ideologically recast as "shameful", but proudly proclaiming its rightful place alongside other "viable and official" languages. The important building blocks would then be in place for the recognition and acceptance of a language the identity of which is reflected in the fabric of three small islands in the West Indies. This should be neither provocative nor controversial, even though some may choose to designate this as such. Thus, while we acknowledge the existence and relevance of numerous languages in the Virgin Islands, we must not reduce the stature and legitimacy of Virgin Islands Creole. Indeed, argues Thiang'o, "[l]language is thus inseparable from ourselves as a community of human beings with a specific form and character, a specific history, a specific relationship to the world" (Thiong'o 16).

Finally, residents themselves will have to see value in such a project, one that goes well beyond the mere level of articulation. Once all of these entities are on the same level with respect to the importance for change, then our Creole would be celebrated and will flourish, in an atmosphere nurtured and fostered by the new participatory trends of our major institutions. U.S. Virgin Islands Creole would have arrived at the level of respectability that it deserves, and having gained this vantage point we would boldly begin to authenticate our proud linguistic identity, an end result that will guarantee new generations of proud speakers and committed preservers of our Virgin Islands Language and culture. There will be born a new vitality for our language, one that would be fostered through intergenerational transmission.

Maybe we can begin the process of re igniting in our young the creative linguistic spirit so endemic in our West Indian culture of realism and magic.[45] In so doing we might, maybe by praxis, recruit a handful of linguistic revolutionaries and guerrilla fighters who see dignity and pride in the process of restoration and reattachment of ourselves, linguistically. Is it possible to redeem ourselves and challenge these antagonistic positions that reject our language as they simultaneously censure our culture? The process of reattachment and rediscovering ourselves can only occur through usage, itself a defiant act that can help us to authenticate who we were and have since become, evolving into our altered ontological selves. It is a process, I hope, that would also encourage us to hold our heads high as we converse using our Virgin Islands Creole, affirming our Virgin Islands and West Indian selves. If we can at least accomplish this initial task, then perhaps the day is not too far away when the Creole of the United States Virgin Islands will be so embraced that it would become an official means of interaction in our community, patronized and promoted at every strata of our Virgin Islands society. We would have achieved a level of institutional trust in our mode of speech. Indeed, we would have begun to embrace the totality of who we are as St. Johnians, Crucians, and St. Thomians and would unapologetically articulate this new self-affirmation using the medium that brands us as Virgin Islanders—that irrepressible Creole fervently percolating in our linguistics souls.

COMPILATION OF SUMMARY CHARTS

I. EXAMPLES OF THE APOCOPATION OF FINAL "D" WHEN PRECEDED BY "N" OR "L"	
"N"	
Standard English	**USVI Creole**
ha<u>n</u>d	han'
understa<u>n</u>d	understan'
compreh<u>en</u>d	comprehen'
pret<u>en</u>d	preten'
wi<u>n</u>d	win'
"L"	
Standard English	**USVI Creole**
mo<u>l</u>d	mol'
co<u>l</u>d	col'
ho<u>l</u>d	hol'
fo<u>l</u>d	fol'
Leopo<u>l</u>d	Leopol'

II. EXAMPLES OF THE APOCOPATION OF FINAL "T" WHEN PRECEDED BY "C," "F," "P," "S," "X"	
Standard English	**USVI Creole**
fact	fac'
lift	lif'

accept	accep'
trust	trus'
next	nex'

III. EXAMPLES OF THE APOCOPATION OF FINAL "T" WHEN PRECEDED BY A VOWEL: EXCEPTIONS

Standard English	USVI Creole
let	le'
get	geh'
put	pu'
but	bu'
at	a' (pronounced "ah")
it	e'
that	da'
what	wa'

IV. EXAMPLES OF THE SUPPRESSION OF THE 'H' IN WORDS WITH 'TH' COMBINATION

Standard English Word	USVI Creole Word
This	Dis
Them	Dem
Three	Tree
Toothache	Tootache
Marathon	Maraton
Faith	Fait
Math	Mat

V. SUMMARY OF NOUN PLURALIZATION

Standard English	USVI Creole
The books	*Deh book (s) dem*
A lot of men	*Ah latah man*

Those houses are pretty.	*Dem house pretty.*

VI. SUMMARY OF THE SUPPRESSION OF THE LINKING VERB

Standard English Statement	USVI Creole Statement
Location: *I **am** here.*	*Ah heh / I heh.*
Origin: *They **are** from New York*	*Dey from New Yark.*
Adjective: *Ellie **is** tall*	*Ellie tall.*
State of being: *He **is** fine.*	*He fine.*
Present Progressive: *Sandy **is** eating.*	*Sandy eatin.'*
Future: *We **are** going to call you.*	*We gon call yoh.*

VII. STANDARD ENGLISH CONJUGATION

I sing	We sing
You sing	You sing
He, she, it sings	They sing

VIII. USVI CREOLE CONJUGATION

Ah (I) duz sing	We duz sing
You/yoh duz sing	Ah you/Ah yoh duz sing
He, she, it duz sing	Dey duz sing

IX. ALTERNATIVE USVI CREOLE CONJUGATION

Ah sing	We sing
You/yoh sing	Ah you/Ah yoh sing
He, she, it sing	Dey sing

X. Subject Pronouns	Object Pronouns
I	Me
You	You
He	Him
She	Her
We	Us

| You | You |
| They | Them |

XI. EXAMPLES OF THE SUPPRESSION OF THE PREPOSITION *"TOH (TO)"*	
USVI CREOLE	**STANDARD ENGLISH**
"She goin' New York."	*{She <u>is</u> going to New York.}*
"We comin' town late."	*{We <u>are</u> going to town late.}*
"Ah gon go soon."	*{I <u>am</u> going to go soon.}*
"Lydia gon do it today."	*{Lydia <u>is</u> going to do it today.}*
"Dey goin' back States nex' week."	*{They <u>are</u> going back to the U.S. next week}*
"Si down close meh."	*{Sit close to me.}*

XII. EXAMPLES OF THE SUPPRESSION OF THE PREPOSITIONS "FOR" AND "AT"	
USVI Creole	**Standard English**
"Ah was lookin' food."	*{"I was looking for food."}*
"Warren was out de beggin' money."	*{"Warren was out there begging for money."}*
"Yoh need toh look wok."	*{"You need to look for work."}*
"Look he, no."	*{"Look at him."}*
"Stop starin' me, no."	*{"Stop staring at me."}*
"He home right now."	*{"He is at home right now."}*
"Benji de' home."	*{"Benji is at home."}*
"Dey don airport."	*{"They are already at the airport."}*

XIII. EXAMPLES OF THE SUPPRESSION OF THE PREPOSITION *"IN"*	
USVI CREOLE	**STANDARD ENGLISH**
"Dey live Tortola."	*{They live in Tortola.}*

"He wokin' Sin Thomas today." *"Tomorrow he wokin' Sin John."*	*{He is working in St. Thomas today.} {Tomorrow he is working in St. John.}*
"Ah stayin' Grove Place tonight."	*{I am staying in Grove Place tonight.}*
"Lydia St. Croix."	*{Lydia is in St. Croix.}*

XIV. EXAMPLES OF PREPOSITION "OF" TO 'AH'	
Sentence in English	**Sentence in USVI Creole**
All of them	*"Arl ah dem"*
All of you	*"Arl ah you/yoh"*
All of us	*"Arl ah we"*
Some of them	*"Some ah dem"*
Which one of these do you want?	*"Out ah dese wich one yoh wan'?"*
Carol is thinking of all kinds of things.	*"Carol tinkin' ah arl kin' ah ting."*

XV. SUBSTITUTION OF PREPOSITION "AT" WITH THE PREPOSITION "TOH"	
Janet: *"Austin don garn?"*	Sammy: *"Yea, he don toh deh airport aready."*
John: *"Way deh party gon be?"*	Cheryl: *"Toh mey sista' Carmen house."*
June: *"Way Ellie dem?"*	Hubert: "Man, *Dey don toh deh house larng time."*

XVI. EXAMPLES OF SHORTENED PREPOSITIONS	
Preposition	**Sentence in USVI Creole**
Unless—less	(*Doan come 'less you have deh ting.*)
Until-til	(Wait **'til** lata'.)
Against—genz'	(Pu' it **'genz'** deh wall.)
Around- roun	(*he live '**roun'** deh fiel.*)
Across-crass	(*pu'it **crass** deh bed.*)
About-bout	(*Stop tarkin' '**bout** people.*)

Among—mong	(*Doan pu'it **mong'** deh good clothes.*)

XVII. ADVERBS WITH SUFFIX "LY"	
Standard English	**USVI Creole**
They were walking *slowly*.	Dey wuz walkin' *slow*.
She was *beautifully* dressed.	She wuz dress' *beautiful*.
Sara speaks *clearly*.	Sara duz speak *clear*.
Run *quickly*.	Run *quick*.

XVIII. FORMATION OF PAST TENSE IN VIRGIN ISLANDS CREOLE	
Some Examples of Verbs conjugated in the present to talk about a PRESENT action	**Some Examples of Verbs conjugated in the present to talk about a PAST action**
Ah see 'im eveyday.	*Yestaday ah see 'im in town.*
We speak toh dem arl deh time.	*We speak toh dem las' night.*
Dey live in Cuba.	*Dey live in Cuba fo' ah year.*
*Notable Exceptions "**to be**," "**to go**," "**to have**"*	
Some Examples of Verbs conjugated in the present to talk about a PRESENT action	**Past Tense Conjugation**
Elena is mey frien'.	*Elena was mey frien'.*
We go chuch every Sunday.	*We went chuch las' Sunday.*
Dey have ah truck.	*Dey had ah truck.*
The Present Tense of These Three Verbs Can Never Be Used For The Past	

XIX. PAST TENSE WITH "DID"	
Standard English	**USVI Creole**
Did you bring the books?	Yoh bring deh books dem?
Did Leroy cook the food already?	Leroy don cook deh food aready?
Did Lisa buy ah house last year?	Lisa buy ah house las' yea'?
Did they go to the movies?	Dey went/garn movies?

XX. SUMMARY OF PRESENT PERFECT, PLUPERFECT & HYPOTHETICAL PROBABILITY

Standard English	USVI Creole
Juan has written the letter.	*Juan ha' write deh letta.*
We had seen them.	*We ha see dem.*
If I knew him, I would talk to him.	*If Ah ha know 'im, Ah wo' tark toh 'im.*
I should have gone with her.	*Ah shoudah <u>go</u> wid ha. ** *Ah shoudah garn wid ha.*
They could have had the money.	*Dey coudah <u>had</u> deh money.** *Dey coudah have deh money.*
That might have been his car.	*Dat might ah <u>be</u>' he ca'. ** *Dat might ah bin (been) he ca'.*

XXI. EXAMPLES OF THE POSSESSIVE ADJECTIVES

Standard English	USVI Creole
my	*mey*
your	*yoh*
his	*he*
her	*she/ha'*
our	*our*
your	*ah you/ah yoh*
their	*dey*

XXII. EXAMPLES OF THE POSSESSIVE PRONOUNS

Standard English	USVI Creole
mine	*Mines/Mine own/My own* "Dat's mine own."
yours	*Your own/Yours own* "Dat truck is yours own?"
his	*Hees own* "Dis TV is hees own."

hers	Her own/Hers own "Deh book is hers own."
ours	Our own "Dis truck is our own."
yours	Ah you/Yoh own "Da' boat is ah you own?"
theirs	Dere own/Deres own "Da house is deres own." Dem own

XXIII. REFLEXIVE PRONOUNS IN V.I. CREOLE	
Meyself	Leave it; ah gon do it myself.
Yohself	Yoh goin' by yohself?
Heself	He fix it heself.
Sheself/Haself	Ah say she gon do it sheself.
Ah you self	Do it ah yoh self.
Ourself*	We gon do it ourself.
Deyself	Dey wan' toh do dat deyself.

XXIV. SAMPLE COMPARATIVE VIEW OF "DEM"	
ADMISSIBLE IN USVI CREOLE	NOT ADMISSIBLE IN USVI CREOLE
Dem is ours	Way _dem_ garn?
Dem de crazy	Why _dem_ do it?
Who _dem_ is, man?	_Dem_ gon leave soon.
Dem boy comin' big	Call meh wen _dem_ reach.

XXV. SUBJECT/VERB ORDER WITH INTERROGATIVES	
Standard English	**USVI Creole**
Where is he?	Way he is?
Where is Phil now?	Way Phil is now?
How old is she?	How ole she is?
Who is that woman?	Who da woman is?

When can they go?	Wen dey cou go?
Why did you go?	Why you/yoh went?
Are thoses` books difficult	Dem books difficult?

XXVI. SUMMARY OF MULTIPLE USAGES OF "AH" AND EXAMPLES

1ST PERSON PERSONAL SUBJECT PRONOUN
Ah live Sin Croix. (I)

PREPOSITION
Mos' ah dem garn. (of)

3RD PERSONAL OBJECT PRONOUN
Call ah tomorrow, man. (her)

ARTICLE
Marlene geh ah house. (*a*)

ADJECTIVE
Me ain goin' ah place. (any)

XXVII. SUMMARY OF MULTIPLE USAGES OF "DEM" AND EXAMPLES

SUBJECT OF SENTENCE
"Dem is too much."
"Who dem is?"

OBJECT OF THE SENTENCE
"Give it toh dem."

DEMONSTRATIVE ADJECTIVE
"Dem tings belong toh you?"

DEMONSTRATIVE PRONOUN
"Meson, dem is mine!"

SUFFIX FOR PLURALIZATION
"Deh bed dem."
"James an' dem garn movies."

ENDNOTES

1   While I certainly cannot be so presumptuous, I suppose in a general sense, if I were to follow the definition of sociolinguistics by the distinguished scholar, R.A. Hudson, this work has some shades of this notion. According to Hudson, "We can define sociolinguistics as the study of language in relation to society" (Hudson 1). I am especially intrigued by Hudson's assertion that "speech has a social function, both as a means of communication and also as a way of identifying social groups, and to study speech without reference to the society that uses it is to exclude the possibility of finding social explanations for the structures that are used" (Hudson 4).

2   In this work my focus is on the United States territories—- St. John, St. Croix, and St. Thomas. To avoid redundancy, at times I may use the designation, "Virgin Islands" to connote "United States Virgin Islands." At other times the designation U.S.V.I. will be used as a convenient designation.

3   "el camino más fácil y llano era contar lo que en mis niñeces oí muchas veces a mi madre y a sus hermanos y tíos y a otros sus mayores…" (Vega 69)

4   The work of these scholars have been groundbreaking. They have looked at the rudiments of the language, its evolution and its eventual decline. What stands out always is the respect and admiration that the scholars themselves exude for this now extinct Dutch based Virgin Islands Creole. My reference to Negerhollands later in the book is not at attempt to give an in-depth look into that important language but to include it in order that more of our residents would at least become aware of it. UVI scholar Dr. Vincent Cooper has contributed greatly to the understanding of the cultural, linguistic, and historical impact of this language.

5   The use of this term itself is elusive, but here I use it to refer to the manner of speaking that is recognized as most represented of the community. In general, its elaboration would infer "correct" grammar usage, spelling, syntax and vocabulary. Spain has the "Real Academia Española," (RAE), [The Royal Spanish Academy] whose main function is to regulate and govern the Spanish language. The Academy's regulatory pronouncements are recognized not only in Spain but

in other Spanish speaking countries, trying to maintain a "standard Spanish." No such regulatory body exists in the United States. Hudson recognizes the "impreciseness" of this notion but nonetheless has identified certain processes through which the "typical standard language" has gone through: 1) selection 2) codification 3) elaboration of function and 4) acceptance (Hudson 32-33).

6   Milroy & Milroy's comments are especially pertinent here: "We will not improve practical language teaching…by maligning…those who study…non-standard vernaculars as 'enemies of standard English' " (Milroy 8).

7   The idea here is that there is no legal requirement to use any particular language in the United States Virgin Islands. The use of the term "de facto" speaks to what is the norm, what is actually in vogue, in spite of stipulated laws, or statutes, what is the reality.

8   Even though it is widely believed that English is the official language of the United States, the truth is there is no such legal designation. The English Only Movement in the U.S. had a political initiative to try to change that situation by pushing for the imposition of English as the only medium of communication in governmental operations. So far this agenda has failed, and in an increasingly pluralistic society the likelihood of eventual success decreases with time.

9   U.S. Census Reports consistently indicate the rapid rise of this population, which conservatively hoovers around 60 million; the projection is that the Hispanic/Latino rate will be around 30% of the U.S. population by 2050.

10   Consider the fact that for some fourteen years the United States Virgin Islands were under the jurisdiction of the Navy (1917-1931), this after being under the Danish rule. The subsequent process of appointed governors to the territory, coupled with the recent vestiges of Danish domination and the military presence created a distinct socio-political situation. It was natural, given this backdrop that there would be a constant fluidity of the English language in its various contours. Americans flocked to the islands from various sectors of the U.S. mainland with a variety of speech patterns.

11   This adjective connotes the idea of "*un habla madrileña.*" I opt to keep the Spanish adjective for emphasis. In general the idea is "Madrilenian speech."

12   Referenced by David Beriss in his excellent work on French West Indians in urban France. CEDAGR is the French acronym for *Centre d'entraide et d'etude des antillais, guyanais, réunionnais* (Beriss 123).

13   The original Spanish: "*Las definiciones que se han propuesto para los conceptos de <<lengua>> y <<dialecto>> han sido muchas y diversas. Desde un punto de vista rigurosamente lingüístico, no existen evidencias que justifiquen la distinción entre lengua y dialecto*" (Fernández 86).

14   Original Spanish: "*muy difícil marcar sus fronteras*" (Fernández 87).

15   Original Spanish: "*Una lengua es el Sistema lingüístico de que se vale una comunidad hablante y que se caracteriza por estar fuertemente diferenciado,….por*

ser un vehículo de una importante tradición literaria y, en ocasiones, por haberse impuesto a sistemas lingüísticos de su mismo origen."

16 Original Spanish: *"{Un dialecto es} un [s]istema de signos desgajado de una lengua común, viva or desaparecida, normalmente con una concreta delimitación geográfica, pero sin una fuerte diferenciación frente a otros de origen común"* (Fernández 88)

17 [Original Spanish *"se hace equivalente a sub-standard o non-standard."* (Fernández 86).

18 The problem arises from the conflicting perceptions of U.S.V.I. Virgin Islands Creole. If one chooses to see it as merely some sort of English "corruption," then the debate becomes stifled in its confused state. No discussion can be advanced nor sustained if opponents insist on adhering to their premise of Virgin Islands Creole as an unmitigated contamination of the English language.

19 Rafael Seco's text "El language es el gran instrumento de comunicación de que dispone la Humanidad, intimamente ligada a la civilización, hasta tal punto, que se ha llegado a discutir si fue el lenguaje que nació de la sociedad, o fue la sociedad la que nació del lenguaje." (Seco XI)

20 I am not ignoring the fact that there are different accents, unique expressions, and cultural particularities reflected in the places cited here. The truth is that Portuguese and Spanish do have a lot in common, enough to allow reasonable exchanges between members of the two group of speakers.

21 I employ this term in the most general sense, of the speaker switching at will, or subconsciously, between two languages

22 Dubois is speaking specifically of the Black individual in the United States and the awkward subject positioning of that citizen, straddling two worlds. This social philosopher's reference, however, is truly applicable to the U.S. Virgin Islands, in its relationship to the United States:
"The Negro is a sort of seventh son,...[born in] a world which yields him no true self-consciousness, but only lets him see himself through the revelation of the other world. It is a peculiar sensation, this double-consciousness, this sense of always looking at one's self through the eyes of others...strivings" (DuBois 38).

23 This of course is in reference to the fact that as inhabitants of an unincorporated territory (looking at all three islands as one territory) of the United States, the Virgin Islands are guaranteed certain rights, yet constitutionally others do not apply, the chief among these is the right to vote in National Elections—Presidential elections.

24 Fanon makes a similar observation of the Martinican who after arriving to France "often he no longer understands Creole" (Fanon 23). Fanon's sarcasm is not lost on the reader. For some people in the Virgin Islands there has been a mistaken and pervasive notion that distancing oneself from the local parlance would somehow move that individual closer to being recognized as an American. It is an argument with no merit, since in fact the United States Virgin Islander

is American, in spite of the paradoxical political and social implications of this categorization.

25 These are all words that over the years have regularly been heard in relationship to U.S.V.I. Virgin Islands Creole. The stigmatization of the language emanates from its perceived association with an inherent flaw.

26 By "linguistic capital" Yosso is referring to the various skills gained through communication in more than one language. In the case of the United States Virgin Islands, the gliding between English and Creole is exactly the type of cultural wealth acquired through the bilingual experience.

27 Here I must make an exception because in U.S.V.I. culture some expressions such as "bad words" or "cussin" certainly are social and cultural taboos, and it would be common for someone to tell a child (or adult) "dat ain appropriate."

28 The island, as we know, is divided in French Saint-Martin and Dutch Sin Maarten. This arrangement began in the mid-17th century. With no physical geographical boundaries on this Caribbean island there is a unique confluence of languages.

29 The Danish took possession of St. Thomas and St. John in the late 17th century and of St. Croix in the first half of the 18th century. The lucrative slave trade naturally provided opportunistic language interchanges and exchanges, not surprising when one considers that slaves were captured from many different zones of the African continent. The confluence of languages clearly had its resonance on Virgin Islands speech, even more so after 1917 when the United States staked its claim.

30 The idea of discourse is in the sense in which Michel Foucault employs the terminology. Ideology imposes itself and over a period of time a kind of "tradition" is created.

31 David Boris' Black Skins, French Voices offers his readers an insight into a similar phenomenon operating in Martinique. Beriss points to the fear of some Martinican citizens as they suspiciously eye their local Creole as a negative influence: "...parents did not want their children studying Creole at School. At meetings with teachers, parents would argue that their children already knew Creole. Creole was not a serious subject" (Beriss 13). Martinique with the inclusion of its Creole as a part of the curriculum has gone much further than we have in the United States Virgin Islands.

32 In her valuable study Teaching Language in Context Omaggio Hadley makes the distinction between "feedback" and "correction." The idea of feedback is especially effective because this would provide a constructive and instrumental basis for a dialogical exchange between teacher and student, in contrast to a dismissive posture engendered by a mere correction. For example, if the student in the classroom uses the word "*tarmon*," the teacher should be careful not to reject this choice simply as "incorrect," citing the word "*tamarind*" as the

"appropriate" word. Such a situation would create an opportune moment for the teacher to explain the usage of the two different words generating from two distinct, yet overlapping communicative mediums (English/V.I. Creole). Here, my notion of 'teacher" can also be extended to include anyone in the position to influence or affect how an individual views his/her own language.

33 Freire's postulates a philosophy that is very useful for educators in any setting; it functions as well in situations that are informal. In this case, we must be careful not to punish the individual for employing what we might consider wrong vocabulary or structure. The problem-posing method would allow the student the opportunity to ask questions, the answers to which might make that student* (*used in the broadest sense of the word) more conscious of the two languages between which he or she oscillates. Of course, the challenge is to convince the entire community that we are indeed speaking of moving between two languages, both of which deserve to be respected.

34 By contemporary I am referring to the emerging Creole made forceful after March 17, 1917, the date that the Danish West Indies were purchased by the United States, already a formidable nation; it is no wonder that the result was a more powerful linguistic imposition (that of American English), that undoubtedly accelerated the declension of Virgin Islands Dutch Creole, already spiraling to oral eradication. In the United States Virgin Islands Transfer Day is celebrated on March 31 of each year, a day that commemorates the transformation of the Danish West Indies into the United States Virgin Islands.

35 Note that there is not a direct translation of *"Who 'e fa'?"* The literal question —*"Who is he for?"* would not capture the essence of the Creolized rendition. This popular question many times suggests that the questioner would very probably know the individual's family.

36 Chomsky defines "generative grammar" as "a system of rules that in some explicit or well-defined way assigns structural descriptions to sentences" (Chomsky 43). Here is where I am allowing some flexibility of Chomsky's theory. Virgin Islands Creole has no explicitly written rules. But there is no question as to the existence of more tacit, or implicit rules that govern articulation. The rules are truly established, even though we certainly cannot consider them as "official." They are, though, adhered to by the speech community.

37 We cannot close our eyes to this important fact, the existence of a governing set of rules. We should never "neglect the fact that non-standard spoken vernaculars have grammars of their own" (Milroy 8). It is natural that those who are speakers of a language do not consciously reflect on the rules while engaged in conversation.

38 Original Spanish: "Nuestra Grecia es preferible a la jure que no es nuestra" (Ureña 223). Greece in the 19th century was seen as the mecca of Western

Civilization. Martí is arguing that Latin America has its own culture that is just as valid and legitimate.

39   I am employing this word as Hudson uses it (cited earlier), as a possible distinguishing feature between language and dialect. Again my allusion to our Creole as a language is as a counter stance, to the position of some who categorically reject this idea.

40   Original Spanish: "El vino, de plátano; y si sale agrio, ¡es nuestro vino!" (Martí 224). What can be more local, more representative of indigenous Caribbean culture than the plantain? Martí's symbolism is quite poignant and relevant to our issue.

41   Domingo Faustino Sarmiento wrote **Facundo: Civilización y la barbarie)** (1845) (Translation: **Facundo: Civilization and Barbarism**) and strongly opposed the indigenous cultures in Latin America. "Facundo" is a reference to Juan Facundo Quiroga, a gaucho, a cowboy (roughly speaking) from the South American regions. Martí offered a counter-ideological position that embraced the cultures of the gaucho and those of various indigenous populations, in opposition to Sarmiento's ideology. He also stressed the importance of acknowledging the African influences in Latin America. Unquestionably, Martí is one whose philosophy Virgin Islanders should endorse.

42   Original Spanish: "Seis ensayos en busca de nuestra expresión" (Ureña 304-310).

43   Original Spanish: "Dirán: la América no ha sacudido aún sus cadenas…"

44   Derrida refers here to the concept of what he calls "play." This is the idea that it is necessary to question what is the "center," the truth; in fact, is the center really the center?—is Derrida's implicit question. This approach should cause us to question the idea of what can be accepted as "language," a challenge of conventionalism. If we expanded the periphery, then the Creole of the United States Virgin Islands can fall under the umbrella of language legitimacy (Derrida 88-103).

45   There is no question that ours is a culture of magical realism in the sense that our "realism" has always been infused with the "unusual" and the inexplicable, given our traumatic history this should not be at all such a surprise. I speak of the same kind of magical realism often used to reference Latin American in its literature.

WORKS CITED

Althusser, Louis. "Ideology and Ideological State Apparatuses." Searle, Hazard Adams & Leroy. *Critical Theory Since 1965*. Tallahassee: University Pressess of Florida, 1992. 239-250.

Bello, Andrés. "Autonomía cultural de América." Filer, Raquel Chang-Rodríguez and Malva E. *Voces de Hispanoamérica*. Boston: Heinle. Cengage Learning, 2017. 107-108.

Beriss, David. *Black Skins, French Voices*. Boulder: Westview Press, 2004.

Chomsky, Noam. "Aspects of the Theory of Syntax." Searle, Hazard Adams & Leroy. *Critical Theory Sibnce 1965*. Tallahassee: Florida State Univesity Press, 1992. p. 40-58.

Chomsky, Noam. "Aspects of the Theory of Syntax." Searle, Hazard Adams & Leroy. *Critical Theory Sibnce 1965*. Tallahassee: Florida State Univesity Press, 1992. p. 40.

Derrida, Jacques. "Structure, Sign, and Play in the Discourse in the Human Sciences." Easthope, A. *Modern Criticism and Theory: A Reader*. New York: Pearson, 1988. 88-103.

DuBois, W.E.B. *The Souls of Black Folk*. Boston: Bedford Books, 1997.

Fanon, Frantz. *Black Skin, White Masks*. New York: Gove Press, Inc, 1967.

Fernández, Francisco Moreno. *Principios de sociolingüística y sociología del lenguaje*. Barcelona: Editorial Ariel, S.A., 1998.

Freire, Paulo. *Pedagogy of the Oppressed*. New YORK: Cintinuum Press, 1990.

Gates, Henry Louis. *"Race," Writing, and Difference*. Chicago: The University of Chicago Press, 1986.

Hadley, Alice Omaggio. *Teaching Language in Context*. Boston: Heinle & Heinle Publishers, 1993.

Hudson, R.A. *Sociolinguistics*. Cambridge: Cambridge University Press, 1990.

Martí, José. "Nuestra América." Filer, Raquel Chang-Rodríguez & Malva E. *Voces de Hispanoamérica*. Boston: Heinle, Cengage Learning, 2013. 221-225.

Milroy, James Milroy and Lesley. *Authority in Language: Investigating Standard English*. London & New York: Routledge, 1999.

Said, Edward. "Orientalism." Ryan, Julie Rivkin & Michael. *Literary Theory: An Anthology*. London: Malden Blackwell, 1998. 874-885.

Saussure, Ferdinand de. "Course in General Linguistgics." McGowan, Antony Easthope & Kate. *A Critical and Cultural Theory Reader*. Toronto: University of Toronto Press, 1997. 7-13.

Seco, Rafael. *Manual de la gramática española*. Madrid: Aguilar, 1971.

Thiong'o, Ngũgĩ wa. *Decolonising The Mind*. Oxford: James Currey Ltd., 2005.

Ureña, Pedro Henríquez. "Nuestra América." Filer, Rafael Chang-Rodríguez and Malva E. *Voces de Hispanoamérica*. Boston: Heinle Cengage Learning, 2013. 304-310.

Vega, Gracilaso de la. "Comentarios reales." V, Raquel Chang-Rodríguez & Malva E. Filer. *Voces de Hispanoamérica*. Boston: Cengage Learning, 2017. 69.

Woodson, Carter G. *Mis-education of the Negro*. Washington, D.c.: The Associated Publishers, INC, 169.

Yosso, Tara. "Whose Culture Has Capital? A Critical Race Theory Discussion of Community Cultural Wealth ." Gillborn, David. *Race, Ethnicity, and Education, Vol. 8, No. 1*. Taylor & Francis Group LTD, 2005. 69-91. On-line.

INDEX

Printed in the United States
By Bookmasters